Learn Spring for Android Application Development

Build robust Android applications with Kotlin 1.3 and Spring 5

S. M. Mohi Us Sunnat
Igor Kucherenko

BIRMINGHAM - MUMBAI

Learn Spring for Android Application Development

Copyright © 2019 Packt Publishing

Commissioning Editor: Aaron Lazar
Acquisition Editor: Sandeep Mishra
Content Development Editor: Manjusha Mantri
Technical Editor: Riddesh Dawne
Copy Editor: Safis Editing
Language Support Editor: Storm Mann
Project Coordinator: Prajakta Naik
Proofreader: Safis Editing
Indexer: Pratik Shirodkar
Graphics: Jisha Chirayil
Production Coordinator: Arvindkumar Gupta

First published: January 2019

Production reference: 1310119

Published by Packt Publishing Ltd.
Livery Place
35 Livery Street
Birmingham
B3 2PB, UK.

ISBN 978-1-78934-925-2

www.packtpub.com

To my beloved parents, Md. Montaz and Taslima Taz, for their benevolent support and countless sacrifices.

To my lovely wife, Chaity, who always supported me and provided motivation whenever I was in trouble.

– S M Mohi Us Sunnat

`mapt.io`

Mapt is an online digital library that gives you full access to over 5,000 books and videos, as well as industry leading tools to help you plan your personal development and advance your career. For more information, please visit our website.

Why subscribe?

- Spend less time learning and more time coding with practical èBooks and Videos from over 4,000 industry professionals

- Improve your learning with Skill Plans built especially for you

- Get a free eBook or video every month

- Mapt is fully searchable

- Copy and paste, print, and bookmark content

Packt.com

Did you know that Packt offers eBook versions of every book published, with PDF and ePub files available? You can upgrade to the eBook version at `www.packt.com` and as a print book customer, you are entitled to a discount on the eBook copy. Get in touch with us at `customercare@packtpub.com` for more details.

At `www.packt.com`, you can also read a collection of free technical articles, sign up for a range of free newsletters, and receive exclusive discounts and offers on Packt books and eBooks.

Contributors

About the authors

S. M. Mohi Us Sunnat is a passionate Android developer and trainer with over 4 years' experience. He has developed applications using Kotlin as the principal programming language. He is the founder of DreamOgrammerS, a small IT company. He is the organizer of Droidcon Dhaka. He loves community engagement and works on a number of open source projects, including Mozilla Firefox and Brave. He is also the community leader of the Bangladesh Kotlin user group and the Dhaka Twitter developer community of Bangladesh.

Writing a book is harder than writing blogs and more gratifying than I could have ever imagined. None of this would have been possible without my family and friends. I will start by thanking my loving wife, Chaity, for her continuous support. She was as important to this book being completed as I was. A special thanks to my friends, Faysal, Hasib, Kiron, Jisan, Mirza, and Zibon. They encouraged me every time I struggled throughout this journey. And finally, my sincere gratitude to everyone on the PacktPub team who helped me so much, especially Manjusha Mantri, for her patience and trust in me. I will not forget all of this help and am indebted to you all.

Igor Kucherenko is an Android developer at Techery, a software development company that uses Kotlin as the main language for Android development. Currently, he lives in Ukraine, where he is a speaker in the Kotlin Dnipro community, which promotes Kotlin, and shares his knowledge with audiences at meetups. You can find his articles concerning Kotlin and Android development on Medium and in a blog for Yalantis, where he worked previously.

I'd like to thank my colleague for imparting his knowledge, and Packt for the opportunity to write this book, as well as my wife for her patience while I was writing it.

About the reviewers

Abid Khan is an application developer and test engineer with over 10 years of experience. He has worked with different programming languages, including C/C++ and Java, and is now working with Kotlin as a primary language for Android development. Abid is also the author of a book, *Hands-On Object-Oriented Programming in Kotlin*. He lives in Stockholm, Sweden, and spends most of his time reading books, learning new technologies, and blogging.

H. M. Mahedi Hasan Jisan is currently pursuing his master's degree in computer science at the University of Regina, Canada. He is working in the research field under the supervision of a professor. He completed his B.Sc. in computer science and engineering at BRAC University in 2017. He previously worked as a junior software engineer at Cramstack Ltd., from June 2017 to December 2018. *Learn Spring for Android Application Development* is the first book that he has worked on as a technical reviewer.

> *I would like to thank S M Mohi Us Sunnat, a writer of this book. He has previously helped me a lot with Android programming, and encouraged me to pursue my dreams. I would like to dedicate this book to my family and friends.*

Packt is searching for authors like you

If you're interested in becoming an author for Packt, please visit `authors.packtpub.com` and apply today. We have worked with thousands of developers and tech professionals, just like you, to help them share their insight with the global tech community. You can make a general application, apply for a specific hot topic that we are recruiting an author for, or submit your own idea.

Table of Contents

Preface

This book is designed to develop both server and client for an application. We have used the Kotlin language for both the server and client sides. In this book, Spring will be the server-side application, and Android the client-side application. Our primary focus is on those areas that will be able to help a developer develop a secure application with the latest architecture. This book describes the basics of Kotlin and Spring, which will be of benefit if you are unfamiliar with these platforms. We also designed the chapters for implementing security and database in a project. This book delves into the use of Retrofit for handling HTTP requests and SQLite Room for storing data in an Android device. You will also be able to find a way of how to develop a robust, reactive project. Then, you will learn how to test a project using JUnit and Espresso for developing a less bug-prone and stable project.

Who this book is for

This book is designed for those developers who are new to Kotlin who wish to develop projects with Spring and Android. Spring for Android provides a functional REST client that supports marshaling objects from JSON. Developers depend on other language platforms, such as PHP and Python for REST API, but Spring comes with Java/Kotlin and a rich content that helps developers to use REST API with the maximum security. There are some dependencies in the application code and Spring removes these dependencies. Nowadays, Java is being replaced by Kotlin, which is lighter and requires fewer lines of code to finish the job.

What this book covers

Chapter 1, *About the Environment*, creates an environment for both the server side and client side. We will also look into the types of tools that will be needed for the project. We will also understand what we can create with a platform using Spring and Android.

Chapter 2, *Overview of Kotlin*, covers the basics of Kotlin and examines how to set up the environment and which tools or IDEs are available for Kotlin, including basic syntax and types. We will see the flow structures, including `if-else` statements, `for` loops, and `while` loops. We will also look into the object-oriented programming for Kotlin and cover classes, interfaces, objects, and so on. Functions will also be covered, along with parameters, constructors, and syntax. We will also explain null safety, reflection, and annotations, which are the core features of Kotlin.

`Chapter` 3, *Overview of Spring Framework*, covers the basics of Spring Framework and readers will learn how to configure Spring and beans. Dependency injection will be explained in this chapter, along with the architecture of Spring. Readers will learn about Spring MVC and Spring Boot, which are helpful for developing the application as quickly as possible. Spring Data modules will also be explained. We will also cover Spring Security, which provides authentication and other securities for the applications.

`Chapter` 4, *Spring Modules for Android*, covers the RestTemplate and Retrofit modules that are connected to the Android projects. An explanation of HTTP clients is provided. Objects to JSON marshaling will also be covered. We will learn how to start and set up the environment. HTTP request methods for both the RestTemplate and Retrofit modules, such as `POST`, `GET`, `UPDATE`, and `DELETE`, will also be covered, along with the common functionality of other Spring modules and Maven dependency management.

`Chapter` 5, *Securing Applications with Spring Security*, covers the requirements for Spring Security. We will learn how to register and configure security and authentication in the web server. We will also learn about the architecture of Spring Security and how to use it for clients. We will see the approach to securing an API for Android application and what the security flow will be. We will learn how to use Spring Security in relation to the REST API. Use of the basic authentication, OAuth2, implicit flow, and the authorization code flow will also be discussed. We will also learn how to connect with Android projects and use basic authentication.

`Chapter` 6, *Accessing the Database*, covers the existing Spring data modules. We will also cover JDBC, JPA, H2, MySQL for Spring, and SQLite Room for Android. We will also learn about the use of JPA to create REST API in Spring and fetch the APIs and handle the contents in Android.

`Chapter` 7, *Concurrency*, covers coroutines, including topics such as concurrency, parallelism, and thread pools. We will also learn about sequential operations and callback hell.

`Chapter` 8, *Reactive Programming*, covers reactive programming-related topics, including Spring Reactor and blocking. Readers will also learn about RxJava and RxAndroid in this chapter.

Chapter 9, *Creating an Application*, starts with the installation of the Android environment. We will then configure Spring on the web server and make a project design. We will then create UI, layout, and RESTful web services and retrieve JSON from the APIs. We will also learn to use Spring Boot and Spring Security for the app. We will then learn how to use Basic Auth to secure the data and give access to users. We will use secured REST API for an Android app and how to handle contents in Android. This application will be based on Kotlin, and we will be taking advantage of the features of Kotlin features, features including null safety, reflection, and annotation, in this application.

Chapter 10, *Testing an Application*, deals with Spring testing. This includes unit, integration, and UI testing, and their uses. We will get to know the test structure for the project, along with the testing tools such as JUnit and Espresso. Test cases for JUnit and JPA will also be discussed. We will learn how to write UI test cases for the Android application. We will also learn to execute these tests via Android Studio. We will also learn how to test UI using Espresso in Kotlin, and its uses in relation to Kotlin in the Android app. We will also look into concurrency and reactive programming in the application.

To get the most out of this book

A basic knowledge of Spring and Kotlin will be helpful, but not essential. MySQL Workbench for the database, Eclipse or IntelliJ IDEA for Spring, Android Studio for Android, and the Postman or Insomnia REST client will be required to run the code samples for this book.

Download the example code files

You can download the example code files for this book from your account at www.packt.com. If you purchased this book elsewhere, you can visit www.packt.com/support and register to have the files emailed directly to you.

You can download the code files by following these steps:

1. Log in or register at www.packt.com.
2. Select the **SUPPORT** tab.
3. Click on **Code Downloads & Errata**.
4. Enter the name of the book in the **Search** box and follow the onscreen instructions.

Once the file is downloaded, please make sure that you unzip or extract the folder using the latest version of:

- WinRAR/7-Zip for Windows
- Zipeg/iZip/UnRarX for Mac
- 7-Zip/PeaZip for Linux

The code bundle for the book is also hosted on GitHub at `https://github.com/PacktPublishing/Learn-Spring-for-Android-Application-Development/`. In case there's an update to the code, it will be updated on the existing GitHub repository.

We also have other code bundles from our rich catalog of books and videos available at `https://github.com/PacktPublishing/`. Check them out!

Download the color images

We also provide a PDF file that has color images of the screenshots/diagrams used in this book. You can download it here: `https://www.packtpub.com/sites/default/files/downloads/9781789349252_ColorImages.pdf`.

Conventions used

There are a number of text conventions used throughout this book.

`CodeInText`: Indicates code words in text, database table names, folder names, filenames, file extensions, pathnames, dummy URLs, user input, and Twitter handles. Here is an example: "The `switch { ... }` control flow element is replaced by `when { ... }`."

A block of code is set as follows:

```
fun test() {
    Bar.NAME
    Bar.printName()
}
```

When we wish to draw your attention to a particular part of a code block, the relevant lines or items are set in bold:

```
<!-- A bean example with singleton scope -->
<bean id = "..." class = "..." scope = "singleton"/>
<!-- You can remove the scope for the singleton -->
<bean id = "..." class = "..."/>
```

Any command-line input or output is written as follows:

```
$ mkdir css
$ cd css
```

Bold: Indicates a new term, an important word, or words that you see onscreen. For example, words in menus or dialog boxes appear in the text like this. Here is an example: "Select **System info** from the **Administration** panel."

Warnings or important notes appear like this.

Tips and tricks appear like this.

Get in touch

Feedback from our readers is always welcome.

General feedback: If you have questions about any aspect of this book, mention the book title in the subject of your message and email us at customercare@packtpub.com.

Errata: Although we have taken every care to ensure the accuracy of our content, mistakes do happen. If you have found a mistake in this book, we would be grateful if you would report this to us. Please visit www.packt.com/submit-errata, selecting your book, clicking on the Errata Submission Form link, and entering the details.

Piracy: If you come across any illegal copies of our works in any form on the internet, we would be grateful if you would provide us with the location address or website name. Please contact us at copyright@packt.com with a link to the material.

If you are interested in becoming an author: If there is a topic that you have expertise in, and you are interested in either writing or contributing to a book, please visit authors.packtpub.com.

Reviews

Please leave a review. Once you have read and used this book, why not leave a review on the site that you purchased it from? Potential readers can then see and use your unbiased opinion to make purchase decisions, we at Packt can understand what you think about our products, and our authors can see your feedback on their book. Thank you!

For more information about Packt, please visit `packt.com`.

About the Environment 1

The title of this book makes reference to two of the greatest stage names—Spring, ostensibly the best framework of Java, and Android, which has the greatest number of clients of any operating system. This book will help to you learn and develop a product-ready application on your own which will be lightweight, secure, powerful, and responsive.

Before start learning about the Spring and Android, we will demonstrate examples and code from Kotlin, as this programming language is very new to developers. These days, Kotlin is so popular that Google has declared it the official language of Android. Moreover, the Spring language also supports Kotlin. In this book, we will figure out how to make a robust, secure, and intense server dependent on Spring in the Kotlin language, and use the substance and utilize of this server in an Android application as a client.

In this chapter, you will learn how to set up the environment to create Spring and Android projects, including the required tools and applications. This will include going through steps with accompanying images for visualization purposes. The developers who know Java, at that point, will have some leeway since it is the common platform among Spring and Kotlin. We will demonstrate the code and models with Kotlin that runs on JVM. The Kotlin is designed by JetBrains. On the off-chance that you are new to Kotlin and Spring, being familiar with Java will allow you to write code in Kotlin with ease.

The following topics will be covered in this chapter:

- Setting up the environment
- Spring
- Java
- Kotlin
- Apache Tomcat
- Integrated development environments
- Android

Technical requirements

To run these frameworks, we need some tools and a specific operating system. Here is the list of these:

- **Operating system:** Linux and macOS are recommended for development because we can find all the required packages for these OSes and they are lighter than Windows.
- **IDE:** My recommended IDE is IntelliJ IDEA (Ultimate version). This is the best IDE for Java, but you have to purchase it to use it. You can also use Eclipse and Netbeans; only one of these is necessary to develop Spring applications. We will show all the projects in IntelliJ, but we will also learn the setup of the environments for Spring in both IntelliJ IDEA and Eclipse.

You can find all the examples from this chapter on CitHub: https://github.com/PacktPublishing/Learn-Spring-for-Android-Application-Development/.

Setting up the environment

An environment setup is one of the prime parts before developing an application. To the developers who are currently working with Spring, feel free to skip this part. This section is for new developers, who need to set up the foundation and the instruments to begin developing.

Here are the steps of how to set up the environment in the accompanying segments.

Spring

Spring is the most powerful Java application framework; it is currently the most popular in the enterprise world. It helps to create high-performing applications that have easily-testable and reusable code. This is open source and was written by Rod Johnson, first released under the Apache 2.0 license in June 2003.

To create and run Spring applications, you need some tools and language supports. You also need a server to test and run your project in your operating system. We will show you how to set up the environment for Spring.

The following software and tools are needed with the current version:

- Java (version 1.8)
- Kotlin (version 1.3)
- Apache Tomcat (version 9.0.11)
- IntelliJ Ultimate (version 2018.2.2) or Eclipse Photon
- Spring Framework Libraries (version 5.0.8.RELEASE)

Java

Java is available in two editions:

- Standard Edition (J2SE)
- Enterprise Edition (J2EE)

Here, we will opt for Standard Edition. Java is free to download and use for all operating systems.

You can download Java 10.0.2 from `http://www.oracle.com/technetwork/java/javase/downloads/index.html`.
Download for your operating system.

After installation, please check whether Java is installed. To check, open your Terminal and type `java --version`. If Java is installed successfully, you will see the following Java version:

```
● ● ●                    ⌂ sunnat629 — -bash — 80×24
Mohis-iMac:~ sunnat629$ java --version
java 10.0.2 2018-07-17
Java(TM) SE Runtime Environment 18.3 (build 10.0.2+13)
Java HotSpot(TM) 64-Bit Server VM 18.3 (build 10.0.2+13, mixed mode)
Mohis-iMac:~ sunnat629$ ▮
```

Check java version

Alternatively, you will see an error. If this occurs, try to install it again to resolve it.

Kotlin

Developed by JetBrains, Kotlin is an open source and statically-typed programming language. It runs on the **Java Virtual Machine** (**JVM**) and can be compiled to JavaScript source code or use the LLVM compiler infrastructure. Kotlin is easy to learn, especially for Java developers.

To use Kotlin, you don't need to download or set it up separately like Java. It comes with the IDEs. Kotlin is a built-in feature of Android Studio, IntelliJ Ultimate, or IntelliJ Community. To use Kotlin in Eclipse, you need to follow these steps:

1. Go to help -> **Eclipse Marketplace** from the Eclipse toolbar.
2. In the search box, write Kotlin, there you will find the **Kotlin** plugin.
3. Install it and you can write code in **Kotlin**:

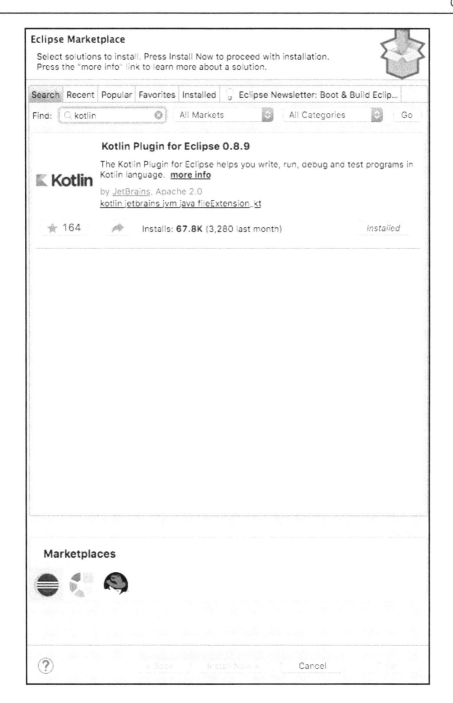

Eclipse Marketplace

We highly recommend using IntelliJ IDE to implement the latest version of Kotlin. The Eclipse plugin does not have the latest version of Kotlin.

Apache Tomcat

We require a steady, free, and open source web server that we can use to create and run Spring-Framework-based ventures. We will utilize Apache Tomcat, which is easy to understand for all developers of Java. You can also use Jetty or Undertow to develop in Spring.

Tomcat is an open source web server. This allows the utilization of Java Servlets and **JavaServer Pages** (**JSP**) for the Java server. The core segment of Tomcat is Catalina.

Apache Tomcat is a web server and not an application server.

You can download Tomcat 9.0.11 from `https://tomcat.apache.org/download-90.cgi`.

If you use Tomcat version 9, you have to use Java version 8 or later. According to the Apache Tomcat source, this version builds on Tomcat 8.0.x and 8.5.x, and implements the Servlet 4.0, JSP 2.3, EL 3.0, WebSocket 1.1, and JASPIC 1.1 specifications (the versions required by the Java EE 8 platform).

Let's see how to configure and verify the Tomcat server.

Configuring Tomcat

You can configure the Tomcat server in two ways—either using the Terminal or from the IDE. To set up the server, you have to download the Tomcat server's content from `https://tomcat.apache.org/download-90.cgi`.

Configuring Tomcat by these following steps:

1. Download a binary distribution of the core module from the link.
2. Extract the file. This creates a folder named `apache-tomcat-9.0.11` (version number can be changed).

3. To access it with ease, rename the folder `Tomcat` and move it to `/usr/local` (for Linux) or `/Library` (for macOS):

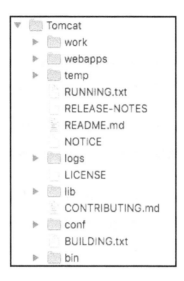

Project files

- For Linux, use these steps:

```
// If you have an older version of Tomcat, then remove it
before using the newer one
sudo rm -rf /usr/local/Tomcat        // To remove exist TomCat

sudo mv ~/Download/Tomcat /usr/local // To move TomCat from the
download directory to your desire direction
```

- For macOS, use these steps:

```
// If you have an older version of Tomcat, then remove it
before using the newer one
sudo rm -rf /Library/Tomcat            // To remove exist
TomCat

sudo mv Downloads/Tomcat /Library/    // To move TomCat from
the download directory to your desire direction
```

To check the current directory, type the following:

- **For Linux:** `cd /usr/local/Tomcat/`
- **For macOS:** `cd /Library/Tomcat/`

4. Type `ls` to see a list of this directory:

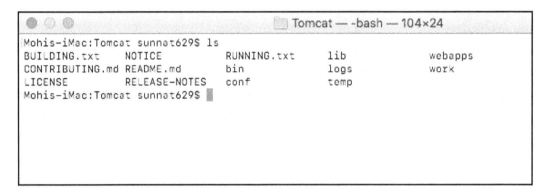

check tomcat files in terminal

5. Change the ownership of the `/usr/local/Tomcat` or `/Library/Tomcat` folder hierarchy:

- **For Linux:** `sudo chown -R <your_username> /usr/local/Tomcat/`
- **For macOS:** `sudo chown -R <your_username> /Library/Tomcat/`

6. Make all scripts executable:

- **For Linux:** `sudo chmod +x /usr/local/Tomcat/bin/*.sh`
- **For macOS:** `sudo chmod +x /Library/Tomcat/bin/*.sh`

7. To check the contents of Tomcat, use the following command:

- **For Linux:** `ls -al /usr/local/Tomcat/bin/*.sh`
- **For macOS:** `ls -al /Library/Tomcat/bin/*.sh`

8. You can see that every file is listed with `-rwxr-xr-x@`, where `-x` means executable. Executable demonstrates to us the authorization status to get to the files:

```
Mohis-iMac:Tomcat sunnat629$ sudo chown -R sunnat629 /Library/Tomcat/
Mohis-iMac:Tomcat sunnat629$ sudo chmod +x /Library/Tomcat/bin/*.sh
Mohis-iMac:Tomcat sunnat629$ ls -al /Library/Tomcat/bin/*.sh
-rwxr-xr-x@ 1 sunnat629   staff   23465 Aug 11 20:48 /Library/Tomcat/bin/catalina.sh
-rwxr-xr-x@ 1 sunnat629   staff    1997 Aug 11 20:48 /Library/Tomcat/bin/ciphers.sh
-rwxr-xr-x@ 1 sunnat629   staff    1922 Aug 11 20:48 /Library/Tomcat/bin/configtest.sh
-rwxr-xr-x@ 1 sunnat629   staff    8513 Aug 11 20:48 /Library/Tomcat/bin/daemon.sh
-rwxr-xr-x@ 1 sunnat629   staff    1965 Aug 11 20:48 /Library/Tomcat/bin/digest.sh
-rwxr-xr-x@ 1 sunnat629   staff    3124 Aug 11 20:48 /Library/Tomcat/bin/makebase.sh
-rwxr-xr-x@ 1 sunnat629   staff    3708 Aug 11 20:48 /Library/Tomcat/bin/setclasspath.sh
-rwxr-xr-x@ 1 sunnat629   staff    1902 Aug 11 20:48 /Library/Tomcat/bin/shutdown.sh
-rwxr-xr-x@ 1 sunnat629   staff    1904 Aug 11 20:48 /Library/Tomcat/bin/startup.sh
-rwxr-xr-x@ 1 sunnat629   staff    5483 Aug 11 20:48 /Library/Tomcat/bin/tool-wrapper.sh
-rwxr-xr-x@ 1 sunnat629   staff    1908 Aug 11 20:48 /Library/Tomcat/bin/version.sh
Mohis-iMac:Tomcat sunnat629$
```

Check the tomcat executable files in terminal

9. To start and stop, type the following:

- **For macOS**:

```
/Library/Tomcat/bin/startup.sh
/Library/Tomcat/bin/shutdown.sh
```

- **For Linux**:

```
/usr/local/Tomcat/bin/startup.sh
/usr/local/Tomcat/bin/shutdown.sh
```

10. To turn on and off the Tomcat server, use this command:

```
Mohis-iMac:~ sunnat629$ /Library/Tomcat/bin/startup.sh
Using CATALINA_BASE:   /Library/Tomcat
Using CATALINA_HOME:   /Library/Tomcat
Using CATALINA_TMPDIR: /Library/Tomcat/temp
Using JRE_HOME:        /Library/Java/JavaVirtualMachines/jdk1.8.0_181.jdk/Contents/Home
Using CLASSPATH:       /Library/Tomcat/bin/bootstrap.jar:/Library/Tomcat/bin/tomcat-juli.jar
Tomcat started.
Mohis-iMac:~ sunnat629$ /Library/Tomcat/bin/shutdown.sh
Using CATALINA_BASE:   /Library/Tomcat
Using CATALINA_HOME:   /Library/Tomcat
Using CATALINA_TMPDIR: /Library/Tomcat/temp
Using JRE_HOME:        /Library/Java/JavaVirtualMachines/jdk1.8.0_181.jdk/Contents/Home
Using CLASSPATH:       /Library/Tomcat/bin/bootstrap.jar:/Library/Tomcat/bin/tomcat-juli.jar
Mohis-iMac:~ sunnat629$
```

Verifying Tomcat

1. After starting the server, go to your browser and
   enter `http://localhost:8080`, which will show you the default page:

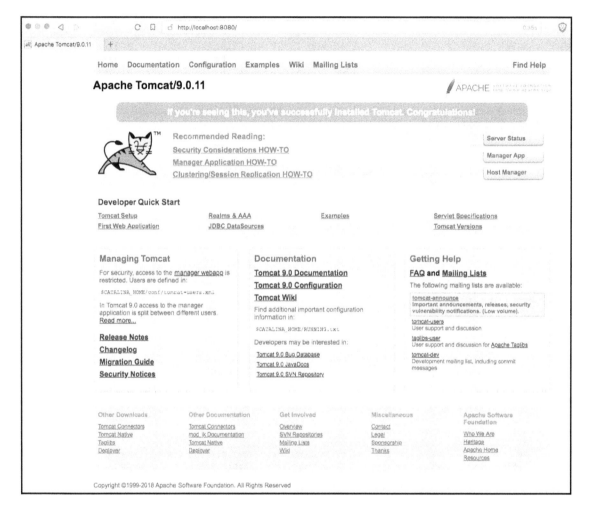

Default tomcat local hosting

This is how we can configure Tomcat from the Terminal.

Integrated development environment

When it comes to writing Java programs, you can use any text editor. However, we encourage you to use an **integrated development environment** (**IDE**) because they provide numerous features. IntelliJ IDEA, Eclipse, and NetBeans are the best of them. IntelliJ is a paid IDE, but you can use Eclipse or NetBeans, which are free.

We can use IDE to do the following:

- Manage Tomcat
- Develop apps and web apps where there is no need to remember the full name of the methods and signatures
- Highlight compile errors

In this book, we will work with Eclipse and IntelliJ IDEA.
You can download the Ultimate version, which has a 30-day free trial, from `https://www.jetbrains.com/idea/download/`.

To download the Eclipse, visit `http://www.eclipse.org/downloads/packages/`.

For Spring, you should download Eclipse IDE for the Java EE Developers version.

For both, once you start IDE, it will ask for a workspace. You can create a folder of your choice and give the path of that folder.

IntelliJ IDEA

IntelliJ IDEA is a Java coordinated development environment for developing computer software. It is developed by JetBrains and is accessible as an Apache 2 Licensed people group release and in a restrictive business version. Both can be utilized for business development.

 The latest version of Kotlin comes built-in with IntelliJ IDEA ultimate and IntelliJ IDEA community.

Eclipse

Eclipse is an incorporated development environment utilized in computer programming and is the most generally-utilized Java IDE. It contains a base workspace and an extensible module framework for tweaking the environment. Eclipse is composed generally in Java and its essential utility is for developing Java applications, yet it might likewise be utilized to develop applications in other programming dialects by means of modules, including Ada, ABAP, C, C++, C#, Clojure, COBOL, D, Erlang, Fortran, Groovy, Haskell, JavaScript, Julia, Lasso, Lua, NATURAL, Perl, PHP, Prolog, Python, R, Ruby (including the Ruby on Rails framework), Rust, Scala, and Scheme.

To use Kotlin in Eclipse, you will need to install the Kotlin plugin.

 Eclipse doesn't have the latest version of Kotlin.

After creating a project, you'll need to integrate the Tomcat server manually. However, if you use Spring Boot, you don't need to do anything because this comes with the Tomcat server.

Follow these steps to create a web project and implement the Tomcat server into your project:

1. Visit new > **New Dynamic Web Project**.
2. Provide a **Project Name**.
3. To integrate Tomcat, click **New Runtime**:

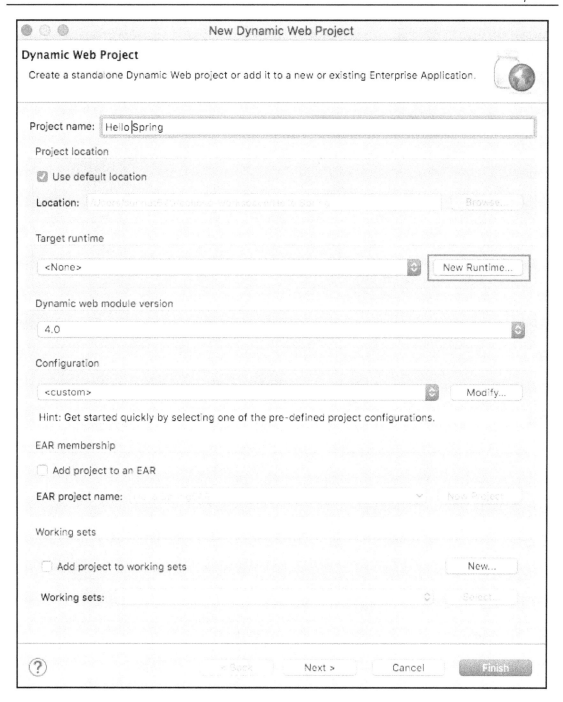

new project create

4. Download version 9+, select **Apache Tomcat v9.0**, and click **Finish**:

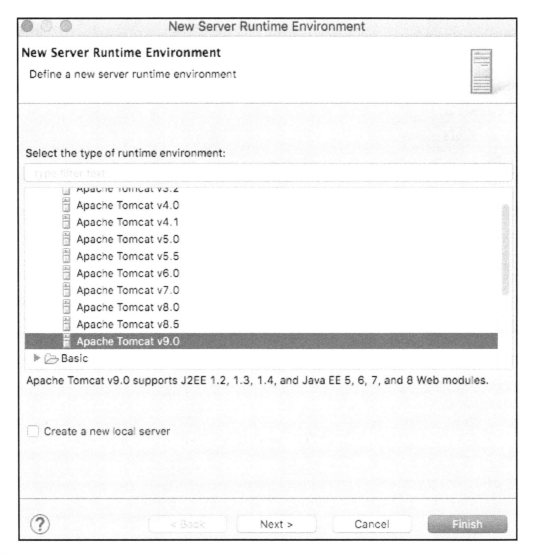

tomcat version selection

5. Select the latest **Dynamic web module version**.
6. Click **Finish**.

You will find these files after creating the project:

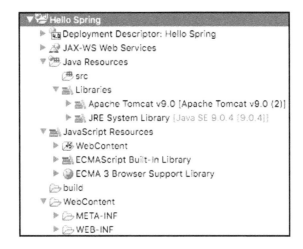

Project files

7. Go to the **Server** tab, which is in the bottom-left window:

project IDE interface

8. Select **Tomcat v9.0 Server at localhost**.
9. Hit the start button.
10. Once the server is started, verify it by visiting `http://localhost:8080` in a browser.
11. If everything is OK, you can start and stop the Tomcat server from here.

Android

Android is a mobile operating system developed by Google, in light of an altered form of the Linux kernel and other open source software and designed basically for touchscreen mobile gadgets, for example, cell phones and tablets. What's more, Google has additionally developed Android TV for televisions, Android Auto for vehicles, and Wear OS for wristwatches, each with a specific UI. Variations of Android are likewise utilized on IoT, advanced cameras, PCs, and various hardware. It was first developed by Android Inc., which Google purchased in 2005, and Android was disclosed in 2007. The first commercial Android devices were launched in September 2008. The current version has since experienced numerous significant discharges, with the present variant being 9 *Pie*, released in August 2018. The core Android source code is known as **Android Open Source Project** (**AOSP**) and is authorized under the Apache License.

In this book, we will figure out how to create a REST API, security, and a database in a Spring platform on a server. We will also learn how to make an Android application and retrieve data from the server, as well as its utilization as a client.

Android Studio is the main IDE among the different IDEs to make an Android application. This is the official IDE for Android. This is based on the IntelliJ IDEA of JetBrains, which is structured especially for Android application development.

To download Android Studio, visit `https://developer.android.com/studio/`. Here, you will find the latest version of Android Studio to download. The best part is that this includes JRE, the latest SDK, and other important plugins to develop.

Install the Android Studio application after downloading it. This tool is very easy to use.

 Don't forget to update and download the latest version of the SDK platform. To update or install a new SDK platform, go to the SDK Manager. In the SDK Platform, you can see the list of all the Android version's platforms.

If you have read and installed the environment without any hassle, you are ready to proceed with learning the information in this book. We have submitted the code on GitHub and shared the link in the *Technical requirements* section, so you can use that example code.

Summary

This chapter is mainly for those developers who are new to this platform. We have shown the setup procedure using some specific tools and applications and you can also develop your project with different tools and applications. We have looked at how to set up an environment to develop Spring and Android. You are now familiar with all the required tools and software. Now can you configure the Tomcat server in your OS and familiarize yourself with how to start and stop the server. You can decide which IDE you need for developing. We also learned the installation procedure for Android Studio without any hassle. Lastly, there are no criteria to use the latest version of the tools or software.

In the next chapter, we will explore Kotlin, which is a statically-typed programming language and the official language for Android.

Questions

1. Is the Spring Framework built on Java SE or Java EE?

2. What are the alternative IDEs of Eclipse and IntelliJ IDEA for developing Spring?

3. Is Tomcat a web server or an application server?

4. What are the alternatives of the Tomcat server for running Spring?

5. Is Android Studio the IDE to develop Android?

Further reading

- *Mastering Spring 5.0* (https://www.packtpub.com/application-development/mastering-spring-50) by Ranga Karanam

2
Overview of Kotlin

Kotlin is the official Android programming language and is statically typed. It is fully interoperable with Java, meaning that any Kotlin user can use the Java framework and mix commands from both Kotlin and Java without any limitations. In this chapter, we will cover the basics of Kotlin and will look at how to set up the environment. We will also look at its flow structures, such as `if { ... } else { ... }` expressions and loops. In addition to this, we will look into object-oriented programming for Kotlin, and we will cover classes, interfaces, and objects. Functions will also be covered, along with parameters, constructors, and syntax.

This chapter will cover the following topics:

- Setting up the environment
- Build tools
- Basic syntax
- Object-oriented programming
- Functions
- Control flow
- Ranges
- String templates
- Null safety, reflection, and annotations

Technical requirements

To run the code in this chapter, you will just need Android Studio and Git installed. This chapter won't require any additional installations.

You can find examples from this chapter on GitHub, at the following link: `https://github.com/PacktPublishing/Learn-Spring-for-Android-Application-Development/tree/master/app/src/main/java/com/packt/learn_spring_for_android_application_development/chapter2`.

Introduction to Kotlin

The 3.0 version of Android Studio was released by Google, and it promoted Kotlin as a first class language for Android development. Kotlin is developed by JetBrains in the same way as the Intellij IDEA platform, which is the basis of Android Studio. This language was released in February 2016, it was in development for five years before it was released. It's easy to gradually convert the code base of a project from Java to Kotlin, and a developer that is familiar with Java can learn Kotlin in a few weeks. Kotlin became popular before its release, because this language is full of features and is designed to interoperate with Java. The following diagram shows how Kotlin and Java code are compiled to the same bytecode:

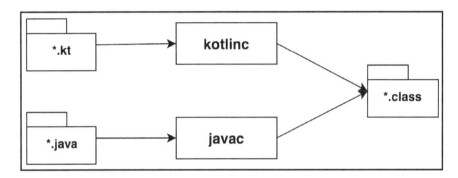

As you can see, part of our application can be written in Java and another part in Kotlin. The **kotlinc** compiler compiles Kotlin source code to the same bytecode as the **javac** compiler.

Setting up the environment

To get started with Android development, you will need to download and install the **Java Development Kit** (**JDK**) from `http://www.oracle.com/technetwork/java/javase/downloads/index.html`. You will also need to download and install the Android Studio **Integrated Development Environment** (**IDE**), from `https://developer.android.com/studio/`.

To create a new project, launch Android Studio and press **Start a new Android Studio project**. Then, you should type a project name and your unique application ID, as shown in the following screenshot:

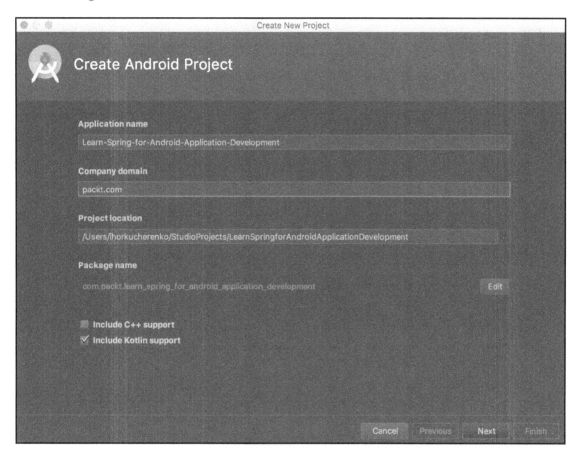

In the preceding screenshot, the **Application name** field is filled according to the name of this book, and the **Company domain** field is `packt.com`. Android Studio concatenates these two values and creates the **Package name** identifier that is equal to the application ID identifier. In our case, the application ID is as follows:

```
com.packt.learn_spring_for_android_application_development
```

Build tools

Android Studio is an official IDE for Android development, and it is based on the Intellij IDEA platform and uses the Gradle build tool system. A typical project structure looks as follows:

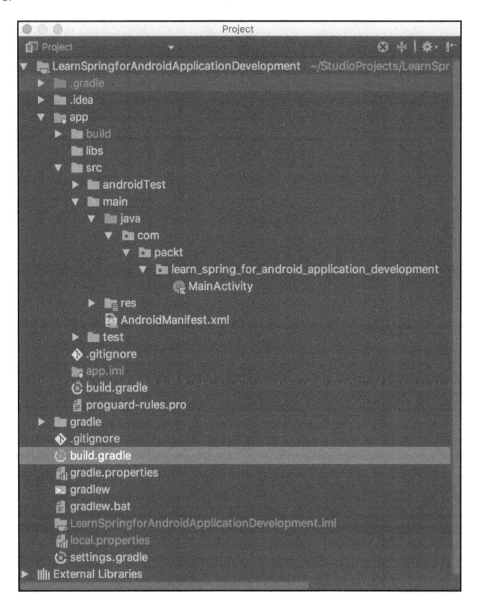

The `build.gradle` file contains the project configuration and manages the library dependencies. To add a dependency to the Spring for Android extension, we should add the following lines:

```
repositories {
    maven {
        url 'https://repo.spring.io/libs-milestone'
    }
}

dependencies {
    //.......
    implementation 'org.springframework.android:spring-android-rest-
template:2.0.0.M3'
}
```

Basic syntax

Syntax is a significant part of the programming language, defining a set of rules that must be applied to combinations of symbols. Otherwise, a program can't be compiled, and will be considered incorrect.

This section will describe the basic syntax of Kotlin, covering the following topics:

- Defining packages
- Defining variables
- Defining functions
- Defining classes

Defining packages

Packaging is a mechanism that allows us to group classes, interfaces, and sub-packages. In our case, a declaration of a package in a file may look as follows:

```
package com.packt.learn_spring_for_android_application_development
```

All citizens of the file belong to this package and must be located in the appropriate folder.

Defining variables

In Kotlin, we can define a read-only variable using the `val` keyword, and we can use the `var` keyword for mutable variables. In Kotlin, a **variable** can be defined as a first class citizen, meaning that we don't have to create a class of a function to hold variables. Instead, we can declare them directly in a file.

The following example shows how to define read-only and mutable variables:

```
val readOnly = 3
var mutable = 3
```

Defining functions

To define a function, we have to use the `fun` keyword; this also can be declared as a first class citizen. This means that a function can only be defined in a file. We will touch on functions in greater detail in the *Functions* section, but for now, let's look at a simple example that changes the value of the `mutable` variable:

```
fun changeMutable() {
    mutable = 4
}
```

In the previous snippet, we can see that the `changeMutable` function can be declared as a first class citizen in the same file as the `mutable` variable, or in any other place.

Defining classes

To define a class, we have to use the `class` keyword. All of the classes in Kotlin are final by default, and if we want to extend a class, we should declare it with the `open` keyword. A class that holds the `readOnly` and `mutable` variables, as well as the `changeMutable` method, may look like this:

```
class Foo {
    val readOnly = 3
    var mutable = 3

    fun changeMutable() {
        mutable = 4
    }
}
```

It is worth mentioning that a function that is a class member is called a **method**. In this way, we can explicitly specify that a function belongs to a class.

Object-oriented programming

Object-oriented programming is a model of programming language that is based on objects that can represent data. Kotlin supports object-oriented programming in the same way that Java does, but even more strictly. This is because Kotlin doesn't have primitive types and static members. Instead, it provides a `companion object`:

```
class Bar {
    companion object {
        const val NAME = "Igor"

        fun printName() = println(NAME)
    }
}
```

The `companion object` is an object that is created once, during class initialization. In Kotlin, we can refer to members of `companion object` in the same way as `static` in Java:

```
fun test() {
    Bar.NAME
    Bar.printName()
}
```

However, under the hood, the nested `Companion` class is created, and we actually use an instance of this class, as follows:

```
Bar.Companion.printName();
```

Moreover, Kotlin supports the following concepts, which make the type system stronger:

- Nullable types
- Read-only and mutable collections
- No raw type of collections

The last point means that we can't compile code, as shown in the following screenshot:

This message means that we have to provide a generic to specify a certain type of this collection.

From the object-oriented programming viewpoint, Kotlin supports the same features as Java. These include encapsulation, inheritance, polymorphism, composition, and delegation. It even provides a language-level construction that helps to implement these concepts.

Functions

To define a function in Kotlin, you have to use the `fun` keyword, as follows:

```
fun firstClass() {
    println("First class function")
}
```

The preceding snippet demonstrates that we can declare functions as first class citizens. We can also define functions as class members, as follows:

```
class A {
    fun classMember() {
        println("Class member")
    }
}
```

A `local` function is a function that is declared in another one, as follows:

```
fun outer() {
    fun local() {
        println("Local")
    }
    local()
}
```

In the preceding snippet, the `local` function is declared inside of the `outer` function. The `local` functions are only available in the scope of a function where they were declared. This approach can be useful if we want to avoid duplicate code inside of a function.

This section will cover the following topics:

- Functional programming
- Higher-order functions
- Lambdas

Functional programming

Kotlin particularly supports a functional style that allows us to operate functions in the same way as variables. This approach brings many features to Kotlin, as well as new ways to describe the flow of a program more concisely.

This subsection will cover the following topics:

- Declarative and imperative styles
- Extension functions
- Collections in Kotlin

Declarative and imperative styles

We used to use the imperative style of programming when writing object-oriented programming, but for functional programming, a more natural style is declarative. The declarative style assumes that our code describes what to do, instead of how to do it, as is usual with imperative programming.

The following example demonstrates how functional programming can be useful in certain cases. Let's imagine that we have a list of numbers, and we want to find the number that is greater than 4. In the imperative style, this may look as follows:

```
fun imperative() {
val numbers = listOf(1, 4, 6, 2, 9)
for (i in 0 until numbers.lastIndex) {
if (numbers[i] > 4) {
println(numbers)
        }
    }
}
```

As you can see, we have to use a lot of control flow statements to implement this simple logic. In the declarative style, it may look as follows:

```
fun declarative() {
    println(listOf(1, 4, 6, 2, 9).find { it > 4 })
}
```

The preceding snippet demonstrates the power of functional programming. This code looks concise and readable. The Kotlin standard library contains a lot of extension functions that extend the functionality of the list type.

Extension functions

The extension functions feature of Kotlin doesn't relate to functional programming, but it's better to explain this concept before moving forward. This feature allows us to extend a class or type with a new functionality, without using inheritance or any software design patterns, such as decorators.

 In object-oriented programming, a decorator is a design pattern that allows us to add a behavior to an object dynamically, without affecting other objects from the same class.

In the following code snippet, the `extension` function is added to the functionality of the A class:

```
fun A.extension() {
    println("Extension")
}
```

As you can see, it's easy to use this feature. We just need to specify a class name and declare a function name after the dot. Now, we can invoke the extension function as usual:

```
fun testExtension() {
    A().extension()
}
```

Collections in Kotlin

The `find` function that we've seen is contained in the `Collections.kt` file from the Kotlin standard library. This file contains a lot of extension functions that bring a functional approach to Kotlin and extend the functionality of Java's collection, in order to simplify work with them.

 A collections is a hierarchy of classes and interfaces that are used to store and manipulate a group of objects.

The most common functions from the `Collections.kt` file are as follows:

- `filter`: This returns a new list that contains elements that only matched a passed predicate
- `find`: This returns an element that matched a passed predicate
- `forEach`: This performs an approved action on each element
- `map`: This returns a new list, where each element was transformed according to the passed function

All of these are referred to as higher-order functions.

Higher-order functions

A function is called **higher-order** if it can take or return another function. The following diagrams show the different cases of higher-order functions.

The first diagram demonstrates a case in which the `f` function takes the lambda and returns a simple object:

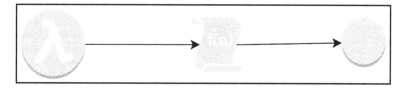

The second diagram demonstrates a case in which the f function takes an object and returns a function:

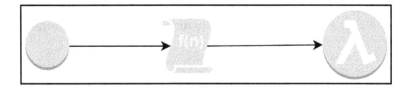

Finally, the third diagram demonstrates a case in which the f function takes and returns lambdas:

Let's look at the implementation of the firstOrNull function, as follows:

```
public inline fun <T> Iterable<T>.firstOrNull(predicate: (T) -> Boolean):
T? {
    for (element in this) if (predicate(element)) return element
    return null
}
```

The firstOrNull function is an extension that takes a lambda as a parameter and invokes it as the usual function—predicate(element). This returns the first element that matches the predicate in a collection; it is null if there is no other element that meets a condition

Lambdas

A lambda is a function that is not declared. This is useful when we need to invoke an action, but we don't need to define a function for it, because we will use it only once, or only in one scope. A lambda is an expression, meaning that it returns a value. All of the functions in Kotlin are expressions, and even a scope of a function doesn't contain the return keyword; it returns a value that is evaluated at the end.

The following lambda expression returns an object of the `Unit` type, implicitly:

```
{x: Int -> println(x)}
```

A declaration of the `Unit` object looks as follows:

```
public object Unit {
    override fun toString() = "kotlin.Unit"
}
```

A reference to a lambda can be saved to a variable:

```
val predicate: (Int) -> Unit = { println(it) }
```

We can use this variable to invoke the saved lambda:

```
predicate(3)
```

Control flow elements

In Kotlin, control flow elements are expressions. This is different from Java, in which they are statements. Statements just specify the flow of a program, and don't return any values. This section will cover the following control flow elements:

- The `if { ... } else { ... }` expression
- The `when { ... }` expression

The if { ... } else { ... } expression

In Kotlin, the `if` control flow element can be used in the same way as it is used in Java. The following example demonstrates the use of `if` as a usual statement:

```
fun ifStatement() {
    val a = 4
    if (a < 5) {
        println(a)
    }
}
```

If you are using the `if { ... } else { ... }` control flow element as an expression, you have to declare the `else` block, as follows:

```
fun ifExpression() {
    val a = 5
    val b = 4
    val max = if (a > b) a else b
}
```

The preceding example shows that `if { ... } else { ... }` returns a value.

The when { ... } expression

The `switch { ... }` control flow element is replaced by `when { ... }`. The `when { ... }` element of Kotlin is much more flexible than the `switch { ... }` element in Java, because it can take a value of any type. A branch only has to contain a matched condition.

The following example demonstrates how to use `when { ... }` as a statement:

```
fun whenStatement() {
    val x = 1
    when (x) {
        1 -> println("1")
        2 -> println("2")
        else -> {
            println("else")
        }
    }
}
```

The preceding code snippet contains the `else` branch, which is optional for a case with a statement. The `else` branch is invoked if all other branches don't have a matching condition. The `else` branch is mandatory if you use `when { ... }` as an expression and the compiler can't be sure that all possible cases are covered. The following expression returns `Unit`:

```
fun whenExpression(x: Int) = when (x) {
    1 -> println("1")
    2 -> println("2")
    else -> {
        println(x)
    }
}
```

As you can see, expressions provide a much more concise way to write code. To be sure that your branches cover all of the possible cases, you can use enums or sealed classes.

 An enum is a special kind of class that is used to define a set of constants. A sealed class is a parent class that has a restricted hierarchy of subclasses. All of the subclasses can only be defined in the same file as a sealed class.

In Kotlin, enums work similarly to how they work in Java. Sealed classes can be used if we want to restrict a class hierarchy. This works in the following way:

1. You should declare a class using the `sealed` keyword
2. All inheritors of your sealed class must be declared in the same file as their parent

The following example demonstrates how this can be implemented:

```
sealed class Method
class POST: Method()
class GET: Method()
```

With the `when { ... }` expression, we can use classes of the `Method` type, in the following way:

```
fun handleRequest(method: Method): String = when(method) {
    is POST -> TODO("Handle POST")
    is GET -> TODO("Handle GET")
}
```

As you can see, using this approach, we don't have to use the `else` branch.

Loops

A loop is a special statement that allows us to execute code repeatedly. Kotlin supports two types of loops, as follows:

- `for`
- `while`

for loops

A `for` loop statement allows us to iterate anything that contains the `iterate()` method. In turn, this provides an instance that matches the iterator interface through the principle of duck typing.

 The duck typing principle means that an interface is implemented implicitly if all of the methods that it contains are implemented.

The `Iterator` interface looks as follows:

```
public interface Iterator<E> {
    boolean hasNext();

    E next();
}
```

If we want to provide the `iterator()`, `hasNext()`, and `next()` methods as class members, we have to declare them with the `operator` keyword. The following example demonstrates a case of this:

```
class Numbers(val numbers: Array<Int>) {

    private var currentIndex: Int = 0

    operator fun iterator(): Numbers = Numbers(numbers)

    operator fun hasNext(): Boolean = currentIndex < numbers.lastIndex

    operator fun next(): Int = numbers[currentIndex ++]
}
```

The `Numbers` class can be used as follows:

```
fun testForLoop() {
    val numbers = Numbers(arrayOf(1, 2, 3))
    for (item in numbers) {
        //......
    }
}
```

An implementation using extension functions is as follows:

```
class Numbers(val numbers: Array<Int>)

private var currentIndex = 0
operator fun Numbers.iterator(): Numbers {
    currentIndex = 0
    return this
}
operator fun Numbers.hasNext(): Boolean = currentIndex < numbers.lastIndex
operator fun Numbers.next(): Int = numbers[currentIndex ++]
```

As you can see, extension functions allow us to make preexisting classes iterable.

while loops

The `while() { ... }` and `do { ... } while()` statements work in the same way that they work in Java. The `while` statement takes a condition, and `do` specifies a block of code that should be invoked while the condition is `true`. The following example demonstrates how `do { ... } while()` looks in Kotlin:

```
fun testWhileLoop() {
    val array = arrayOf(1, 2, 3)
    do {
        var index = 0
        println(array[index++])
    } while (index < array.lastIndex)
}
```

As you can see, the `do { ... } while` construction works in the same way that it does in other C-like languages.

Ranges

Kotlin supports the concept of ranges, which represent sequences of comparable types. To create a range, we can use the `rangeTo` methods that are implemented in classes, such as `Int`, in the following way:

```
public operator fun rangeTo(other: Byte): LongRange = LongRange(this,
other)

public operator fun rangeTo(other: Short): LongRange = LongRange(this,
other)

public operator fun rangeTo(other: Int): LongRange = LongRange(this, other)

public operator fun rangeTo(other: Long): LongRange = LongRange(this,
other)
```

So, we have two options for creating a range, as follows:

- Using the `rangeTo` method. This may look as follows—`1.rangeTo(100)`.
- Using the `..` operator. This may look as follows—`1..100`.

Ranges are extremely useful when we work with loops:

```
for (i in 0..100) {
    // .....
}
```

The `0..100` range is equal to the `1 <= i && i <= 100` statement.

If you want to exclude the last value, you can use the `until` function, in the following way:

```
0 until 100
```

We can also use the `step` function, as follows:

```
1..100 step 2
```

The preceding snippet represents a range like the following:

```
[1, 3, 5, 7, 9, 11, 13, 15, 17, 19, 21, 23, 25, 27, ... 99]
```

It's worth mentioning that ranges support a lot of `until` functions, such as `filter` or `map`:

```
(0..100)
        .filter { it > 50 }
        .map { it * 2 }
```

String templates

Kotlin supports one more powerful feature—string templates. Strings can contain code expressions that can be executed, and their results concatenated to the string. The syntax of the string template assumes that we use the $ symbol at the start of an expression. If the expression contains some evaluation, it has to be surrounded by curly braces.
The simplest use of string templates looks like the following:

```
var number = 1
val string = "number is $number"
```

A more advanced example that contains an expression is as follows:

```
val name = "Igor"
val lengthOfName = "length is ${name.length}"
```

As you can see, the string templates feature allows us to write code in a more concise way than the usual concatenation or the `StringBuilder` class.

Null safety, reflection, and annotations

Although we have already covered the most common topics that relate to a basic overview of Kotlin, there are a few more topics that have to be touched upon.

This section will introduce the following topics:

- Null safety
- Reflection
- Annotations

Null safety

Kotlin supports a more strict type system when compared to Java, and divides all types into two groups, as follows:

- Nullable
- No-nullable

One of the most popular causes of an app crashing is the `NullPointerException`. This happens as a result of accessing a member of a `null` reference. Kotlin provides a mechanism that helps us to avoid this error by using a type system.

The following diagram shows what the class hierarchy looks like in Kotlin:

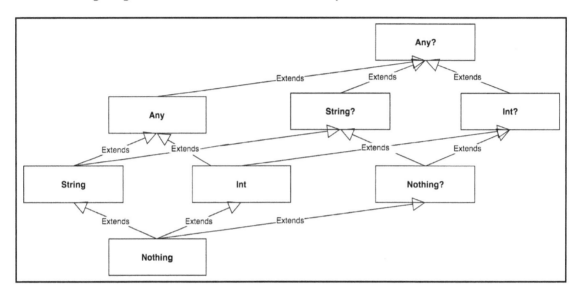

In Kotlin, nullable types have the same names as no-nullable types, except with the `?` character at the end.

If we use a no-nullable variable, we can't assign `null` to it, and the following code can't be compiled:

```
var name = "Igor"
name = null
```

To be able to compile this code, we have to explicitly declare the `name` variable as nullable:

```
var name: String? = "Igor"
name = null
```

After doing this, we cannot compile the following code:

```
name.length
```

To access members of nullable types, we have to use the ?. operator, like in the following example:

```
name?.length
```

One expression can contain the ?. operator as many times as needed:

```
name?.length?.compareTo(4)
```

If a member in this chain is `null`, the next member can't be invoked.

To provide an alternative program flow, if `null` is encountered, we can use the Elvis operator (?:). This can be used in the following way:

```
name?.length?.compareTo(4) ?: { println("name is null") }()
```

The preceding snippet demonstrates that the Elvis operator can be used if we want invoke a block of code if an expression returns as `null`.

Reflection

Reflection allows us to introspect code at runtime; this is implemented by a set of languages and standard library features. The Kotlin standard library contains the `kotlin.reflect` package that, in turn, contains classes that represent references to elements, such as classes, functions, or properties.

To obtain a reference to an element, we should use the :: operator. The following example demonstrates how to obtain a reference to a class:

```
val reference: KClass<String> = String::class
```

As you can see, references to classes are represented by the `KClass` class.

References to functions can also be passed to high-order functions. The following example shows how this may look:

```
fun isOdd(number: Int): Boolean = number % 2 == 0
val odds = listOf(1, 2, 3, 4, 5).filter(::isOdd)
```

A reference to a property is represented by the `KProperty` class, and this can be obtained in the following way:

```
val referenceToOddsPreperty = ::odds
```

`KProperty` is a class that represents a property of a class, and it can be used to retrieve metadata, such as names or types.

Annotations

Annotations are used to attach metadata to code. This is created using the `annotation` keyword:

```
public annotation class JvmStatic
```

In the most common cases, annotations are used by annotation processing tools to generate or modify code. Let's look at the following example:

```
class Example1 {
    companion object {
        fun companionClassMember() {}
    }
}
```

The Kotlin bytecode viewer shows the following code:

```
public final class Example1 {
   public static final Example1.Companion Companion = new
Example1.Companion((DefaultConstructorMarker)null);

   public static final class Companion {
      public final void companionClassMember() {
      }

      private Companion() {
      }

      // $FF: synthetic method
      public Companion(DefaultConstructorMarker $constructor_marker) {
         this();
      }
   }
}
```

As you can see, the `Example1` class contains the nested `Companion` class that contains the `companionClassMember` method. We can mark the `companionClassMember` method when the `@JvmStatic` annotation and the decompiled code to Java code version looks as follows:

```java
public final class Example1 {
    public static final Example1.Companion Companion = new
Example1.Companion((DefaultConstructorMarker)null);

    @JvmStatic
    public static final void companionClassMember() {
       Companion.companionClassMember();
    }

    public static final class Companion {
       @JvmStatic
       public final void companionClassMember() {}

       private Companion() {}

       // $FF: synthetic method
       public Companion(DefaultConstructorMarker $constructor_marker) {
          this();
       }
    }
}
```

The preceding snippet contains the additional static `companionClassMember` function in the `Example1` class that invokes the method of the `Companion` class. Using the `@JvmStatic` annotation, we tell the compiler to generate an additional method that can be used from the Java side.

Summary

In this chapter, we took a close look at the basic syntax of Kotlin. We also introduced and looked at examples of some features, such as lambdas, string templates, and ranges. Furthermore, you learned that control flow elements, such as `if { ... } else { ... }` and `when { ... }`, can be used as expressions that can make our code more concise and readable.

In the next chapter, we will take a look at an overview of the Spring framework.

Questions

1. What is Kotlin?
2. How does Kotlin support object-oriented programming?
3. How does Kotlin support functional programming?
4. How do we define variables in Kotlin?
5. How do we define functions in Kotlin?

Further reading

Kotlin Quick Start Guide (`https://www.packtpub.com/application-development/kotlin-quick-start-guide`) by Marko Devcic, published by Packt.

Overview of Spring Framework 3

Spring is a powerful, lightweight application framework that provides support for various frameworks, such as Hibernate, Struts, and JSF. Spring Framework is one of the top enterprise frameworks for building the most complex, secure and robust products. This framework is very popular for Java developers, as most developers working in Java Enterprise are working with Spring. Nowadays, Spring supports the Kotlin language, so it's becoming more popular with other language users. In this book, we'll develop Spring projects in Kotlin.

In this chapter, we'll learn about the basics of Spring Framework. We'll discuss the basics of Spring and also see some examples of how to implement them with Spring MVC and SpringBoot.

This chapter covers the following topics:

- Introduction to Spring
- The advantages of Spring
- Spring architecture
- Configuring beans
- Spring MVC
- SpringBoot

Technical requirements

In Chapter 1, *About the Environment*, we demonstrated how to set up the environment and what tools, software, and IDE are needed in order to develop Spring. To begin, visit https://start.spring.io/ and create your very first project. The following options will be available there:

- A Maven project or a Gradle project (we've chosen Maven)
- **Language**: Java or Kotlin (we've chosen Kotlin)
- **Spring Boot version**: 2.1.1 (SNAPSHOT)

Once you click on **Create**, you need to give information, such as **Group**, **Artifact**, **Name**, **Description**, **Package Name**, **Packaging**, and **Java Version**.

For this stage, there's no need to add any dependencies. Lastly, generate the project and import this into your IDE.

The source code with an example for this chapter is available on GitHub: https://github.com/PacktPublishing/Learn-Spring-for-Android-Application-Development/tree/master/Chapter03.

Introduction to Spring

Spring Framework is an open source framework. This is written in Java and developed by Pivotal software. Any Java-based enterprise applications can use the core of this framework. Spring Framework uses the **Plain Old Java Object** (**POJO**), which makes it easier to build an enterprise application.

A POJO is a Java object that isn't bound by any restriction other than those forced by the Java language specification. POJOs are used to increase the readability and reusability of an application.

Let's learn the advantages of Spring and architectures in the following sections.

The advantages of Spring

Spring Framework is a component-rich framework with the following advantages:

- Spring can be utilized for independent applications, web applications, and mobile applications.
- Spring has given an answer for free coupling through the creation of **dependency injection** (**DI**). This gives a configuration file (or annotation) to rearrange the conditions.
- It utilizes **aspect-oriented programming** (**AOP**) and makes it possible to isolate cross-cutting concerns, such as logging, reserving, and security.
- It limits boilerplate code. Spring has a huge amount of bundles and classes that decrease coding and keep away from the boilerplate code.
- It bolsters different frameworks, such as *ORM*, *Hibernate*, *Logging*, and *JEE*.
- Spring provides a simple and secure approach to dealing with login frameworks, forms, and so on.
- It handles *autowiring*, which can be a nightmare when building a complex web application.
- Spring Web Framework has a web *MVC framework*, which gives leverage, rather than a legacy web framework.
- It has the ability to take out the creation of singleton and factory classes.
- Spring Framework incorporates support for overseeing business objects and presenting their administrations to the introduction-level segments with the aim.
- It underpins both *XML* and *annotation* arrangements.

Spring Architecture

Spring Framework is a layered architecture that's composed of a few modules. All modules are based on the highest point of its core container. These modules give a developer everything they may require for use in the enterprise application development. In any case, developers allowed to pick the highlights they need and dispose of the modules that are of no use.

 Modular programming is a software design technique. This separates the functionality of a program into independent modules so that each contains one specific functionality.

Here's a diagram of the Spring architecture:

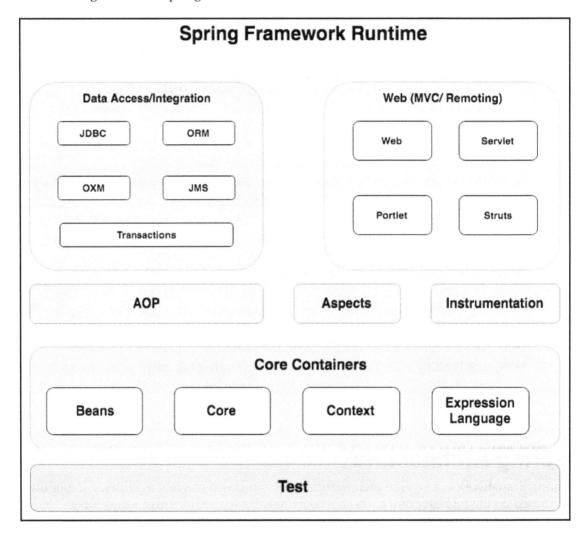

Spring Framework has about 20 modules, which are grouped into **Core Containers**, **Data Access/Integration**, **Web**, **AOP**, **Instrumentation**, and **Test**.

Let's learn about the components of Spring architecture.

Core containers

This section consists of **Core**, **Beans**, **Context**, and **Expression Language** modules.

The **Core** module is the center of the Spring architecture. This provides the implementation for features such as **Inversion of Control (IoC)** and **Dependency Injection (DI)**. IoC is one of the center containers of the Spring core. DI is another known name of IoC. This container is responsible for creating forms of objects and controls the complete life cycle. During this life cycle, the system creates a dependency and the container injects those dependencies while it creates the bean. This inverse process of DI is basically called IoC.

`org.springframework.beans` and `org.springframework.context` are the two containers of Spring Framework's IoC. IoC has a root interface, called `BeanFactory`, which is executed by the items and holds various bean definitions, each bean being recognized by a String name. A propelled configuration component is given by this interface to deal with items. `ApplicationContext` is a sub-interface of `BeanFactory`, which includes more application-layer settings. For example, it includes `WebApplicationContext` for use in web applications. `ApplicationContext` is in charge of instantiating, designing, and collecting the beans.

The tasks of object instantiation, configuration, and object assembling are specified for the container in the configuration metadata. There are three ways to configure the metadata: through XML, annotation, or code. This occurs in spite of the way that we work with Kotlin, so we'll write code and metadata in the Kotlin language.

Here's a simple diagram of the flow of the **Core** container:

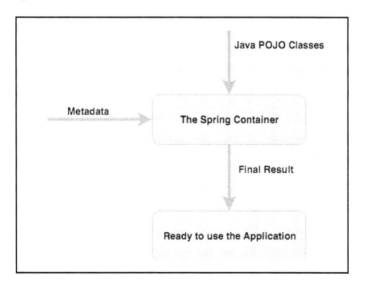

The core container is the process of getting the Spring project ready to see the output. With the help of **Java POJO Classes**, which are mainly the business objects and the **Metadata** (the configuration metadata), the **Spring Container** represents the ready application as output.

The **Bean** module represents a bean, which is an object that's assembled, managed, and instantiated by the IoC Container.

The **Context** module supports EJB, JMS, Basic Remoting, and so on. The `ApplicationContext` interface is the point of concurrence of the **Context** module.

The **Expression Language** module is normally used to execute logic, such as data query, sum, divide, and mod, in the application. To execute the logic, this module provides powerful expressions, as listed here:

Arithmetic	+, −, *, /, %, ^
Relational	<=, >=,<, >, ==, !=
Logical	&&, ||, !
Conditional	?, :
Regex	matches

Data Access/Integration

Data Access/Integration is responsible for setting and getting public or private data. It acts as a bridge between the data-access layer and the business layer. Here are some names of the data modules:

- **JDBC**: **Java Database Connectivity** (**JDBC**) helps the application to connect with the database.
- **Object-relational mapping**: This uses as an integration layer for **object-relational mapping** (**ORM**) APIs.
- **Object/XML mapping:** This uses as an integration layer for **object/XML mapping** (**OXM**) implementations.
- **Java Messaging Service**: This is used to provide support in Spring for the **Java Messaging Service** (**JMS**).
- **Transactions**: This is used to provide programmatic and declarative transaction management for the POJO classes.

Web

The **web** is the center of the Spring MVC framework. We can also integrate other technologies, such as JSF and Spring MVC. The web provides some basic integration features, such as login, logout, and uploading or downloading files. The web layer has four modules:

- **Web**: This provides the basic web-oriented integration features.
- **Web-servlet**: This module contains Spring's MVC implementation for the web application.
- **Web-struts**: This module provides an enhanced and improved framework to make web development easier.
- **Web-portlet**: This module is an identical representation of the web MVC framework.

Aspect-oriented programming

Aspect-oriented programming (**AOP**) is a key component of Spring Framework. This provides a new way to think about the structure of a program. AOP can be implemented in Java and Kotlin. It can be configured in the bean.

AOP splits program logic into certain parts, called **affirmed concerns**. In any enterprise application, there are cross-cutting concerns, which should to be separate from the basic business logic. Logging, transaction handling, performance observing, and security are known as cross-cutting concerns within the application.

Instrumentation

Instrumentation is the capacity to screen the level of an item's performance, to analyze mistakes, and to compose the trace information. Instrumentation is one of the key highlights of Spring Framework for auditing application performance. Spring supports instrumentation through AOP and logging.

Test

One of the essential parts of an enterprise software development is **testing**. JUnit or TestNG can be used to test Spring components. This supports the unit and integration testing of Spring elements.

Configuring beans

A bean is an object that can be instantiated and assembled by the Spring IoC. These beans are created by configuring Spring's metadata. Here's a set of properties that represent each bean definition:

- Class
- Name
- Scope
- Constructor-arg

Let's learn about the configured metadata's uses in the following sections.

Spring configuration metadata

The three major functions that provide configuration metadata with the Spring container are as follows:

- XML-based configuration
- Kotlin/Java-annotation-based configuration
- Kotlin/Java-code-based configuration

XML-based configuration

The XML-based configuration was introduced in Spring 2.0, and enhanced and extended in Spring 2.5 and 3.0. The main reason for moving to XML-based configuration files was to make Spring XML configuration easier. The *classic* <bean/> based approach is good, but also adds some more configuration that can become complex in the big project.

Let's take a look at an example of an XML-based setup document with various bean definitions, including the scope, initialization technique, and destruction strategy, and then we'll discuss this. Here's a piece of code for bean.xml:

```
<!-- A simple bean definition -->
<bean id = "..." class = "...">
<!-- collaborators and configuration-->
</bean>

<!-- A bean example with prototype scope -->
<bean id = "..." class = "..." scope = "prototype">
<!-- collaborators and configuration-->
```

```
</bean>

<!-- A bean definition with initialization function -->
<bean id = "..." class = "..." init-function = "...">
<!-- collaborators and configuration-->
</bean>

<!-- A bean definition with destruction function -->
<bean id = "..." class = "..." destroy-function = "...">
<!-- collaborators and configuration for this bean go here -->
</bean>
```

Bean scopes

We can choose to proclaim an extension for a bean while defining it. For instance, if we constrain Spring to deliver another bean occasion each time, we can initialize a prototype scope as an attribute of a bean. Additionally, if we need Spring to restore a similar bean example, we should proclaim the bean's scope attribute to be a *singleton*.

Spring Framework underpins the accompanying five scopes, three of which are accessible in the event that we utilize a web-aware `ApplicationContext`. Here are some common scopes:

- **Singleton**: Returns the same instance that's used by default every time
- **Prototype**: Returns a different instance every time
- **Request**: Defines an HTTP request that's visible in a single JSP page of the application
- **Session**: Defines an HTTP session that's visible in all JSP pages of the application

Singleton scope

The default scope is always a `singleton`. This is a bean definition of the Spring IoC container that returns a single object instance in every object initialization. Here's a piece of code for the singleton scope:

```
<!-- A bean example with singleton scope -->
<bean id = "..." class = "..." scope = "singleton"/>
<!-- You can remove the scope for the singleton -->
<bean id = "..." class = "..."/>
```

Let's take a look at an example of a `singleton` scope.

Create a Spring project in the IDE. To do this, create two `kt` files and a bean XML configuration file under the `src` folder.

Here's a piece of the code of `CreateUserGreeting.kt`:

```
class UserGreeting {
    private var globalGreeting: String? = "Sasuke Uchiha"

    fun setGreeting(greeting: String) {
        globalGreeting = greeting
    }

    fun getGreeting() {
        println("Welcome, " + globalGreeting!! + "!!")
    }
}
```

The content of `BeansScopeApplication.kt` is as follows:

```
fun main(args: Array<String>) {
    val context = ClassPathXmlApplicationContext("Beans.xml")
// first object
    val objectA = context.getBean("userGreeting", UserGreeting::class.java)

// set a value for greeting
    objectA.setGreeting("Naruto Uzumaki")

    objectA.getGreeting()

    val objectB = context.getBean("userGreeting", UserGreeting::class.java)
    objectB.getGreeting()
}
```

The following is the `beans.xml` configuration file:

```
<?xml version = "1.0" encoding = "UTF-8"?>
<beans xmlns = "http://www.springframework.org/schema/beans"
       xmlns:xsi = "http://www.w3.org/2001/XMLSchema-instance"
       xsi:schemaLocation = "http://www.springframework.org/schema/beans
    http://www.springframework.org/schema/beans/spring-beans-3.0.xsd">

    <bean id="userGreeting" class ="ktPackage.UserGreeting"
scope="singleton"/>

</beans>
```

After running this project, you will find this output:

```
Welcome, Naruto Uzumaki!!  <--- value of objectA
Welcome, Naruto Uzumaki!!  <--- value of objectB
```

Prototype scope

A `prototype` scope creates a new instance of a bean in every object initialization. This scope is preferred for the stateful beans. The container doesn't manage the full life cycle of this `prototype` scope. Here's a code piece for a `prototype` scope:

```
<!-- A bean example with prototype scope -->
<bean id = "..." class = "..." scope = "prototype"/>
```

Let's look at an example of a `prototype` scope.

Reuse the previous project and modify the bean XML configuration file, as follows:

```
<?xml version = "1.0" encoding = "UTF-8"?>
<beans xmlns = "http://www.springframework.org/schema/beans"
       xmlns:xsi = "http://www.w3.org/2001/XMLSchema-instance"
       xsi:schemaLocation = "http://www.springframework.org/schema/beans
   http://www.springframework.org/schema/beans/spring-beans-3.0.xsd">

    <bean id="userGreeting" class ="ktPackage.UserGreeting"
scope="prototype"/>

</beans>
```

Once we finish creating the source and bean configuration files, we can run the application. If there's no error, we'll get the following message:

```
Welcome, Naruto Uzumaki!!  <--- value of objectA
Welcome, Sasuke Uchiha!!  <--- value of objectB
```

Bean life cycle

Occasionally, we need to instate assets in the bean classes. For instance, this is possible by making database associations or approving third-party services at the season of initialization before any customer request. Spring Framework gives distinctive courses through which we can give post-introduction and pre-annihilation techniques in a Spring bean life cycle.

These are as follows:

- By actualizing the `InitializingBean` and `DisposableBean` interfaces—both of these interfaces announce a solitary strategy where we can instate/close assets in the bean. For `post-instatement`, we can execute the `InitializingBean` interface and provide an implementation of the `afterPropertiesSet()` function. For `pre-destroy`, we can actualize the `DisposableBean` interface and provide an implementation of the `destroy()` function. These functions are the callback techniques, which are similar to servlet audience implementations. This functionality is easy to utilize, yet it's not recommended, as it will cause tight coupling with Spring Framework in our bean implementations.
- Giving `init-function` and `destroy-function` quality values for the bean in the Spring bean configuration file. This is the prescribed functionality as there's no immediate dependency to Spring Framework. We can also make our own functions.

 Both the `post-init` and `pre-destroy` functions shouldn't have any contentions, but they can throw exceptions. We would also have to get the bean occasion from the Spring application setting for these functions.

Let's see an example of the life cycle of a bean. Here, we'll look at how to initialize and destroy the bean function. Reuse the previous project and modify the bean XML configuration file as follows:

```
<?xml version = "1.0" encoding = "UTF-8"?>
<beans xmlns = "http://www.springframework.org/schema/beans"
        xmlns:xsi = "http://www.w3.org/2001/XMLSchema-instance"
        xsi:schemaLocation = "http://www.springframework.org/schema/beans
    http://www.springframework.org/schema/beans/spring-beans-3.0.xsd">

    <bean id="userGreeting" class ="ktPackage.UserGreeting" init-function =
"afterPropertiesSet"
        destroy-function = "destroy"/>

</beans>
```

Now add two functions in `UserGreeting.kt`:

```
class UserGreeting {
    private var globalGreeting: String? = "Sasuke Uchiha"

    fun setGreeting(greeting: String) {
        globalGreeting = greeting
    }
```

```
    fun getGreeting() {
        println("Welcome, " + globalGreeting!! + "!!")
    }

    fun afterPropertiesSet(){
        println("Bean is going to start.")
    }

    fun destroy(){
        println("Bean is going to destroy.")
    }
}
```

Call `registerShutdownHook()` after the task is completed in the `main` function of the class:

```
fun main(args: Array<String>) {
    val context = ClassPathXmlApplicationContext("Beans.xml")
    val objectA = context.getBean("userGreeting", UserGreeting::class.java)

    objectA.setGreeting("Naruto Uzumaki")
    objectA.getGreeting()
    context.registerShutdownHook()
}
```

The output will be as follows:

```
Bean is going to start.
Welcome, Naruto Uzumaki!!
Bean is going to destroy.
```

Dependency injection

DI is a system where dependencies of an object are provided by outside containers. Spring DI helps in wiring a class with its dependencies and keeping them decoupled so that we can inject these dependencies at runtime.

The dependencies are characterized in the bean configuration. The two most common approaches to injecting objects utilizing XML are *constructor injection and setter injection,* which we'll take a look at now:Constructor injection

Constructor injections inject dependencies to the class constructor. Let's take a look at an example of the constructor injection. Reuse the previous project and modify the content of `beans.xml`:

```xml
<?xml version = "1.0" encoding = "UTF-8"?>
<beans xmlns="http://www.springframework.org/schema/beans"
       xmlns:xsi="http://www.w3.org/2001/XMLSchema-instance"
       xsi:schemaLocation="http://www.springframework.org/schema/beans
    http://www.springframework.org/schema/beans/spring-beans-3.0.xsd">
    <!--Constructor-based Dependency Injection Example Start-->
    <bean id="userGreeting" class="ktPackage.UserGreeting">
        <constructor-arg ref="userSurname" />
    </bean>
    <bean id="userSurname" class="ktPackage.UserSurname"/>
    <!--Constructor-based Dependency Injection Example End-->
</beans>
```

`constructor-arg` is utilized to inject dependencies. The reference of `constructor-arg` is an object of the constructor.

Create a class of `UserSurname.kt` to see the use of the constructor injection. We'll get the surname from this class, as follows:

```kotlin
class UserSurname {
    init {
        println("This is init of UserSurname")
    }

    fun getSurname(){
        println("This is the surname of user")
    }
}
```

Initialize `UserSurname` and add the `getUserSurname()` function to `CreateUserGreeting.kt`:

```kotlin
// added a constractor of UserSurname
class UserGreeting(surname: UserSurname) {
    private var userSurname: UserSurname ?= surname
    init {
        println("It is a constructor for user's surname")
    }

    private var globalGreeting: String? = "Sasuke Uchiha"

    fun setGreeting(greeting: String) {
        globalGreeting = greeting
```

```
    }

    fun getGreeting() {
        println("Welcome, " + globalGreeting!! + "!!")
    }

    fun afterPropertiesSet(){
        println("Bean is going to start.")
    }

    fun destroy(){
        println("Bean is going to destroy.")
    }

    fun getUserSurname(){
        userSurname?.getSurname()
    }
}
```

Now, if we call the `getUserSurname()` function in `BeansScopeApplication`, we'll get the `UserSurname` class.

Here's the sample code of `BeansScopeApplication.kt`:

```
fun main(args: Array<String>) {
    val context = ClassPathXmlApplicationContext("Beans.xml")
    val objectA = context.getBean("userGreeting", UserGreeting::class.java)
    objectA.getUserSurname()

//    objectA.setGreeting("Naruto Uzumaki")
//    objectA.getGreeting()
//    context.registerShutdownHook()
}
```

The output will be as follows:

```
This is init of UserSurname            <------ init from UserSurname.kt
It is a constructor for user's surname  <------ init from
UserGreeting.kt
This is the surname of user            <------ getUserSurname() of
UserGreeting.kt
```

Setter injection

In Spring, a setter injection is a kind of DI in which the framework injects the objects that are dependent on another object into the customer using a `setter` function. The container first calls the no contention constructor and then calls the setters. The setter-based injection will work regardless of whether a few dependencies have been injected utilizing the constructor.

Let's see an example of the `setter` injection. Here, reuse the previous project and modify the content of `beans.xml`:

```xml
<?xml version = "1.0" encoding = "UTF-8"?>
<beans xmlns="http://www.springframework.org/schema/beans"
       xmlns:xsi="http://www.w3.org/2001/XMLSchema-instance"
       xsi:schemaLocation="http://www.springframework.org/schema/beans
    http://www.springframework.org/schema/beans/spring-beans-3.0.xsd">
<!--Setter Injection Example Start-->
    <bean id="userGreeting" class="ktPackage.UserGreeting">
        <property name="userSurnameClass" ref="userSurname"/>
    </bean>
    <bean id="userSurname" class="ktPackage.UserSurname"/>
    <!--Setter Injection Example End-->
</beans>
```

After modifying the bean file, add a setter and getter of `UserSurname` to the `CreateUserGreeting.kt` file:

```kotlin
class UserGreeting {
    private var userSurname: UserSurname? = null

    fun setUserSurnameClass(surname: UserSurname) {
        userSurname = surname
    }

    fun getUserSurnameClass(): UserSurname? {
        return userSurname
    }

    private var globalGreeting: String? = "Sasuke Uchiha"

    fun setGreeting(greeting: String) {
        globalGreeting = greeting
    }

    fun getGreeting() {
        println("Welcome, " + globalGreeting!! + "!!")
    }
```

```
fun afterPropertiesSet() {
    println("Bean is going to start.")
}

fun destroy() {
    println("Bean is going to destroy.")
}

fun getUserSurname() {
    userSurname?.getSurname()
}
}
```

The result will be as follows:

```
This is init of UserSurname
Setting User Surname in UserGreeting
This is the surname of user
```

An example of an empty string or null value is as follows:

```
<bean id="app" class="App">
<property name="name" value=""/>
</bean>
<!-- If we need to pass an empty string or null as a value -->
<bean id="app" class="App">
<property name="name"><null/></property>
</bean>
```

Auto-wiring beans

We've been utilizing <constructor-arg> and <property> to inject dependencies. Instead, we can autowire the dependencies, which helps to diminish the measure of configurations that should be composed.

There are diverse choices for auto-wiring that manage the Spring container on the most proficient method to infuse the conditions. A bean has no auto-wiring by default.

Here are the two major types of auto-wiring:

- byName: To autowire a bean, the Spring container chooses the bean by the class name. Here's an example of the use of byName:

```
<bean id="app" class="App" autowire="byName"/>
```

- `byType`: To autowire a bean, the Spring container chooses the bean according to the class type. Here is an example of the use of `byType`:

```
<bean id="app" class="App" autowire="byType"/>
```

If there are multiple implementing classes for a `Service` interface, you'll find two types of scenario.

In the case of `services` (a cluster of `services` execute the `Service` interface), bean won't allow us to execute the `autowire` of `byName`. If there isn't an occurrence of `byName`, it will inject all the executing objects.

In the case of `mainService` (an object actualizes the `Service` interface), for the `byType`/constructor, allocate the autowire-applicant attribute in the `<bean>` tag of all executing classes as `false`, keeping one of them as `true`.

Here's an example of how to handle multiple implementing classes for a `Service` interface in `beans.xml`:

```xml
<?xml version = "1.0" encoding = "UTF-8"?>
<beans xmlns="http://www.springframework.org/schema/beans"
       xmlns:xsi="http://www.w3.org/2001/XMLSchema-instance"
       xsi:schemaLocation="http://www.springframework.org/schema/beans
    http://www.springframework.org/schema/beans/spring-beans-3.0.xsd">

    <!--Beans Auto-Wiring Example Start-->
    <bean id="userGreeting" class="ktPackage.UserGreeting"
autowire="byType"/>
    <bean id="userSurname" class="ktPackage.UserSurname" autowire-
candidate="true"/>
    <bean id="xxxxx" class="ktPackage.XXXX" autowire-candidate="false"/>
<!--demoClass-->
    <bean id="yyyyy" class="ktPackage.YYYY" autowire-candidate="false"/>
<!--demoClass-->
    <!--SBeans Auto-Wiring Example End-->
</beans>
```

For `byName`, either rename `mainService` in the application class to one of the actualizing classes (that is, `userSurname`), or rename the bean `id` of that class in the XML configuration to `mainService`:

```xml
<?xml version = "1.0" encoding = "UTF-8"?>
<beans xmlns="http://www.springframework.org/schema/beans"
       xmlns:xsi="http://www.w3.org/2001/XMLSchema-instance"
       xsi:schemaLocation="http://www.springframework.org/schema/beans
    http://www.springframework.org/schema/beans/spring-beans-3.0.xsd">
```

```
    <!--Beans Auto-Wiring Example Start-->
    <bean id="userGreeting" class="ktPackage.UserGreeting"
autowire="byName"/>
    <bean id="mainService" class="ktPackage.UserSurname"/>
    <bean id="xxxxx" class="ktPackage.XXXX"/> <!--demoClass-->
    <bean id="yyyyy" class="ktPackage.YYYY"/> <!--demoClass-->
    <!--SBeans Auto-Wiring Example End-->
</beans>
```

Here are some limitations of auto-wiring:

- **Overriding possibility**: To specify the dependencies, you can use the `<constructor-arg>` and `<property>` settings, which will override auto-wiring.
- **Primitive data types**: Primitives, strings, and classes can't be called.
- **Confusing nature**: Auto-wiring is less accurate than unequivocal wiring.

Annotation-based configuration

Annotations are the new technology of DI. This started being used with Spring 2.5. There was no need for any XML files to maintain the configuration. To use the annotation-based configuration, you need to create a component class in which you can implement bean configurations. Annotations are unique names or markers on the pertinent class, function, or field revelation.

Presumably, you're familiar with `@Override`, which is an annotation that tells the compiler that this annotation is an abrogated function.

In the preceding annotations, the conduct of Spring Framework was to a great extent controlled through XML configuration. Today, the utilization of annotations gives us many advantages through the way we design the practices of Spring Framework.

Here's a piece of `bean.xml` code:

```
<?xml version = "1.0" encoding = "UTF-8"?>
<beans xmlns="http://www.springframework.org/schema/beans"
       xmlns:xsi="http://www.w3.org/2001/XMLSchema-instance"
       xmlns:context="http://www.springframework.org/schema/context"
       xsi:schemaLocation="http://www.springframework.org/schema/beans
    http://www.springframework.org/schema/beans/spring-beans-3.0.xsd
    http://www.springframework.org/schema/context
    http://www.springframework.org/schema/context/spring-context.xsd">

    <context:annotation-config/>
```

```
    <!-- bean definitions will be from here -->
</beans>
```

If we use `<context:annotation-config/>` in `bean.xml`, we can begin annotating the code to wire values into properties, functions, or constructors. We'll learn about a few essential annotations in the following sections.

The @Required annotation

The `@Required` annotation is applied to bean property-setter functions. The bean property must be populated in the XML configuration file at configuration-time. This annotation essentially shows that the setter function must be arranged to be dependency-injected with a value at configuration-time.

Add a user model and the `Main` class with a `bean.xml` configuration file.

The content of the `bean.xml` configuration file is as follows:

```
<?xml version = "1.0" encoding = "UTF-8"?>
<beans xmlns="http://www.springframework.org/schema/beans"
       xmlns:xsi="http://www.w3.org/2001/XMLSchema-instance"
       xmlns:context="http://www.springframework.org/schema/context"
       xsi:schemaLocation="http://www.springframework.org/schema/beans
    http://www.springframework.org/schema/beans/spring-beans-3.0.xsd
    http://www.springframework.org/schema/context
    http://www.springframework.org/schema/context/spring-context.xsd">

    <context:annotation-config/>  <!--after this tag, we have to write the
beans-->

    <bean id="users" class="requiredAnnotation.UsersForReq">
        <property name="name" value="Naruto Uzumaki"/>
        <property name="village" value="Konohagakure"/>
    </bean>
</beans>
```

The content of `UsersForReq.kt` is as follows:

```
class Users{
    private var village: String? = null
    private var name: String? = null

    @Required
    fun setVillage(village: String?) {
        this.village = village
    }
```

```kotlin
    fun getVillage(): String? {
        return village
    }

    @Required
    fun setName(name: String) {
        this.name = name
    }

    fun getName(): String? {
        return name
    }
}
```

The content of `AnnotationBasedReqApp.kt` is as follows:

```kotlin
fun main(args: Array<String>) {
    val context =
ClassPathXmlApplicationContext("requiredAnnotation/beans_for_req.xml")
    val users = context.getBean("users") as UsersForReq

    println("Name: "+users.getName())
    println("Village: "+users.getVillage())
}
```

The output of this project will be as follows:

```
Name: Naruto Uzumaki
Village: Konohagakure
```

The @Autowired annotation

The `@Autowired` annotation helps us to connect constructors, fields, and setter functions. This annotation injects object dependencies.

Here's the sample code of how to use `@Autowired` on a property:

```kotlin
class User(val name: String,
          val id: String)

class Users{
    @Autowired
    val user:User ?= null
}
```

Here's the sample code of how to use `@Autowired` on a property:

```
class UsersForAutowired{
    private lateinit var userDetails: UserDetails

    @Autowired
    fun setUserDetails(userDetails: UserDetails){
        this.userDetails = userDetails
    }

    fun getUserDetails(){
        this.userDetails.getDetails()
    }
}
```

The content of `UserDetails.kt` is as follows:

```
class UserDetails{
    init {
        println("This class has all the details of the user")
    }

    fun getDetails(){
        println("Name: Naruto Uzumaki")
        println("Village: Konohagakure")
    }
}
```

The output of the project will be as follows:

```
This class has all the details of the user
Name: Naruto Uzumaki
Village. Konohagakure
```

We can utilize the `@Autowired` annotation on properties to dispose of the setter functions. When we pass values of autowired properties utilizing `<property>`, Spring will allocate those properties with the passed values or references. So with the utilization of `@Autowired` on properties, the `UsersForAutowired.kt` file will become as follows:

```
class UsersForAutowired{
    init {
        println("UsersForAutowired constructor." )
    }

    @Autowired
    private lateinit var userDetails: UserDetails

    fun getUserDetails(){
```

```
        this.userDetails.getDetails()
    }
}
```

The result will be as follows:

```
UsersForAutowired constructor.
This class has all the details of the user
Name: Naruto Uzumaki
Village: Konohagakure
```

You can also apply `@Autowired` to constructors. An `@Autowired` constructor annotation demonstrates that the constructor should be autowired when making the bean. This should be the case regardless of whether any `<constructor-arg>` components are utilized when configuring the bean in the XML file.

Here is the modified content of `UsersForAutowired.kt`:

```
class UsersForAutowired @Autowired constructor(private var userDetails:
UserDetails) {
    init {
        println("UsersForAutowired constructor.")
    }

    fun getUserDetails() {
        this.userDetails.getDetails()
    }
}
```

The result will be as follows:

```
This class has all the details of the user
UsersForAutowired constructor.
Name: Naruto Uzumaki
Village: Konohagakure
```

The @Qualifier annotation

You might create an excess of one bean of a similar type and need to wire just a single one of them with the property. In such cases, you can utilize the `@Qualifier` annotation alongside `@Autowired` to evacuate the disarray by determining which correct bean will be wired. In this section, we'll look at a precedent to demonstrate the utilization of a `@Qualifier` annotation.

The content of the `bean.xml` configuration file is as follows:

```xml
<?xml version = "1.0" encoding = "UTF-8"?>
<beans xmlns="http://www.springframework.org/schema/beans"
       xmlns:xsi="http://www.w3.org/2001/XMLSchema-instance"
       xmlns:context="http://www.springframework.org/schema/context"
       xsi:schemaLocation="http://www.springframework.org/schema/beans
   http://www.springframework.org/schema/beans/spring-beans-3.0.xsd
   http://www.springframework.org/schema/context
   http://www.springframework.org/schema/context/spring-context.xsd">

    <context:annotation-config/>  <!--after this tag, you have to write the
beans-->

    <!-- Definition for Fighters bean without constructor-arg  -->
    <bean id="fighters" class="qualifierAnnotation.Fighters"/>

    <!--fighter 1-->
    <bean id="fighter1" class="qualifierAnnotation.UsersForQualifier">
        <property name="name" value="Naruto Uzumaki"/>
        <property name="village" value="Konohagakure"/>
    </bean>

  <!--fighter 2-->
    <bean id="fighter2" class="qualifierAnnotation.UsersForQualifier">
        <property name="name" value="Gaara"/>
        <property name="village" value="Sunagakure"/>
    </bean>
</beans>
```

Here's the content of `AnnotationBasedQualifierApp.kt`:

```kotlin
fun main(args: Array<String>) {
    val context =
ClassPathXmlApplicationContext("qualifierAnnotation/beans_for_qualifier.xml
")
    val fighters = context.getBean("fighters") as Fighters
    fighters.getName()
    fighters.getVillage()
}
```

Now, add another class. Here's the content for `UsersForQualifier.kt`:

```kotlin
class UsersForQualifier{
    private var village: String? = null
    private var name: String? = null

    fun setVillage(village: String?) {
```

```
        this.village = village
    }

    fun getVillage(): String? {
        return village
    }

    fun setName(name: String) {
        this.name = name
    }

    fun getName(): String? {
        return name
    }
}
```

Finally, add the `Fighters.kt` class. Here's the content of this class:

```
class Fighters {
    @Autowired
    @Qualifier("fighter1")
    lateinit var usersForQualifier: UsersForQualifier

    init {
        println("Fighters constructor.")
    }

    fun getName() {
        println("Name: " + usersForQualifier.getName())
    }

    fun getVillage() {
        println("Village: " + usersForQualifier.getVillage())
    }
}
```

If you run the output, it will be as follows:

```
Fighters constructor.
Name: Naruto Uzumaki
Village: Konohagakure
```

Modify the qualifier value like so:

```
@Qualifier("fighter2")
```

It will create the following output:

```
Fighters constructor.
Name: Gaara
Village: Sunagakure
```

Code-based configuration

We saw how to design Spring beans by utilizing the XML configuration file. If you are used to XML configuration, you can ignore this topic.

The code-based configuration alternative empowers you to compose the majority of your Spring configuration without XML.

The @Configuration and @Bean annotations

The use of the @Configuration annotation on a class, implies that this class will be utilized by the Spring IoC container and will be considered a source of bean definitions.

The use of a @Bean annotation on a function means the function will return an object that's enrolled as a bean in the Spring application context.

Here's a sample code of @Configuration and @Bean:

```
@Configuration
open class CodeBasedConfiguration{
  @Bean
  open fun mainApp(): MainApp{
      return MainApp()
  }
}
```

The previous code will be equivalent to the following XML configuration:

```
<beans>
  <bean id = "mainApp" class = "MainApp"/>
</beans>
```

Here, the function name is commented on with the @Bean annotation, which creates and returns the bean definition. Your configuration class can have a presentation for in excess of one @Bean.

The content of GreetingConfigurationConfBean.kt is as follows:

```
@Configuration
open class GreetingConfigurationConfBean{
  @Bean
  open fun greeting(): GreetingConfBean{
      return GreetingConfBean()
  }
}
```

The content of GreetingConfBean.kt is as follows:

```
class GreetingConfBean{
    private var users: String? = null
    fun setUsers(users: String) {
        this.users = users
    }
    fun getUsers() {
        println("Welcome, $users!!")
    }
}
```

The content of MainAppConfBean.kt is as follows:

```
fun main(args: Array<String>) {
    val applicationContext =
AnnotationConfigApplicationContext(GreetingConfigurationConfBean::class.java)

    val greeting = applicationContext.getBean(GreetingConfBean::class.java)
    greeting.setUsers("Naruto Uzumaki")
    greeting.getUsers()
}
```

The result will be as follows:

```
Welcome, Naruto Uzumaki!!
```

Dependency injection bean

Annotate the `@Bean` annotation to inject dependencies. Here's the content of `GreetingConfigurationDIBean.kt`:

```
@Configuration
open class GreetingConfigurationDIBean{
    @Bean
    open fun greeting(): GreetingDIBean {
        return GreetingDIBean(getUserDetails())
    }

    @Bean
    open fun getUserDetails(): GreetingDetailsDIBean {
        return GreetingDetailsDIBean()
    }
}
```

When two `@Beans` are dependent on each other, the dependency is as simplistic as having one bean method call another.

The content of `GreetingDIBean.kt` is as follows:

```
class GreetingDIBean (private val userDetails: GreetingDetailsDIBean){
    init {
        println("Inside DependenciesInjectBean.GreetingDIBean
constructor.")
    }

    fun getGreeting() {
        userDetails.getGreetingDetails()
    }
}
```

The content of `GreetingDetailsDIBean.kt` is as follows:

```
class GreetingDetailsDIBean{
    init {
        println("This class has all the details of the user")
    }

    fun getGreetingDetails(){
        println("Welcome, Naruto Uzumaki!!")
    }
}
```

The content of `MainApp.kt` is as follows:

```kotlin
fun main(args: Array<String>) {
    val applicationContext =
AnnotationConfigApplicationContext(GreetingConfigurationDIBean::class.java)

    val greeting = applicationContext.getBean(GreetingDIBean::class.java)
    greeting.getGreeting()
}
```

The result will be the following:

```
This class has all the details of the user
Inside Greeting constructor.
Welcome, Naruto Uzumaki!!
```

The @Import annotation

Spring's `@Import` annotation offers functions such as `<import/>` an element in Spring XML. By utilizing the `@Import` annotation, you can import at least one `@Configuration` class. It can also import classes that contain no less than one `@Bean` function.

The content of `Boo.kt` is as follows:

```kotlin
class Foo{
    init {
        println("This is class Foo")
    }
}
class Boo{
    init {
        println("This is class Boo")
    }
}
```

The content of `ConfigBoo.kt` is as follows:

```kotlin
@Configuration
class ConfigFoo {
    @Bean
    fun foo(): Foo{
        return Foo()
    }
}

@Configuration
@Import(ConfigFoo::class)
```

```
class ConfigBoo {
    @Bean
    fun foo(): Boo {
        return Boo()
    }
}
```

You don't need to specify both `ConfigFoo.class` and `ConfigBoo.class` when instantiating the context, so the following code isn't required when you initialize `AnnotationConfigApplicationContext`:

```
val applicationContext =
AnnotationConfigApplicationContext(ConfigBoo::class.java,
ConfigFoo::class.java)
```

As bean definitions of `ConfigFoo` are already loaded by using the `@Import` annotation with the `ConfigBoo` bean, only `ConfigBoo` needs to be explicitly specified:

```
val applicationContext =
AnnotationConfigApplicationContext(ConfigBoo::class.java)
```

Here's the modified complete code of the `main` function of `MainAppImport.kt`:

```
fun main(args: Array<String>) {
    val applicationContext =
AnnotationConfigApplicationContext(ConfigBoo::class.java)

    //both beans Boo and Foo will be available...
    val boo: Boo = applicationContext.getBean(Boo::class.java)
    val foo: Foo = applicationContext.getBean(Foo::class.java)
}
```

The result will be as follows:

```
This is class Boo
This is class Foo
```

Life cycle callbacks

A `@Bean` annotation supports determining discretionary introductions and obliteration callback functions. If you noticed `beans.xml` in the `XMLBasedSpringConfiguration` project, you can find the `init-method` and `destroy-method` attributes. Here's an example of how to initialize the `init-method` and `destroy-method` attributes:

```
<bean id="userGreeting" class="ktPackage.UserGreeting" init-
method="afterPropertiesSet" destroy-method="destroy"/>
```

Here's the modified code of `MainAppLifeCall.kt`:

```
fun main(args: Array<String>) {
    val applicationContext =
AnnotationConfigApplicationContext(ConfigFoo::class.java)

    val foo: Foo = applicationContext.getBean(Foo::class.java)
    applicationContext.registerShutdownHook()
}
```

The modified code of `Foo.kt` is as follows:

```
class Foo{
    fun init(){
        println("Foo is initializing...")
    }

    fun destroy(){
        println("Foo is destroying...")
    }
}
```

Now create a configuration class for `Foo`. The modified code of `ConfigFoo.kt` is as follows:

```
@Configuration
open class ConfigFoo {
    @Bean(initMethod = "init", destroyMethod = "destroy")
    open fun foo(): Foo {
        return Foo()
    }
}
```

The output of this project will be as follows:

```
Foo is initializing...
Foo is destroying...
```

Creating a scope bean

Create a `@Scope` bean to make a prototype scope with `@Configuration`. `@Configuration` represents the configure file of a SpringBoot project. Here's a piece of code that shows how to use the `@Scope` prototype annotation:

```
@Configuration
public class ConfigFoo {
```

```
@Bean
@Scope("prototype")
public Foo foo() {
    return new Foo();
}
}
```

Spring MVC

The Spring Web MVC framework uses the **model-view-controller** (**MVC**) architecture, which manages the web applications. This provides a ready component that can be used by developers to develop a robust and loosely-coupled web application. With the presentation of Spring 3.0, the `@Controller` component additionally enables you to make peaceful web locales and applications through the `@PathVariable` annotation and different features. The MVC pattern separates the different aspects, such as input, business, and UI logic of the application.

There are three parts to MVC:

- The **model** is at the core of MVC applications. This is where the primary logic and information objects that comprise the core usefulness of the application are produced.
- The **view** is the place the information given by the model is introduced to the client. A view regulates the visual (or other) interface components – it chooses, filters, and arranges data provided by the model.
- The **controller** is in charge of preparing client requests, building a proper model, and passing it to the view for rendering.

Here are some of the advantages of Spring MVC framework:

- Spring MVC helps to separate each role, such as the model object and controller.
- When developing and deploying an application, it helps developers to use the lightweight servlet container.
- It provides a robust and powerful configuration for the project.
- You can develop a project very quickly and in parallel.
- Testing is very easy and you can inject test data using a setter function.

DispatcherServlet

DispatcherServlet is one of the core components of the Spring MVC. This works as a front-controller in an application. A front-controller means the Spring MVC receives all incoming requests and forwards these to the Spring MVC controller for processing. This is totally coordinated with the Spring IoC container and accordingly enables you to utilize each element of Spring.

DispatcherServlet handles all the HTTP requests and responses that are designed under the Spring MVC.

Here's a diagram to illustrate DispatcherServlet:

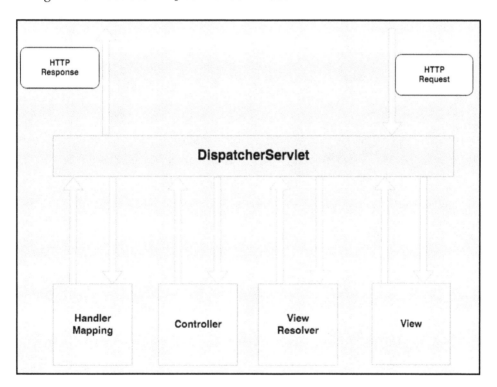

The succession of occasions relating to an approaching HTTP request to DispatcherServlet is as follows:

1. The application (as a client) sends a request to DispatcherServlet.
2. DispatcherServlet asks the related Handler Mapping to call the Controller.

3. The `Controller` takes requests from `DispatcherServlet` and calls a relevant service function based on the `GET` or `POST` function. The service function sets the model data based on the business logic.

4. `ViewResolver` selects the defined `View`.

5. The defined `View` is executed on the application.

Creating a project

Now, we'll learn about the MVC framework with Kotlin. Although this project is a web application and we need to utilize Maven for dependencies administration, we need to make a dynamic web application and then change it to a Maven venture first. The following screenshot demonstrates how to prepare our task skeleton structure:

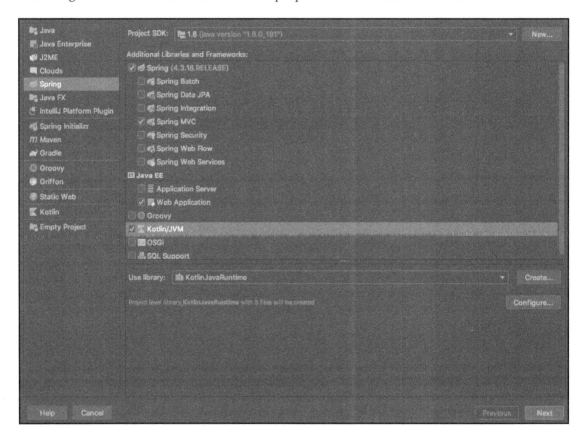

Now we're going to learn how to convert this project into a Maven project.

Converting to a Maven project

Now that the skeleton code for our Maven web-application venture is prepared, we can begin rolling out improvements to it, as well as making our Spring MVC HELLO WORLD application.

The created project is a non-Maven project. We need to convert the project into the Maven project.

To convert this project into a Maven project, open the existing project. In the project tool window, right-click your project and select **Add Framework Support**.

In the dialog that opens, select **Maven** from the options on the left and click **OK**:

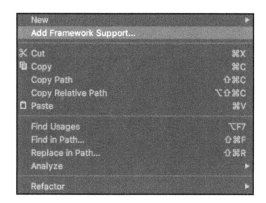

Spring MVC dependencies to pom.xml

We have to include `spring-web` and `spring-webmvc` dependencies in `pom.xml`, as well as including a servlet-programming interface, JSP-programming interface, and JSTL dependencies. Here's part of the `pom.xml` file (the full version is on GitHub) of our project with the `Spring Core`, `Kotlin`, and `Web` dependencies:

```
<?xml version="1.0" encoding="UTF-8"?>
<project xmlns="http://maven.apache.org/POM/4.0.0"
        xmlns:xsi="http://www.w3.org/2001/XMLSchema-instance"
        xsi:schemaLocation="http://maven.apache.org/POM/4.0.0
http://maven.apache.org/xsd/maven-4.0.0.xsd">
    <modelVersion>4.0.0</modelVersion>
    ----
    ----
    <properties>
```

```
    <springframework.version>5.0.8.RELEASE</springframework.version>
     <kotlin.version>1.3.0</kotlin.version>
     <jstl.version>1.2</jstl.version>
</properties>

<dependencies>
    <!--Spring dependencies-->
    <dependency>
        <groupId>org.springframework</groupId>
        <artifactId>spring-core</artifactId>
    </dependency>
    ----
    ----
    ----

    <!--We need to add the following Kotlin dependencies-->
    <dependency>
        <groupId>org.jetbrains.kotlin</groupId>
        <artifactId>kotlin-stdlib-jdk8</artifactId>
    </dependency>
</dependencies>
<build>
<plugins>
    ----
    ----
</plugins>
</build>
</project>
```

Creating Spring configuration beans

Go to the `/WebContent/WEB-INF/` directory and create an XML file called `spring-mvc-kotlin-servlet.xml`:

```
<?xml version="1.0" encoding="UTF-8"?>
<beans xmlns="http://www.springframework.org/schema/beans"
       xmlns:mvc="http://www.springframework.org/schema/mvc"
       xmlns:context="http://www.springframework.org/schema/context"
       xmlns:xsi="http://www.w3.org/2001/XMLSchema-instance"
       xsi:schemaLocation="
        http://www.springframework.org/schema/beans
        http://www.springframework.org/schema/beans/spring-beans.xsd
        http://www.springframework.org/schema/mvc
        http://www.springframework.org/schema/mvc/spring-mvc.xsd
        http://www.springframework.org/schema/context
        http://www.springframework.org/schema/context/spring-context.xsd">
```

```
    <mvc:annotation-driven />
    <context:component-scan
            base-package="mvckotlin" />
    <mvc:default-servlet-handler />

    <bean id="viewResolver"
 class="org.springframework.web.servlet.view.UrlBasedViewResolver">
        <property name="viewClass"
                value="org.springframework.web.servlet.view.JstlView" />
        <property name="prefix" value="/WEB-INF/jsp/" />
        <property name="suffix" value=".jsp" />
    </bean>
</beans>
```

In the `spring-mvc-kotlin-servlet.xml` configuration file, we mentioned a `<context:component-scan>` tag. All the components from the `mvckotlin` package and all its child packages will now be loaded by the Spring:

- This will load our `MVCKotlinApp.class` and also assign a `viewResolver` bean.
- `<property name="prefix" value="/WEB-INF/jsp/" />` will resolve the view and add a prefix string named `/WEB-INF/jsp/`.
- Note that we have returned a `ModelAndView` object with the view name `welcome` in our `MVCKotlinApp` class.
- This will be resolved to the `/WEB-INF/jsp/greeting.jsp` path.
- There's a `web.xml` file under the `/WebContent/WEB-INF/` directory. If you don't find it, create it in the `/WebContent/WEB-INF/` directory. Here's a piece of code from `web.xml`:

```
<?xml version="1.0" encoding="UTF-8"?>
<web-app xmlns:xsi="http://www.w3.org/2001/XMLSchema-instance"
        xmlns="http://xmlns.jcp.org/xml/ns/javaee"
        xsi:schemaLocation="http://xmlns.jcp.org/xml/ns/javaee
http://xmlns.jcp.org/xml/ns/javaee/web-app_4_0.xsd"
        version="4.0">
    <display-name>spring-mvc-kotlin</display-name>
    <welcome-file-list>
        <welcome-file>index.jsp</welcome-file>
        <welcome-file>default.jsp</welcome-file>
        <welcome-file>default.html</welcome-file>
        <welcome-file>index.html</welcome-file>

    </welcome-file-list>
    <servlet>
  <servlet-name>spring-mvc-kotlin</servlet-name>
        <servlet-
```

```
class>org.springframework.web.servlet.DispatcherServlet</servlet-class>
        <load-on-startup>1</load-on-startup>
    </servlet>
    <servlet-mapping>
        <servlet-name>spring-mvc-kotlin</servlet-name>
        <url-pattern>/index.jsp</url-pattern>
        <url-pattern>/greeting.jsp</url-pattern>
    </servlet-mapping>
</web-app>
```

`web.xml` will map `DispatcherServlet` with the `/greeting.jsp` URL pattern. Furthermore, note that we have mentioned `index.jsp` as a greeting file.

After initialization, `DispatcherServlet` will look for a file named `[servlet-name]-servlet.xml` in the `WEB-INF` folder. The value of the servlet XML file prefix name, and value of the `<servlet-name>` tag in `web.xml`, have to be the same. In our example, the name of the servlet is `spring-mvc-kotlin-servlet.xml`.

Creating a controller class

Go to `src | main | java` in the project and create the package name that we mentioned in `spring-mvc-kotlin-servlet.xml`. Assume that our package name is `mvckotlin`:

Create a controller .kt file. We call this MVCKotlinAppController.kt:

```kotlin
@Controller
class MVCKotlinAppController {
    @RequestMapping("/greeting")
    fun greetingMessage(): ModelAndView {
        val message =
            "<div style='text-align:center;'>" +
                "<h3>Welcome to Learn Spring for Android Application
Development</h3>" +
            "</div>"
        return ModelAndView("greeting", "message", message)
    }
}
```

We have a class named MVCKotlinAppController.kt and annotated this with
@Controller, which means that this class is a controller class. After initializing the project,
Spring starts to search the bundle from here.

The @RequestMapping("/greeting") annotation will map a web request and
/greeting will create a base URI.

We have created a function named greetingMessage() that will return a ModelAndView
object. Here we just create a sample HTML code for greeting. If we go to
http://localhost:8080/greeting, this will return a view based
on greetingMessage().

The view

Create a new file named /WebContent/index.jsp, with the following content:

```jsp
<%@ page contentType="text/html;charset=UTF-8" language="kotlin" %>
<html>
<head>
    <title>Spring MVC Kotlin</title>
</head>
<body>
<br>
<div style="text-align: center">
    <h2>
        Hey You..!! This is your 1st Spring MCV Tutorial..<br> <br>
    </h2>
    <h3>
        <a href="greeting.html">Click here to See Welcome Message...
</a>(to
```

```
          check Spring MVC Controller... @RequestMapping("/greeting"))
     </h3>
</div>
</body>
</html>
```

Then create another file named `/WebContent/WEB-INF/jsp/greeting.jsp`, with the following content:

```
<html>
<head>
    <title>Spring MVC Kotlin</title>
</head>
<body>
${message}
</body>
</html>
```

IntelliJ Ultimate

To run the project, you need to set up the run configuration. Follow these steps to do so:

1. Click the **Run...** button from the toolbar and then add Maven with the `clean install` comment:

2. Add `TomCat Server --> Local` and add the `SpringMVCKotlin:war` build from **Deployment**:

3. Click the **RUN** button on the menu bar to start the project.

Eclipse

Here are the steps to build the project:

1. To run the project, right-click on **Project** | **Run As** | **Maven Build....**
2. Add Goals—**clean install.**
3. Click **Apply** and **Run**.

If there are no errors, you'll see the following **BUILD SUCCESS** message:

```
[INFO]
[INFO] ------------------------------------------------------------------
[INFO] Building Spring MVC Kotlin 1.0-SNAPSHOT
[INFO] ------------------------------------------------------------------
[INFO]
[INFO] --- maven-clean-plugin:2.5:clean (default-clean) @ SpringMVCKotlin ---
[INFO] Deleting /Users/sunnat629/Book/Learn-Spring-for-Android-Application-Development/app/src/main/java/(
[INFO] ------------------------------------------------------------------
[INFO] BUILD SUCCESS
[INFO] ------------------------------------------------------------------
[INFO] Total time: 0.203 s
[INFO] Finished at: 2018-11-05T11:39:03+06:00
[INFO] Final Memory: 9M/309M
[INFO] ------------------------------------------------------------------

Process finished with exit code 0
```

Visit `http://localhost:8080/SpringMVCKotlin/`, where you'll see the following output of the demo code:

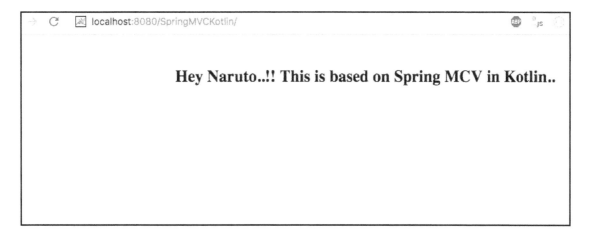

SpringBoot

SpringBoot is a Spring Framework module that has some features to help developers create a production-class application. SpringBoot is a combination of two words—**BOOT** is from bootstrap, while **SPRING** is a framework used to build Java enterprise applications. This is a large framework that's also supported by numerous other frameworks. SpringBoot is similar in that it lets you bootstrap a spring application from scratch, which is how it gets the name SpringBoot. According to spring.io, here's the definition of SpringBoot—"Spring Boot makes it easy to create stand-alone, production-grade, Spring-based applications that you can just run." This means that it helps you to create a runnable project without the help of others. In addition, we showed a **production-grade** project here, which is a ready-product application. SpringBoot minimizes the pain of setting up an application.

The features of SpringBoot are as follows:

- It helps to create a standalone Spring application.
- It comes with Tomcat, Jetty, or Undertow, and so there's no need to worry about setting up the server environment.
- With the use of SpringBoot, you don't need to deploy WAR files.
- Third-party frameworks can be imported automatically with their configurations.
- XML configuration isn't required if you use SpringBoot.

 SpringBoot doesn't produce code or make changes to your files. Instead, when you start up your application, SpringBoot dynamically wires up beans and settings, and applies them to your application context.

Let's create a SpringBoot project to learn about its dependencies and features.

Creating a project

To create a Spring Boot project, let's generate a sample project from https://start.spring.io/. Here, you can add your required dependencies, such as Web, Thymeleaf, JPA, and DevTools. This can be done as follows:

1. In the drop-down menus at the top, select **Maven Project** with **Kotlin** and Spring Boot **2.1.1 (SNAPSHOT)**:

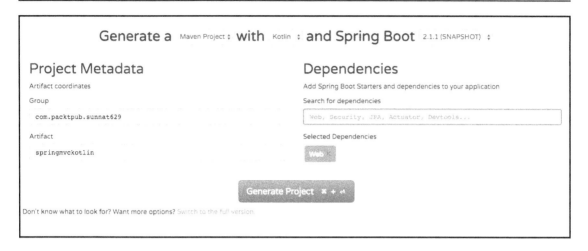

2. Give the name of **Group**, **Artifact**, **Package Name**, and add **Dependencies**. Then hit **Generate Project**.
3. Download and unzip the project.
4. Import the downloaded project into your IDE.

After following these steps, you're ready to use and modify the project. Let's see what's inside this project. You'll find a controller file
under `src/main/kotlin/{packageName}/AppController.kt`.

Here's a piece of code from the `controller` file:

```
@RestController
class HtmlController {
    @GetMapping("/")
    fun blog(model: Model): String {
        model["title"] = "Greeting"
        return "index"
    }
}
```

Create a class named `HtmlController.kt` and annotate it with the `@RestController` annotation to make it a controller class in which we'll deal with web requests. `@RestController` is the combination of `@Controller` and `@ResponseBody`.

Create a function named `blog(model: Model)` and annotate it with `@GetMappingmaps("/")`. This will return `index.xml` as output.

Creating an application class

Under `src/main/kotlin/{packageName}`, create an application class named `SpringBootKotlinApplication.kt`:

```kotlin
@SpringBootApplication
class SpringBootKotlinApplication

fun main(args: Array<String>) {
    runApplication<SpringBootKotlinApplication>(*args)
}
```

`@SpringBootApplication` is utilized to empower the following three features:

- `@Configuration` enables Java-based configuration.
- `@EnableAutoConfiguration` enables the auto-configuration feature of SpringBoot.
- `@ComponentScan` enables component scanning.

The `main()` function utilizes SpringBoot's `SpringApplication.run()` method to dispatch an application. This web application is 100% unadulterated Kotlin and there's no need to arrange any pipes or foundations here.

Similarly, there's a `CommandLineRunner` function set apart as `@Bean` and this keeps running on startup. It recovers every one of the beans that were made either by your application or were naturally added by SpringBoot. It then sorts and prints these out.

In the code of the `SpringBootKotlinApplication` class, in contrast with Java, you can see the absence of semicolons, the absence of sections in an empty class (you can add a few, in case you have to proclaim beans by means of a `@Bean` annotation), and the utilization of a `runApplication` top-level function. `runApplication<SpringBootKotlinApplication>(*args)` is Kotlin's informal option in contrast to `SpringApplication.run(SpringBootKotlinApplication::class.java, *args)`, and this can be utilized to customize the application.

Now create an HTML file in the folder underneath `src/main/resources/templates/`.

The content of `index.html` is as follows:

```html
<!DOCTYPE html>
<html lang="en">
<head>
    <meta charset="UTF-8"/>
```

```
    <title>Spring Boot Kotlin</title>
</head>
<body>
    <p>Welcome, Naruto. This project is based on Spring Boot in Kotlin</p>
</body>
</html>
```

Start the web application by running the `main` function of
`SpringBootKotlinApplication.kt`. If everything is fine, you'll see this in the logcat:

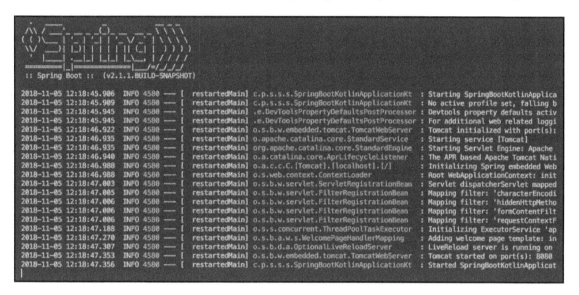

Next, go to `http://localhost:8080/`. Here, you should see a web page with a
SpringBoot Kotlin application headline:

We've covered the basics of SpringBoot. Later, we'll go into this in more depth with more
dependencies.

Summary

In this chapter, we explored Spring and its modules, dependencies, and use of functions. We attempted to cover all the essential information that will be required for the rest of this book. We looked at the steady and solid architecture of Spring Framework with Core, Information Access, Web, AOP, Instrumentation, and Test. Furthermore, we figured out the life cycle of a bean and how to design beans in three different ways. We found out about the depth of bean configurations, and we learned about the use of beans in XML, annotation, and code. Now we know how to inject the dependencies into the tasks.

We explored two noteworthy frameworks: Spring MVC and SpringBoot. We'll now be able to make an MVC-based venture with its dependencies and modules. In addition, we learned out about the use of SpringBoot and created a web application that uses Boot, allowing us to make a web page without an HTML file. We also explored the contrasts between Spring MVC and SpringBoot. You can now create a Spring project in the Kotlin language.

In the next chapter, we'll learn about the required Android and Spring modules to build a client application on the Android platform.

Questions

1. What is Spring Framework?
2. What is dependency injection?
3. What is aspect-oriented programming?
4. What is the Spring IoC container?
5. What is a Spring bean?
6. What is a controller in Spring MVC?
7. What is `DispatcherServlet`?
8. What is `ContextLoaderListener`?
9. What is the boilerplate code?

Further reading

- *Learning Spring Application Development* (`https://www.packtpub.com/application-development/learning-spring-application-development`)
- *Spring MVC: Beginner's Guide - Second Edition* (`https://www.packtpub.com/application-development/spring-mvc-beginners-guide-second-edition`)
- *Spring: Microservices with Spring Boot* (`https://www.packtpub.com/application-development/spring-microservices-spring-boot`)

Spring Modules for Android

4

This chapter will cover the modules and features that support Spring for Android and use REST in Android as a client. There are some modules that help request and retrieve REST APIs. They also provide security, such as *basic authentication* and *OAuth2*. Because of these securities, the resources of the server are secured and are therefore difficult to hack. Even a client needs to be granted permission from the owner to use the resources from the protected server. The modules also incorporate a strong OAuth-based authorization client and implementations for mainstream social websites, such as Google, Twitter, Facebook, and so on.

This chapter covers the following topics:

- The `RestTemplate` module.
- The Gradle and Maven repository
- `RestTemplate` module
- Retrofit
- Creating an Android app

Technical requirements

The Android SDK is required to develop Android applications. The developers used Eclipse and the Android plugin to develop Android applications at the beginning of the Android development. But later, Google announced that Android Studio is the official tool for Android application development. It has all the vital modules, such as Gradle, Maven, Android SDK, NDK, Java JDK, and so on, so we don't have to utilize the Terminal command line. In `Chapter 1`, *About the Environment*, we demonstrated how to download and create a sample Android application using Android Studio.

The source code with an example for this chapter is available on GitHub at the following link: `https://github.com/PacktPublishing/Learn-Spring-for-Android-Application-Development/tree/master/Chapter04`

REST client module

Representational State Transfer (**REST**) is designed to take advantage of the existing protocols. The consistent systems of REST are often called **RESTful systems**. It can be used over almost every protocol, but it normally takes advantage of HTTP during the use of web APIs. It makes it simpler for systems to speak with one another. These systems are portrayed by how they are stateless and separate the concerns of the client and server. We will go in depth into what these terms mean and why they are advantageous qualities for services on the web.

A RESTful web service is responded to with a payload formatted in either HTML, XML, JSON, or some other format. The response can affirm that a change has been made to the requested response, and the reaction can give hypertext links that are related to other resources, or a bundle of resources. At the point in which HTTP is utilized, as is normal, the tasks that are accessible are `GET`, `POST`, `PUT`, `DELETE`, and other predefined HTTP functions.

To use Spring for Android, you can use different HTTP libraries. Spring has suggested using `RestTemplate` for Android. This is now outdated and may not be supported for the newer Android version. However, now, you can find some libraries that are easier and more powerful, with lots of features. You can use a different HTTP library, such as one of the following:

- `RestTemplate`
- Retrofit
- Volley

We will explore the use of all of these libraries in this chapter. In our upcoming chapters, we will use Retrofit because it's easier, updated, robust, and requires less code to be written. However, you can use any of them in your projects.

The RestTemplate module

`RestTemplate` is a robust and Java-based REST client. In Android application development, we can use the `RestTemplate` module, which will provide a template to request and retrieve a REST API. `RestTemplate` is Spring's core class for synchronous client-side HTTP access. It's intended to disentangle correspondence with HTTP servers and authorize RESTful standards.

`RestTemplate` is the main class for synchronous RESTful HTTP requests. A native Android HTTP client library is used to retrieve requests. The default `ClientHttpRequestFactory`, which is utilized when you make another `RestTemplate` example, varies depending on the adaptation of Android on which your application is running.

Gradle and Maven repository

To develop an Android application, we have to implement or compile a few dependencies. Android officially supports Gradle to implement or compile dependencies. Android also supports Maven, so if you want to use Maven, then you need to modify `pom.xml`.

You can check the latest version of the dependency at `https://mvnrepository.com/artifact/org.springframework.android/spring-android-core` for implementing `spring-android-core`, which has the core modules for Android.

You can check the latest version of the dependency at `https://mvnrepository.com/artifact/org.springframework.android/spring-android-rest-template` for implementing `spring-android-rest-template`, which has the all modules for `RestTemplate`.

Now, we will look at the use of Gradle and Maven for the Android project.

Gradle

Gradle is a build system that's used to build Android bundles (APK files) by overseeing conditions and giving custom build logic. It is a JVM-based form framework, meaning that you can compose your own content in Java, which Android Studio makes use of.

In Android Studio, Gradle is a custom form apparatus that's used to fabricate Android bundles (APK files) by overseeing dependencies and giving custom form rationale. An APK file (Android application bundle) is an extraordinarily formatted compressed file that contains bytecode, resources (pictures, UI, XML, and so on), and manifest files.

The dependency command of how to implement these dependencies is shown in the following code:

```
dependencies {
    //
https://mvnrepository.com/artifact/org.springframework.android/spring-andro
id-rest-template
    implementation 'org.springframework.android:spring-android-rest-
template:2.0.0.M3'

    //
https://mvnrepository.com/artifact/org.springframework.android/spring-andro
id-core
    implementation 'org.springframework.android:spring-android-
core:2.0.0.M3'
}

repositories {
    maven {
        url 'https://repo.spring.io/libs-snapshot'
    }
}
```

Maven

The Android Maven module is used to build applications for the Android OS and assemble libraries. These are to be used to create the **Android Archive Library** (**AAR**) and the inheritance APKLIB format, thus utilizing Apache Maven.

Here is a code sample of how to add a dependency of Android in `pom.xml`:

```
<dependencies>
    <!--
https://mvnrepository.com/artifact/org.springframework.android/spring-andro
id-rest-template -->
    <dependency>
        <groupId>org.springframework.android</groupId>
        <artifactId>spring-android-rest-template</artifactId>
        <version>2.0.0.BUILD-SNAPSHOT</version>
    </dependency>

<!--
https://mvnrepository.com/artifact/org.springframework.android/spring-andro
id-core -->
    <dependency>
        <groupId>org.springframework.android</groupId>
        <artifactId>spring-android-core</artifactId>
        <version>1.0.1.RELEASE</version>
    </dependency>
</dependencies>
<repositories>
    <repository>
        <id>spring-snapshots</id>
        <name>Spring Snapshots</name>
        <url>https://repo.spring.io/libs-snapshot</url>
        <snapshots>
            <enabled>true</enabled>
        </snapshots>
    </repository>
</repositories>
```

RestTemplate constructors

The four `RestTemplate` constructors are listed in the following code:

```
RestTemplate();
RestTemplate(boolean includeDefaultConverters);
RestTemplate(ClientHttpRequestFactory requestFactory);
RestTemplate(boolean includeDefaultConverters, ClientHttpRequestFactory
requestFactory);
```

This constructor has no parameter, by default. If you want to use a default set of message converters with another `RestTemplate` example, you can pass `TRUE` as a parameter. If you want to use another `ClientHttpRequestFactory`, then you need to pass it as a parameter.

RestTemplate functions

`RestTemplate` gives a larger amount of functions. It has six primary HTTP functions, which makes it simple to conjure numerous RESTful services and authorize REST best practices. `RestTemplate`'s strategy name pursues a naming tradition; the initial segment demonstrates what the HTTP strategy is and the second part shows what will be returned. There is an interface called `ResponseErrorHandler` in `RestTemplate` which is used to determine whether a particular response has an error or not. Here are the descriptions of the six HTTP functions.

HTTP GET

HTTP characterizes an arrangement of request functions to demonstrate the coveted activity to be performed for a given resource. The `GET` function requests a description of the predetermined resource and requests that utilizing `GET` should just retrieve data. `GET` is a standout among the most well-known HTTP functions.

Here are the common functions of HTTP `GET`:

```
@Throws(RestClientException::class)
fun <T> getForObject(url: String, responseType: Class<T>, vararg
urlVariables. Any). T

@Throws(RestClientException::class)
fun <T> getForObject(url: String, responseType: Class<T>, urlVariables:
Map<String, *>): T

@Throws(RestClientException::class)
fun <T> getForObject(url: URI, responseType: Class<T>): T

fun <T> getForEntity(url: String, responseType: Class<T>, vararg
urlVariables: Any): ResponseEntity<T>

fun <T> getForEntity(url: String, responseType: Class<T>, urlVariables:
Map<String, *>): ResponseEntity<T>
```

```
@Throws(RestClientException::class)
fun <T> getForEntity(url: URI, responseType: Class<T>): ResponseEntity<T>
```

Here is an example of how to call these functions:

```
val restTemplate = RestTemplate()

val baseUrl: String ?= "YOUR_URL" // API URL as String
val response = restTemplate.getForEntity(baseUrl, String::class.java)

val uri = URI(baseUrl) // API URL as URL format
val responseURI = restTemplate.getForEntity(uri, String::class.java)Auth
Module
```

HTTP POST

HTTP POST requests that the asset at the URI accomplishes something with the given substance. POST is often utilized to make another substance; however, it can likewise be utilized to refresh an element.

Here are the common functions of HTTP POST:

```
@Throws(RestClientException::class)
fun postForLocation(url: String, request: Any, vararg urlVariables: Any):
URI

fun postForLocation(url: String, request: Any, urlVariables: Map<String,
*>): URI

@Throws(RestClientException::class)
fun postForLocation(url: URI, request: Any): URI

fun <T> postForObject(url: String, request: Any, responseType: Class<T>,
vararg uriVariables: Any): T

fun <T> postForObject(url: String, request: Any, responseType: Class<T>,
uriVariables: Map<String, *>): T

@Throws(RestClientException::class)
fun <T> postForObject(url: URI, request: Any, responseType: Class<T>): T

fun <T> postForEntity(url: String, request: Any, responseType: Class<T>,
vararg uriVariables: Any): ResponseEntity<T>

@Throws(RestClientException::class)
fun <T> postForEntity(url: String, request: Any, responseType: Class<T>,
```

```
uriVariables: Map<String, *>): ResponseEntity<T>
```

@Throws(RestClientException::class)
```
fun <T> postForEntity(url: URI, request: Any, responseType: Class<T>):
ResponseEntity<T>
```

Here is an example of how to call these functions:

```
/** POST **/

val restTemplate = RestTemplate()

val baseUrl: String ?= "YOUR_URL"
val uri = URI(baseUrl)
val body = "The Body"

val response = restTemplate.postForEntity(baseUrl, body,
String::class.java)

val request = HttpEntity(body)
val responseExchange = restTemplate.exchange(baseUrl, HttpMethod.POST,
request, String::class.java)

val responseURI = restTemplate.postForEntity(uri, body, String::class.java)
val responseExchangeURI = restTemplate.exchange(uri, HttpMethod.POST,
request, String::class.java)
```

HTTP PUT

To store an element at a URI, the PUT function can create a new element or update a current one. A PUT request is idempotent. Idempotency is the fundamental contrast between the desires for PUT versus a POST request.

Here are the common functions of HTTP PUT:

```
Here are the common functions -
@Throws(RestClientException::class)
fun put(url: String, request: Any, vararg urlVariables: Any)

@Throws(RestClientException::class)
fun put(url: String, request: Any, urlVariables: Map<String, *>)

@Throws(RestClientException::class)
fun put(url: String, request: Any, urlVariables: Map<String, *>)
```

Here is an example of how to call the functions of HTTP PUT:

```
val baseUrl: String ?= "YOUR_URL"
val restTemplate = RestTemplate()
val uri = URI(baseUrl)

val body = "The Body"

restTemplate.put(baseUrl, body)
restTemplate.put(uri, body)
```

HTTP DELETE

HTTP DELETE is a request function that is used to remove a resource. However, the resource does not have to be removed immediately. DELETE could be an asynchronous or long-running request.

Here are the common functions of HTTP DELETE:

```
@Throws(RestClientException::class)
fun delete(url: String, vararg urlVariables: Any)

@Throws(RestClientException::class)
fun delete(url: String, urlVariables: Map<String, *>)

@Throws(RestClientException::class)
fun delete(url: URI)
```

Here is an example of how to call these functions:

```
val baseUrl: String ?= "YOUR_URL"
val restTemplate = RestTemplate()
val uri = URI(baseUrl)

restTemplate.delete(baseUrl)
restTemplate.delete(uri)
```

HTTP OPTIONS

The HTTP OPTIONS function is utilized to depict the correspondence options for the target resource. The client can indicate a URL for the OPTIONS method, or a reference mark, (*), to allude to the whole server.

Here are the common functions of HTTP OPTIONS:

```
@Throws(RestClientException::class)
fun optionsForAllow(url: String, vararg urlVariables: Any): Set<HttpMethod>

@Throws(RestClientException::class)
fun optionsForAllow(url: String, urlVariables: Map<String, *>):
Set<HttpMethod>

@Throws(RestClientException::class)
fun optionsForAllow(url: URI): Set<HttpMethod>
```

Here is an example of how to call the functions:

```
val baseUrl: String ?= "YOUR_URL"
val restTemplate = RestTemplate()
val allowHeaders = restTemplate.optionsForAllow(baseUrl)

val uri = URI(baseUrl)
val allowHeadersURI = restTemplate.optionsForAllow(uri)
```

HTTP HEAD

In the current version of Spring (4.3.10), HEAD is automatically supported.

@RequestMapping functions mapped to GET are also implicitly mapped to HEAD, meaning that there is no need to have HEAD explicitly declared. An HTTP HEAD request is processed as if it were an HTTP GET, but instead of writing the body, only the number of bytes is counted, as well as the Content-Length header set.

Here are the common functions of HTTP HEAD:

```
@Throws(RestClientException::class)
fun headForHeaders(url: String, vararg urlVariables: Any): HttpHeaders

@Throws(RestClientException::class)
fun headForHeaders(url: String, urlVariables: Map<String, *>): HttpHeaders

@Throws(RestClientException::class)
fun headForHeaders(url: URI): HttpHeaders
```

Retrofit

Retrofit is a library that makes parsing an API reaction simple and better for utilization in the application. Retrofit is a REST client for Java and Android that makes it moderately simple to recover and transfer JSON by means of a REST-based web service. In Retrofit, you can arrange which converter is utilized for the information serialization. Normally, for JSON, you utilize Gson, but you can add custom converters to process XML or different conventions. Retrofit utilizes the `OkHttp` library for HTTP requests.

The use of Retrofit

To work with Retrofit, you will require the following three classes:

- A model class, which is utilized as a JSON model
- Interfaces that characterize the conceivable HTTP activities
- The `Retrofit.Builder` class, which utilizes the interface and the developer programming interface to permit characterizing the URL endpoint for HTTP activities.

Each function of an interface speaks to one conceivable programming interface call. It must have an HTTP annotation (`GET`, `POST`, `DELETE`, and so on) to determine the request type and the relative URL.

Advantages of Retrofit

Retrofit is very easy to utilize. It basically gives you a chance to regard programming interface calls as straightforward Java method calls, so you just characterize which URLs to hit and the request/reaction parameters as Java classes.

The whole system call, plus JSON/XML parsing, is totally taken care of by Retrofit (with assistance from Gson for JSON parsing), alongside support for self-assertive formats with pluggable serialization/deserialization.

Configuring Retrofit

Of course, Retrofit can just deserialize HTTP bodies into `OkHttp`'s `ResponseBody` type and it can acknowledge its `RequestBody` type for `@Body`.

Converters can be added in order to support different sorts. Seven kinds of modules adjust mainstream serialization libraries for your benefit. These include the following libraries:

- **Gson**: `com.squareup.retrofit2:converter-gson`
- **Jackson**: `com.squareup.retrofit2:converter-jackson`
- **Moshi**: `com.squareup.retrofit2:converter-moshi`
- **Protobuf**: `com.squareup.retrofit2:converter-protobuf`
- **Wire**: `com.squareup.retrofit2:converter-wire`
- **Simple XML**: `com.squareup.retrofit2:converter-simplexml`
- **Scalars (primitives, boxed, and String)**:
  `com.squareup.retrofit2:converter-scalars`

Downloading Retrofit

Download the latest JAR from `https://search.maven.org/remote_content?g=com.squareup.retrofit2a=retrofitv=LATEST`.

Alternatively, you can inject the dependency via Maven with the following code:

```
<dependency>
    <groupId>com.squareup.retrofit2</groupId>
    <artifactId>retrofit</artifactId>
    <version>2.4.0</version>
</dependency>
```

Alternatively, you can use Gradle, as per the following code:

```
implementation 'com.squareup.retrofit2:retrofit:2.4.0'
implementation 'com.squareup.retrofit2:converter-gson:2.3.0'
compile 'com.jakewharton.picasso:picasso2-okhttp3-downloader:1.1.0'
```

HTTP request functions

Each function must have an HTTP annotation that gives the request function and relative URL. There are five built-in annotations—`GET`, `POST`, `PUT`, `DELETE`, and `HEAD`. The overall URL of the asset is indicated in the annotation.

Let's take a look at the use of these annotations. We are considering all the URLs based on GitHub API v3 (`https://developer.github.com/v3/`).

GET

Let's assume that you want to get a response to your details from your GitHub account. You need to use the following endpoint with the @GET function to get the user's info:

```
@GET("group/{id}/users")
Call<List<Users>> groupList(@Path("id") int id);
```

Let's assume that you want to create a new repo in your GitHub account. Here, you need to use the following endpoint with the @POST function:

```
@POST("user/repos")
fun createRepo(@Body repo:Repository,
               @Header("Authorization") accessToken: String,
               @Header("Accept") apiVersionSpec: String,
               @Header("Content-Type") contentType: String):
Call<Repository>
```

PUT

Let's assume that you want to update a GitHub Gist object. You need to use the following endpoint with the @PUT function:

```
@PUT("gists/{id}")
fun updateGist(@Path("id") id: String,
               @Body gist: Gist): Call<ResponseBody>
```

DELETE

Let's assume that you want to delete a repository from your GitHub account. In this case, you need to use the following endpoint with the @DELETE function:

```
@DELETE("repos/{owner}/{repo}")
    fun deleteRepo(@Header("Authorization") accessToken: String,
               @Header("Accept") apiVersionSpec: String,
               @Path("repo") repo: String,
               @Path("owner") owner: String): Call<DeleteRepos>
```

HEAD

A request header can be refreshed progressively using the @Header annotation. If the value is invalid, the header will be overlooked:

```
// example one
```

```
@GET("user")
Call<User> getUser(@Header("Authorization") String authorization)

// example two
@Headers("Accept: application/vnd.github.v3.full+json", "User-Agent: Spring
for Android")
@GET("users/{username}")
fun getUser(@Path("username") username: String): Call<Users>
```

Creating an Android app

Let's create a simple Android app as a client that will retrieve the REST API using the GitHub API. First of all, we need to create an app from Android Studio and put down our project and the company domain. Don't forget to check **Include Kotlin support**. It will include all of the support of Kotlin. The following screenshot shows the **Create Android Project** window:

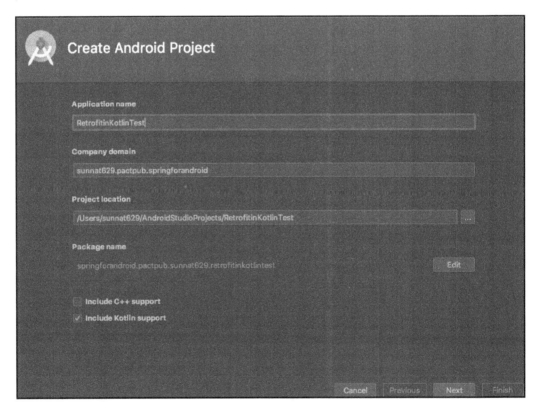

Then, select the minimum API version from the **Phone and Tablet** option. There is no need to add other options for this project. After clicking **Next**, in the **Add an Activity to Mobile** section, you can select **Empty Activity** and then, after renaming the **Activity Name** and layout, click **Finish**. After the build, you will be ready to start creating an Android app.

The final files of this project are shown in the following screenshot:

Gradle information

Here are the details of my Android Studio's Gradle file:

```
buildscript {
    ext.kotlin_version = '1.3.10'
    repositories {
        google()
        jcenter()
    }
    dependencies {
        classpath 'com.android.tools.build:gradle:3.2.1'
        classpath "org.jetbrains.kotlin:kotlin-gradle-
plugin:$kotlin_version"

        // NOTE: Do not place your application dependencies here; they
belong
        // in the individual module build.gradle files
    }
}

allprojects {
    repositories {
        google()
        jcenter()
    }
}

task clean(type: Delete) {
    delete rootProject.buildDir
}
```

Gradle dependencies

We will use Retrofit and its features, so we need to implement all the dependencies, as shown in the following code:

```
implementation 'com.squareup.retrofit2:retrofit:2.4.0'
implementation 'com.squareup.retrofit2:converter-gson:2.4.0'

implementation 'com.squareup.retrofit2:retrofit-converters:2.5.0'
implementation 'com.squareup.retrofit2:retrofit-adapters:2.5.0'
implementation 'com.squareup.okhttp3:logging-interceptor:3.12.0'
implementation 'com.google.code.gson:gson:2.8.5'
```

Creating a model

We will use the GitHub API. You can check all the REST API URLs at `https://api.github.com/`. We will use the simplest API, which has no security issues. We will show the list of a user's repositories. The API is `https://api.github.com/users/{user}/repos`. You need a `GET` HTTP function with a username parameter.

The following screenshot shows the output of the REST API:

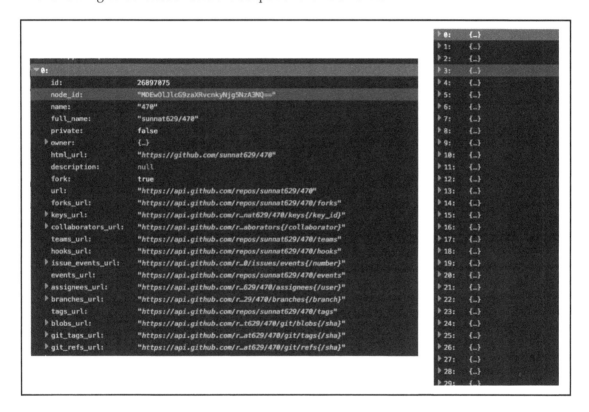

The left-hand side of the preceding screenshot shows part of the content of a repo and the right-hand side is the collapsed total repo list.

So, according to the API, we will create a user model for the client side. Here is the model class named `GitHubUserModel.kt`, where we will show only the name of the list of all the repos:

```
class GitHubUserModel {
    val name: String? = null
}
```

Create an interface that will have the HTTP request functions. In this project, we will only use a `GET` function that retrieves all the details of the users. Here, we are using the `GET` Retrofit annotation to encode details about the parameters and the request function. For this function, our endpoint is `/users/{user}/repos`, where you need to add a parameter of the `userName` and it will provide a list of `UserModel`.

Here is the code of the `GithubService` interface:

```
interface GithubService {
    @GET("/users/{user}/repos")
    fun reposOfUser(@Path("user") user: String):
Call<List<GitHubUserModel>>
}
```

Implementing a service

This class is responsible for the main task. It will be responsive for the control of all the tasks using the `Retrofit.builder` class and will configure it with the base of the given URL.

Here is the code of `UserServiceImpl.kt`:

```
class GithubServiceImpl{
    fun getGithubServiceFactory(): GithubService {
        val retrofit = Retrofit.Builder()
                .baseUrl("https://api.github.com/")
                .addConverterFactory(GsonConverterFactory.create())
                .build()
        return retrofit.create(GithubService::class.java)
    }
}
```

Here, our `baseUrl()` is `https://api.github.com/`.

Calling callback

Here, we are calling `CallBack<>` from the `MainActivity`. This callback will have the response of the REST API request.

Let's check the `MainActivity.kt` code:

```kotlin
class MainActivity : AppCompatActivity() {
    override fun onCreate(savedInstanceState: Bundle?) {
        super.onCreate(savedInstanceState)
        setContentView(R.layout.activity_main)

        val githubService: GithubService =
GithubServiceImpl().getGithubServiceFactory()

        val call: Call<List<GitHubUserModel>> =
githubService.reposOfUser("sunnat629")
        call.enqueue(object: Callback<List<GitHubUserModel>>{
            override fun onFailure(call: Call<List<GitHubUserModel>>, t:
Throwable) {
                Log.wtf("PACKTPUB", t.message)
            }

            override fun onResponse(call: Call<List<GitHubUserModel>>,
response: Response<List<GitHubUserModel>>) {
                val listItems = arrayOfNulls<String>(
response.body()!!.size)
                for (i in 0 until response.body()!!.size) {
                    val recipe = response.body()!![i]
                    listItems[i] = recipe.name
                }
                val adapter = ArrayAdapter<String>(this@MainActivity,
android.R.layout.simple_list_item_1, listItems)
                displayList.adapter = adapter
            }
        })
    }
}
```

First of all, we need to initialize
`GithubServiceImpl().getGithubServiceImpl(username,password)` so that we can
call `reposOfUser()` from `UserService`. Here, I add my GitHub username in the
parameter. Then, we will call `enqueue(retrofit2.Callback<T>)`, which will
be executed asynchronously and send the request and get the response. It has two
functions—`onResponse()` and `onFailure()`. If there is any server-related error, then it
will call `onFailure()`, and if it gets the response and the resources, it will
call `onResponse()`. We can use the resources of the `onResponse()` function for this.

Here, we will get a response of the `UserModel` list. So, we can use this list to show our
REST output in our application UI.

Creating an interface

We will show a list of the user's details and the names of all the repos. Here, we will use
`ListView`.

Here is the code of the `acitivity_main.xml` file:

```
<?xml version="1.0" encoding="utf-8"?>
<android.support.constraint.ConstraintLayout
xmlns:android="http://schemas.android.com/apk/res/android"
    xmlns:app="http://schemas.android.com/apk/res-auto"
    xmlns:tools="http://schemas.android.com/tools"
    android:layout_width="match_parent"
    android:layout_height="match_parent"
    tools:context=".MainActivity">

    <ListView
        android:id="@+id/displayList"
        android:layout_width="wrap_content"
        android:layout_height="wrap_content"
        app:layout_constraintBottom_toBottomOf="parent"
        app:layout_constraintLeft_toLeftOf="parent"
        app:layout_constraintRight_toRightOf="parent"
        app:layout_constraintTop_toTopOf="parent" />

</android.support.constraint.ConstraintLayout>
```

We will use this `listview` in the `onResponse()` function of `MainActivity`.

We will get the list and create a custom adapter to show the user list, as shown in the following code:

```
val listItems = arrayOfNulls<String>( response.body()!!.size)
for (i in 0 until response.body()!!.size) {
    val recipe = response.body()!![i]
    listItems[i] = recipe.name
}
val adapter = ArrayAdapter<String>(this@MainActivity,
android.R.layout.simple_list_item_1, listItems)
displayList.adapter = adapter
```

Here, we get the list of repos and convert them into an array. Then, we create the native adapter for the list with `val adapter = ArrayAdapter<String>(this@MainActivity, android.R.layout.simple_list_item_1, listItems)` and set the adapter in our list with `displayList.adapter = adapter`.

You should never perform long-running tasks on the main thread. It will incur an **Application Not Responding (ANR)** message.

Mobile applications

So, after everything, run your server. Then, run your app. The following screenshot shows the output of our app:

 You can modify this as you wish, although you have to be careful about the endpoint and the model.

Summary

In this chapter, we have given a quick presentation of the ideas driving REST and the REST client modules. The RESTful HTTP way of dealing with uncovering functionality is unique. We have seen the different libraries of REST client functions. First, we saw what RestTemplate is and its implementation in an Android application. Now, we know about the constructors of RestTemplate and its functionalities. Furthermore, we have learned about Retrofit, allowing us to actualize Retrofit in an Android application. We have also seen the utilization of its functionalities. Lastly, we look at how to implement Retrofit to get data from a REST API.

In the following chapters, we will develop a total project, including security, authorization/authentication, a database, and a custom REST API, with the Spring and Android application to deal with the API as a client. In these chapters, you will explore the full usage of the API and prepare to figure out how to make an API for a server and recover it from the client.

Questions

1. What is the difference between REST and RESTful?
2. What is the architectural style for creating a web API?
3. What tools are required to test your web API?
4. What are RESTful web services?
5. What is a URI? What is the purpose of a URI in REST-based web services?
6. What does the HTTP Status Code `200` state?
7. What does the HTTP Status Code `404` state?

Further reading

- *Hands-On RESTful API Design Patterns and Best Practices* (`https://www.packtpub.com/application-development/hands-restful-api-design-patterns-and-best-practices`), by Pethuru Raj, Anupama Raman, and Harihara Subramanian
- *Building a RESTful Web Service with Spring* (`https://www.packtpub.com/web-development/building-restful-web-service-spring`), by Ludovic Dewailly

5
Securing Applications with Spring Security

Security is one of the first priorities for the enterprise, e-commerce, and banking projects. These projects need to create a security system since they exchange millions of dollars and store the protected resources of an organization.

Spring Security is a sub-task of the immense Spring Framework portfolio. It has been upgraded to be utilized with a Spring MVC web application framework, yet can similarly be utilized with Java servlets. This supports authentication incorporation with a long list of other technologies, such as **Lightweight Directory Access Protocol (LDAP)**, **Java Authentication and Authorization Service (JAAS)**, and OpenID. It was developed as a complete security solution for Java-based enterprise environments.

In this chapter, we'll learn about Spring Security and its modules and learn how to implement security in a Spring-based project. The following topics will be covered in this chapter:

- Spring Security architecture
- The advantages of Spring Security
- Spring Security features
- Spring Security modules
- Implementing Spring Security
- Securing REST with Spring Security basic authentication
- Securing REST with Spring Security OAuth2

Technical requirements

You need to add these dependencies to enable and use the features of Spring Security. Here are the dependencies that need to be added to the `pom.xml` file of the Spring project:

```
<dependency>
    <groupId>org.springframework.security</groupId>
    <artifactId>Spring_Security_SUB_Module_Name</artifactId>
    <version>CURRENT_RELEASE_VERSION</version>
</dependency>

<dependency>
    <groupId>org.springframework.security</groupId>
    <artifactId>spring-security-core</artifactId>
    <version>5.1.1.RELEASE</version>
</dependency>
```

You can find all the examples from this chapter on GitHub at `https://github.com/PacktPublishing/Learn-Spring-for-Android-Application-Development/tree/master/Chapter05`.

Spring Security architecture

Spring Security is the security service solution for a J2EE-based enterprise production. This helps to develop a secured application in a faster and easier way with the use of its particular dependency-injection principles. To develop a secure J2EE-based enterprise application, Spring Security is an incredible and flexible authentication and authorization framework. Authentication is the process of checking the identity of a procedure or a client. On the other hand, authorization implies a procedure of checking the authority of a client to perform activities in the application.

Authentication

Authentication is the process that identifies a user or client based on their username and password. It helps a user to get the access protected system objects based on their identity. For the authentication procedure, spring security gives us the `AuthenticationManager` interface. This interface has just a single capacity, named `validate()`.

The accompanying snippet of code is an example of the `AuthenticationManager` interface:

```
interface AuthenticationManager {
    @Throws(AuthenticationException::class)
    fun authenticate(authentication: Authentication): Authentication
}
```

Three tasks are completed by the `authenticate()` in this `AuthenticationManager` interface:

- `authenticate()` returns `Authentication` on the off-chance that its capacity can check that the input represents a valid principle. The previously-mentioned code generally returns `authenticated=true`.
- In the event that the capacity finds that the input doesn't speak to a substantial rule, it tosses `AuthenticationException`.
- In the event that the capacity can't choose anything, it will return `null`.

`AuthenticationException` is a runtime exception. An application handles this exception in a conventional way.

`ProviderManager` is often used to implement `AuthenticationManager`, and represents a chain of `AuthenticationProvider` objects. If there's no parent accessible, it throws `AuthenticationException`.

`AuthenticationProvider` resembles `AuthenticationManager`, but has an additional function. This additional function enables the client to query on the off-chance that it supports a given `Authentication` type.

Here's some code of the `AuthenticationProvider` interface:

```
interface AuthenticationProvider {
    @Throws(AuthenticationException::class)
    fun authenticate(authentication:Authentication):Authentication
    fun supports(authentication: Class<*>): Boolean
}
```

This interface has two functions—`authenticate()` returns the user's authentication details and `supports()` returns a `Boolean` if the authentication and given username-password pair matches, or doesn't.

Here is a diagram of the `AuthenticationManager` hierarchy utilizing `ProviderManager`:

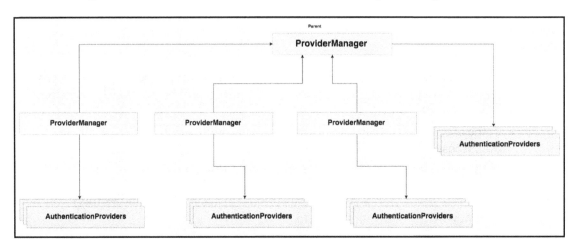

According to this diagram, in an application, `ProviderManager` may have a group of other `ProviderManager` instances but the first one will behave as a parent.
Every `ProviderManager` may have multiple `AuthenticationManager`. For example, if all web resources are under the same path, every group will have its own dedicated `AuthenticationManager`. However, there will be only one common parent, which will act as a global resource and will be shared by these dedicated `AuthenticationManager` instances. Now, let's see how to modify the authentication manager.

Modifying authentication managers

Spring Security provides some configuration helpers to set up authentication manager features in your application. This will help to get the features quickly. `AuthenticationManagerBuilder` helps to modify the authentication managers.

Here is an example of how to implement `AuthenticationManagerBuilder` in the `ApplicationSecurity.kt` class:

```
class ApplicationSecurity: WebSecurityConfigurerAdapter() {
    @Autowired
    fun initialize(builder: AuthenticationManagerBuilder, dataSource:
```

```
DataSource) {
builder.jdbcAuthentication().dataSource(dataSource).withUser("Sunnat629").p
assword("packtPub").roles("USER")
 }
}
```

Here, we have given a username, `sunnat629`, and a password, `packtPub`, as a `USER` role in this application.

 Spring Boot accompanies a default global `AuthenticationManager`, which is sufficiently secure. You can supplant it by giving your own `AuthenticationManager` bean.

Authorization

Authorization is the process of accepting or rejecting access to network resources. It will grant access to utilize the data from the resources. After the `Authentication` process, the `Authorization` process begins. `Authorization` is used to deal with controlling access. `AccessDecisionManager` is one of the core entities of this.

Web security

The servlet channels of spring security provide web security. The `@WebSecurityConfigurer` annotation is used to enable the web security and override `WebSecurityConfigurerAdapter` in the web security class.

Method Security

This is a module of a security method that's provided by Spring Security. We can provide a role in a particular function so that role-based users can access the function.

The following annotation is used to enable this feature:

```
@EnableGlobalMethodSecurity(securedEnabled = true)
```

Here's an example of how to enable method security in the
`SpringSecurityApplication.kt` class, which is the main application class of our demo
project:

```
@SpringBootApplication
@EnableGlobalMethodSecurity(securedEnabled = true)
class SpringSecurityApplication{

    fun main(args: Array<String>) {
        runApplication<SpringSecurityApplication>(*args)
    }
}
```

Now you can create the method resources, such as the following code:

```
@Secured
class CustomService{
    @Secured
    fun secure(): String{
        return "The is Secured..."
    }
}
```

Here, we created a secured class named `CustomService` using the `@Secured` annotation,
and then created a secured function that will return a spring. The `@Secured` annotation is
used to specify a list of roles on a function.

The advantages of Spring Security

The Spring Security framework provides the following advantages:

- Spring Security is an open source security framework
- It supports authentication and authorization
- It protects against common tasks
- It can be integrated with Spring MVC and the Servlet API
- It supports Java and Kotlin configuration support
- It's easy to develop and unit-test the applications
- Spring dependency injection and AOP can be used with ease
- It develops loosely-coupled applications

Spring Security features

There are a lot of features that are implemented in Spring Security.

Here, we have explained some common and major features:

- **LDAP**: LDAP is an open application protocol. This maintains and accesses distributed directory data services over the internet.
- **OAuth 2.0 login**: This component makes it possible for the client to log into the application by utilizing their existing accounts on Google, Facebook, Twitter, or GitHub.
- **Basic access authentication**: This gives a username and password when a client requests them over the network.
- **Digest access authentication**: This asks the program to affirm the identity of the client before sending personal information over the system.
- **Web form authentication**: In this authentication system, a web form collects and authenticates user credentials from the web browser.
- **Authorization**: Spring Security offers this feature to approve of the client before getting the assets.
- **HTTP authorization**: This refers to the HTTP authorization of web request URLs. It uses Apache Ant paths or regular expressions.
- **Reactive support**: This provides reactive programming and web runtime support.
- **Modernized password encoding**: A new password encoder, named `DelegatingPasswordEncoder`, is introduced from Spring Security 5.0.
- **Single sign-on**: This feature allows a client to access multiple applications with a single account.
- **JAAS**: JAAS is a Pluggable Authentication Module that's implemented in Java.
- **Remember-me**: Spring Security utilizes HTTP cookies, which remember a client's login ID and password in order to maintain a strategic distance from login again until the client logs out.
- **Software localization**: You can create the user interface of an application in any human language.

Spring Security modules

The Spring Security module has been isolated into a few sub-modules in Spring Security 3.0. However, in the present version, there are 12 submodules. To support these modules, the code is sub-partitioned into isolated containers. These containers are currently disengaged, where every submodule has a diverse useful area and third-party dependencies.

Here is a list of sub-module jars:

- `spring-security-core.jar`
- `spring-security-remoting.jar`
- `spring-security-web.jar`
- `spring-security-config.jar`
- `spring-security-ldap.jar`
- `spring-security-oauth2-core.jar`
- `spring-security-oauth2-client.jar`
- `spring-security-oauth2-jose.jar`
- `spring-security-acl.jar`
- `spring-security-cas.jar`
- `spring-security-openid.jar`
- `spring-security-test.jar`

 The Spring Security Core sub-module is the base module for the rest of the Security sub-modules, such as `web`, `config`, and `oauth2`.

Implementing Spring Security

If you want to use Spring Security in your project, you need to implement the Spring Security dependencies that you want to use in both Maven and Gradle.

Let's take a look at how to implement the Spring Security dependencies in both Maven and Gradle.

Maven

To implement the security dependencies, you need to implement `spring-security-core` in `pom.xml`:

```xml
<dependency>
 <groupId>org.springframework.security</groupId>
 <artifactId>Spring_Security_SUB_Module_Name</artifactId>
 <version>CURRENT_RELEASE_VERSION</version>
</dependency>

<!--here is an example of a security core sub-modules-->
<dependency>
 <groupId>org.springframework.security</groupId>
 <artifactId>spring-security-core</artifactId>
 <version>5.1.1.RELEASE</version>
</dependency>
```

Gradle

To implement the dependencies, you need to put the following code in `build.gradle`:

```groovy
dependencies {
    implementation
'org.springframework.security:[Spring_Security_SUB_Module_Name]:CURRENT_REL
EASE_VERSION'
}

// here is an example of a security core sub-modules
dependencies {
    implementation 'org.springframework.security:[spring-security-
core]:5.1.1.RELEASE'
}
```

Securing REST with basic authentication

Within this topic, we'll learn basic authentication with a simple project. Here, we'll create an example where you'll build a secure REST API. We'll make a project and implement the basic authentication. This will help us to avoid the basic configuration and complete Kotlin config duration. For this project, you must enter your username and password to access the content. This project has no UI and therefore you need to use an HTTP client to test the project. Here, we're using Insomnia (`https://insomnia.rest/download/`). You can test your project and access the content from here.

Before starting with our project, we'll learn about basic authentication and its use.

What is basic authentication?

Basic authentication is the simplest authentication scheme, which is built into the HTTP protocol. To use it, the client needs to send HTTP requests with the authentication header, which contains the word *Basic* followed by a space. Then, the given string of username and password will be considered as `username/password` and encoded into Base64. For example, if the username and password are `Sunnat629` and `pa$$worD`, these will be converted into Base64 encoding, which will be `U3VubmF0NjI5L3BhcyQkd29yRA==` as authorized. Finally, the client will send `Authorization:` `Basic  U3VubmF0NjI5L3BhcyQkd29yRA==` to the server.

> Base64 can easily be decoded. This is neither encrypted nor hashed. If you want to use the basic authentication, we highly recommend using this together with other security tools, such as HTTPS/SSL.

Creating a project

We'll create a small project where we'll implement the basic authentication security to protect the data. A user needs to be accepted by our security system to access the data. Let's create the project with the given steps:

1. To create the project, go to the `https://start.spring.io/` and modify the given field with your requirement. You can check our project information in the following screenshot:

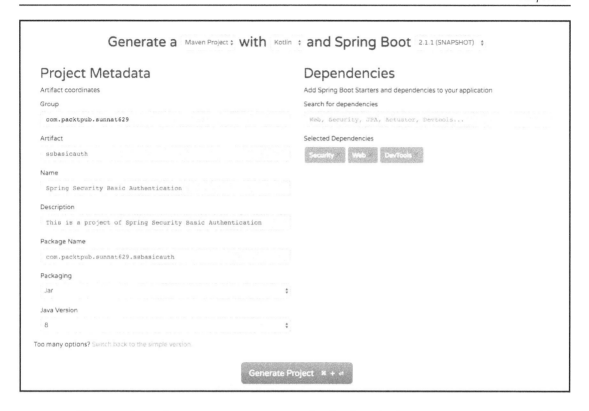

Here, we're using `Maven Project` and selecting the language as `Kotlin` and the Spring Boot version as `2.1.1 (SNAPSHOT)`.

We've added the `Security`, `Web`, and `DevTools` dependencies. You can check the list in `pom.xml`.

3. When you select `Generate Project`, you'll get the project as a ZIP file. Unzip and open this project with your IDE.

4. It will take a moment to download and update the Maven dependencies. Here's a screenshot of your project's content:

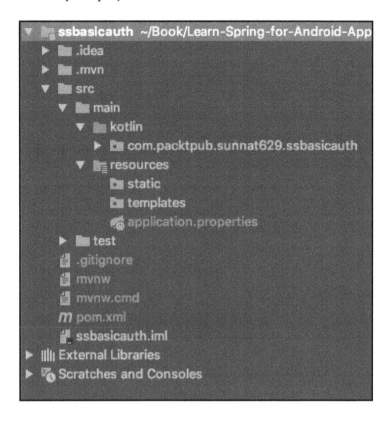

If you need to add new dependencies or update the versions, modify pom.xml. If you want to create kotlin files, you need to create files under the src->main->kotlin->{Package_NAME} folder.

Configuring pom.xml

In this pom.xml, you'll have all the information regarding the project. Here, you can insert new dependencies, update versions, and so on. Here is the sample pom.xml (the full code is on the GitHub, at https://github.com/PacktPublishing/Learn-Spring-for-Android-Application-Development/tree/master/Chapter05:

```
<groupId>com.packtpub.sunnat629</groupId>
<artifactId>ssbasicauth</artifactId>
<version>0.0.1-SNAPSHOT</version>
```

```xml
<packaging>jar</packaging>

<name>Spring Security Basic Authentication</name>
<description>A sample project of Spring Security Basic
Authentication</description>

----
----

<properties>
    <project.build.sourceEncoding>UTF-8</project.build.sourceEncoding>
<project.reporting.outputEncoding>UTF-8</project.reporting.outputEncoding>
    <java.version>1.8</java.version>
    <kotlin.version>1.3.0</kotlin.version>
</properties>

<dependencies>
    <dependency>
        <groupId>org.springframework.boot</groupId>
        <artifactId>spring-boot-starter-security</artifactId>
    </dependency>
    <dependency>
        <groupId>org.springframework.boot</groupId>
        <artifactId>spring-boot-starter-web</artifactId>
    </dependency>
    <dependency>
        <groupId>com.fasterxml.jackson.module</groupId>
        <artifactId>jackson-module-kotlin</artifactId>
    </dependency>
    <dependency>
        <groupId>org.jetbrains.kotlin</groupId>
        <artifactId>kotlin-stdlib-jdk8</artifactId>
    </dependency>
    <dependency>
        <groupId>org.jetbrains.kotlin</groupId>
        <artifactId>kotlin-reflect</artifactId>
    </dependency>

    <dependency>
        <groupId>org.springframework.boot</groupId>
        <artifactId>spring-boot-starter-test</artifactId>
        <scope>test</scope>
    </dependency>
    <dependency>
        <groupId>org.springframework.security</groupId>
        <artifactId>spring-security-test</artifactId>
        <scope>test</scope>
    </dependency>
</dependency>
```

```
</dependencies>

---
---
---
```

Configuring a Spring bean

To configure a Spring bean, we'll create an application file named
SSBasicAuthApplication.kt and use Java configuration, which configures Spring
Security without writing any XML code.

Here's a simple code for the application file (SSBasicAuthApplication.kt):

```
@ComponentScan(basePackages = ["com.packtpub.sunnat629.ssbasicauth"])
@SpringBootApplication
class SSBasicAuthApplication: SpringBootServletInitializer()

fun main(args: Array<String>) {
 runApplication<SSBasicAuthApplication>(*args)
}
```

Here, we've extended SpringBootServletInitializer. This runs SpringApplication
from a traditional WAR archive. This class is responsible for binding the Servlet, Filter,
and ServletContextInitializer beans from the application context to the server.

@SpringBootApplication is a convenience annotation that's equivalent to declaring
@Configuration and @EnableAutoConfiguration for this SSBasicAuthApplication
class.

Mention a package name or a collection of package names in the
@ComponentScan annotation to specify the base packages. This is used with the
@Configuration annotation to tell Spring packages to scan for annotated components.

Configuration for Spring Security

To add the configuration for Spring Security of our project, create a file
named SSConfig.kt in the application package using the following code:

```
@Configuration
@EnableWebSecurity
class SSConfig: WebSecurityConfigurerAdapter() {

    @Autowired
```

```
private val authEntryPoint: AuthenticationEntryPoint? = null

@Throws(Exception::class)
override fun configure(http: HttpSecurity) {
    http.csrf().disable().authorizeRequests()
            .anyRequest().authenticated()
            .and().httpBasic()
            .authenticationEntryPoint(authEntryPoint)
}

@Autowired
@Throws(Exception::class)
fun configureGlobal(auth: AuthenticationManagerBuilder) {
    auth.inMemoryAuthentication()
            .withUser("sunnat629")
.password(PasswordEncoderFactories.createDelegatingPasswordEncoder()
                    .encode("password"))
            .roles("USER")
    }
}
```

We've annotated this class with `@Configuration`, which helps in the Spring annotation-based configuration. `@EnableWebSecurity` will enable the web security support of Spring Security.

We've extended `WebSecurityConfigurerAdapter` and this will give us access to overriding and customizing the Spring features. We're using HTTP Basic Authentication and all of our requests will be authenticated using this.

If the authentication fails, we need to handle this. To do so, create an authentication entry point class named `AuthenticationEntryPoint.kt` and `autowire` it. It will help to retry this process again in case of the failure.

Here we are using the `sunnat629` username, the `password` password, and the `USER` role.

Configuring an authentication entry point

Configure the authentication entry point to handle the failed authentication. When the credentials aren't authorized, this class is mainly responsible for sending the response.

Here's the code of an authentication entry point class named `AuthenticationEntryPoint.kt`:

```
@Component
class AuthenticationEntryPoint : BasicAuthenticationEntryPoint() {
```

```
@Throws(IOException::class, ServletException::class)
override fun commence(request: HttpServletRequest,
                      response: HttpServletResponse,
                      authEx: AuthenticationException) {
    response.addHeader("WWW-Authenticate", "Basic realm=$realmName")
    response.status = HttpServletResponse.SC_UNAUTHORIZED
    val writer = response.writer
    writer.println("HTTP Status 401 - " + authEx.message)
}

@Throws(Exception::class)
override fun afterPropertiesSet() {
    realmName = "packtpub ssbasicauth"
    super.afterPropertiesSet()
}
}
```

Here, we've extended `BasicAuthenticationEntryPoint()`. This will return a full description of a `401 Unauthorized` response to the client.

`401 Unauthorized Error` is an HTTP response status code. This indicates that the request sent by the client couldn't be authenticated.

Configuring Spring WebApplicationInitializer

A Spring `WebApplicationInitializer` uses a Servlet 3.0+ implementation to configure `ServletContext` programmatically.

Here's the sample code of the `WebApplicationInitializer` class, called `MyApplicationInitializer.kt`:

```
class MyApplicationInitializer: WebApplicationInitializer {

    @Throws(ServletException::class)
    override fun onStartup(container: ServletContext) {

        val ctx = AnnotationConfigWebApplicationContext()
        ctx.servletContext = container
        val servlet = container.addServlet("dispatcher",
DispatcherServlet(ctx))
        servlet.setLoadOnStartup(1)
        servlet.addMapping("/")
    }
}
```

This class will help to map the project URL path, "\", using start. As we are using a code-based annotation in place of an XML configuration, we are using `AnnotationConfigWebApplicationContext`.

Then we have created and registered the dispatcher servlet.

Creating a user model

By accessing a simple REST API, we're creating a user model class. When the client inputs a correct username and password, this will return a simple JSON output of some user details.

Here is the code of `Users.kt`:

```
class Users(val id: String,
           val name: String,
           val email: String,
           val contactNumber: String)
```

In this user model, we have an id, a name, an email, and a `contactNumber`. We'll create a JSON-type REST API that will be protected by our security system.

Creating a controller

The controller class will map the URL path of the project. Here, we will use the GET or POST HTTP request functions to create the REST API. Here's a sample code of the controller of the project, named `UserController.kt`:

```
@RestController
class UserController {

    @GetMapping(path = ["/users"])
    fun userList(): ResponseEntity<List<Users>>{
        return ResponseEntity(getUsers(), HttpStatus.OK)
    }

    private fun getUsers(): List<Users> {
        val user = Users("1","Sunnat", "sunnat123@gmail.com", "0123456789")
        val user1 = Users("2","Chaity", "chaity123@gmail.com",
"1234567890")
        val user2 = Users("3","Jisan", "jisan123@gmail.com", "9876543210")
        val user3 = Users("4","Mirza", "mirza123@gmail.com", "5412309876")
        val user4 = Users("5","Hasib", "hasib123@gmail.com", "5678901234")

        return Arrays.asList<Users>(user, user1, user2, user3, user4)
```

```
    }
  }
```

Here, we've created a user list of five people with the user model. In a controller, the `@RequestMapping` annotation is applied to the class level and/or the method level. This maps a particular request path onto a controller. With the `@GetMapping(path = ["/users"])` annotation, the client will send a `GET` request to get the list of the users if the Http status is `OK`.

Using the HTTP client

To see the output, open your third-party HTTP client tools. Here, we're using Insomnia.

After you run the project, open Insomnia.

Please follow these steps to test the project:

1. Create a **New Request** with a name.
2. In the **GET** input box, put the `http://localhost:8080/user` URL. Here, `localhost:8080` is the root URL and as we use `@RequestMapping(path = ["/user"], method = [RequestMethod.GET])` in the controller class, the project will work under the `http://localhost:8080/user` path.
3. If you hit the **Send** button, you'll see an `HTTP Status 401 – Bad credentials` error, as shown in the following screenshot:

Although you're using the basic authentication, you have to input a **Username** and **Password** to complete this request. You need to click on the **Auth** (second tab) and select `Basic` auth; you can enter the **Username** and **Password** there. If you input a random username and password, you'll also get the same error.

After entering the correct **Username** and **Password**, you'll get the list of the users in JSON format as output, as shown in the following screenshot:

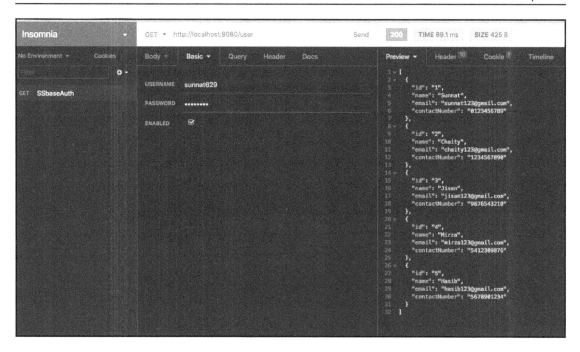

You can also test in the browser. There, you'll be asked to input the **Username** and **Password**.

You can also use the browser to see the REST API:

After inserting the username and password, we can see the user list:

You've created a very simple project using Spring Security basic authentication. We hope that from now on you can write your own auth-based project with the help of Spring Security.

Creating an Android app

It's time to create a simple Android app as a client that will retrieve the REST API from our base authentication server. First of all, we need to create an app from Android Studio and fill in your project name and the company domain. Don't forget to check `Include Kotlin support`. Here's a screenshot of the create application project window:

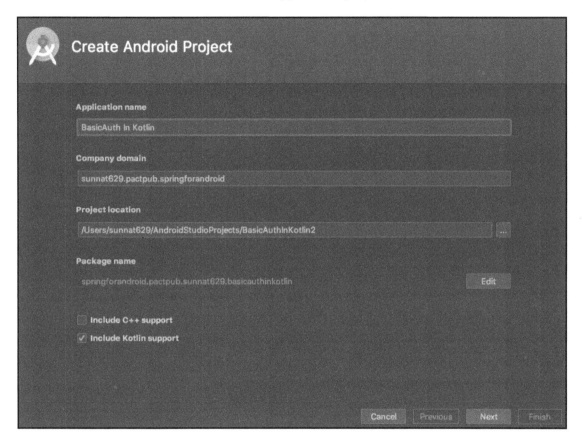

Select the minimum API version from the **Phone and Tablet** option. There's no need to add other options for this project. After clicking **Next**, you can select **Empty Activity** in the **Add an Activity to Mobile** window. After renaming the **Activity Name** and **layout**, click **Finish**. After building the gradle, you'll be ready to start creating an Android app.

Now, let's see how to implement the project's dependencies in Gradle.

Gradle information

In the Gradle file, mention the Kotlin dependency and the application Gradle version. Here are the details of my Android Studio's Gradle file:

```
buildscript {
    ext.kotlin_version = '1.3.10'
    repositories {
        google()
        jcenter()
    }
    dependencies {
        classpath 'com.android.tools.build:gradle:3.2.1'
        classpath "org.jetbrains.kotlin:kotlin-gradle-
plugin:$kotlin_version"

        // NOTE: Do not place your application dependencies here; they
belong
        // in the individual module build.gradle files
    }
}

allprojects {
    repositories {
        google()
        jcenter()
    }
}

task clean(type: Delete) {
    delete rootProject.buildDir
}
```

Here, our Gradle version is `3.2.1` and the Kotlin version is `1.3.10`

Gradle dependencies

In this Gradle file, we'll implement the dependencies of Retrofit, which will help us to fetch the JSON-type REST API from our previous project. Here are all the dependencies:

```
implementation 'com.android.support:appcompat-v7:27.1.1'
implementation 'com.android.support.constraint:constraint-layout:1.1.3'

implementation 'com.google.code.gson:gson:2.8.5'

implementation 'com.squareup.retrofit2:retrofit:2.4.0'
```

```
implementation 'com.squareup.retrofit2:converter-gson:2.4.0'
implementation 'com.squareup.retrofit2:retrofit-converters:2.5.0'
implementation 'com.squareup.retrofit2:retrofit-adapters:2.5.0'
implementation 'com.squareup.okhttp3:logging-interceptor:3.12.0'
```

Creating a user model

We'll fetch the REST API of our basic authentication-based Spring project, which was created using basic authentication. Although the REST API has four entities (`id`, `name`, `email`, and `contactNumber`), we'll create a model based on this REST API.

Here's the output of the REST API where we can see five users' details:

```
▼ 0:
    id:              "1"
    name:            "Sunnat"
    email:           "sunnat123@gmail.com"
    contactNumber:   "0123456789"
▼ 1:
    id:              "2"
    name:            "Chaity"
    email:           "chaity123@gmail.com"
    contactNumber:   "1234567890"
▼ 2:
    id:              "3"
    name:            "Jisan"
    email:           "jisan123@gmail.com"
    contactNumber:   "9876543210"
▼ 3:
    id:              "4"
    name:            "Mirza"
    email:           "mirza123@gmail.com"
    contactNumber:   "5412309876"
▼ 4:
    id:              "5"
    name:            "Hasib"
    email:           "hasib123@gmail.com"
    contactNumber:   "5678901234"
```

According to the API, we'll create a user model for the client side. Here's the model class, named `UserModel`:

```
class UserModel (val id: String
                 val name: String,
                 val contactNumber: String,
                 val id: String,
                 val email: String)
```

Now, we need to create an interface that will have the HTTP request functions. In this project, we'll only use a GET function that retrieves all the details of users. Here, we're using the GET retrofit annotation to encode details about the parameters and request function.

Here's the code of the `UserService` interface:

```
interface UserService {
    @GET("/user")
    fun getUserList(): Call<List<UserModel>>
}
```

We'll search the `/user` endpoint and this will provide a list of user models.

Implementing the user service

Retrofit client calls the Gerrit API and handles the result by printing the result of the call to the console.

Create a class where we'll build a Retrofit client, and this will call the API and handle the result. This will be responsible for controlling all the tasks using the `Retrofit.builder` class and configuring it with the base of the given URL.

Here's the code of `UserServiceImpl.kt`:

```
class UserServiceImpl{
    fun getGithubServiceImpl(username:String, password:String): UserService
{
        val retrofit = Retrofit.Builder()
                .client(getOkhttpClient(username, password))
                .baseUrl(YOUR_SERVER_DOMAIN)
                .addConverterFactory(GsonConverterFactory.create())
                .build()
        return retrofit.create(UserService::class.java)
    }

    private fun getOkhttpClient(username:String, password:String):
OkHttpClient{
        return OkHttpClient.Builder()
                .addInterceptor(BasicAuthInterceptor(username, password))
                .build()
    }
}
```

According to this code, we set `.client()` with `username` and `password`. Then we implemented the `YOUR_SERVER_DOMAIN` (assume the URL of the Rest API server is `http://localhost:8080`), `baseUrl()` , and we've used `OkHttpClient` as the client.

Authenticating with OkHttp interceptors

Although we're using a base authentication security, we need a `username` and `password` to grant access to this REST API. Here, we're using `OkHttp` interceptors for authentication. This will help you to send a request and get the auth permission to access the resources.

Here, we've called the `BasicAuthInterceptor` class in `OkHttpClient.Builder()`:

```
 private fun getOkhttpClient(username:String, password:String):
OkHttpClient{
        return OkHttpClient.Builder()
                .addInterceptor(BasicAuthInterceptor(username, password))
                .build()
    }
```

Here's the class of `BasicAuthInterceptor.kt`:

```
class BasicAuthInterceptor(user: String, password: String) : Interceptor {

    private val credentials: String = Credentials.basic(user, password)
```

```
@Throws(IOException::class)
override fun intercept(chain: Interceptor.Chain): Response {
    val request = chain.request()
    val authenticatedRequest = request.newBuilder()
            .header("Authorization", credentials).build()
    return chain.proceed(authenticatedRequest)
    }
}
```

In this class, only the credentials are added as your user details. Here, a client will make a request using the `username` and `password` credentials. During every request, this interceptor acts before it's performed and alters the request header. Consequently, you don't need to add `@HEADER("Authorization")` to the API function.

Calling callbacks

Here, we're calling `CallBack<>` from `MainActivity`. This callback response comes from a server or offline requests. This means returning the result of a long-running function at a later moment in time.

Check the `MainActivity.kt` code to use the `CallBack` function and handle the result:

```
class MainActivity : AppCompatActivity() {

    var username: String = "sunnat629"
    var password: String = "password"

    override fun onCreate(savedInstanceState: Bundle?) {
        super.onCreate(savedInstanceState)
        setContentView(R.layout.activity_main)

        val githubService: UserService =
UserServiceImpl().getGithubServiceImpl(username,password)

        val call: Call<List<UserModel>> = githubService.getUserList()
        call.enqueue(object: Callback<List<UserModel>> {
            override fun onFailure(call: Call<List<UserModel>>, t:
Throwable) {
                Log.wtf("PACKTPUB", t.message)
            }

            override fun onResponse(call: Call<List<UserModel>>, response:
Response<List<UserModel>>) {
                val adapter = UserListAdapter(this@MainActivity,
response.body())
```

```
                displayList.adapter = adapter
            }
        })
    }
}
```

Let's discuss the preceding code as follows:

1. First, we need to initialize `UserServiceImpl().getGithubServiceImpl(username,passwor d)` so that we can call `getUserList()` from `UserService`.
2. Then we'll call `enqueue(retrofit2.Callback<T>)`, which will be executed asynchronously, send the request, and get the response.
3. `enqueue()` has two functions: `onResponse()` and `onFailure()`. If there are any server-related errors, it will call `onFailure()`, and if it gets the response and the resources, it will call `onResponse()`. We can also use the resource of the `onResponse()` function.

Here, we'll get a response of the `UserModel` list. We can show the list in our application UI.

Creating the UI

In the created `main_activity` layout, we'll show a list of the user details where we show the name, email ID, and contact number of a user—we'll use `ListView`.

Here's the code of the `mainActivity` layout of the `MainActivity` class:

```xml
<?xml version="1.0" encoding="utf-8"?>
<android.support.constraint.ConstraintLayout
xmlns:android="http://schemas.android.com/apk/res/android"
    xmlns:app="http://schemas.android.com/apk/res-auto"
    xmlns:tools="http://schemas.android.com/tools"
    android:layout_width="match_parent"
    android:layout_height="match_parent"
    tools:context=".MainActivity">

    <TextView
        android:id="@+id/textView"
        android:layout_width="match_parent"
        android:layout_height="wrap_content"
        android:text="@string/user_title"
        app:layout_constraintEnd_toEndOf="parent"
        android:textStyle="bold"
        android:padding="5dp"
```

```
        android:gravity="center_horizontal"
        android:textAppearance="?android:textAppearanceLarge"
        app:layout_constraintStart_toStartOf="parent"
        app:layout_constraintTop_toTopOf="parent" />

    <ListView
        android:id="@+id/displayList"
        android:layout_width="match_parent"
        android:layout_height="wrap_content"
        android:layout_marginStart="8dp"
        android:layout_marginLeft="8dp"
        android:layout_marginTop="8dp"
        android:layout_marginEnd="8dp"
        android:layout_marginRight="8dp"
        app:layout_constraintEnd_toEndOf="parent"
        app:layout_constraintStart_toStartOf="parent"
        app:layout_constraintTop_toBottomOf="@+id/textView" />

</android.support.constraint.ConstraintLayout>
```

In this layout, we have one `TextView` and one `ListView`.

We'll use this `ListView` in the `onResponse()` function of `MainActivity`.

We'll get the list and create a custom adapter to show the user list, as follows:

```
val adapter = UserListAdapter(this@MainActivity,
response.body()//this is a arraylist
)
```

Here, we have a custom adapter where we'll send the context and the `Array` list of the users.

Creating a custom list adapter

To show the output of the REST API, we need to create a custom list adapter and so we need to design an XML file of the custom list adapter. Here's the XML code for each row in the list:

```
<?xml version="1.0" encoding="utf-8"?>
<android.support.constraint.ConstraintLayout
xmlns:android="http://schemas.android.com/apk/res/android"
    xmlns:app="http://schemas.android.com/apk/res-auto"
    xmlns:tools="http://schemas.android.com/tools"
    android:layout_width="match_parent"
    android:layout_height="match_parent"
```

```
android:padding="10dp">

<TextView
    android:id="@+id/name"
    android:layout_width="match_parent"
    android:layout_height="wrap_content"
    android:gravity="center_horizontal"
    android:padding="5dp"
    android:textAppearance="?android:textAppearanceMedium"
    android:textStyle="bold"
    app:layout_constraintBottom_toTopOf="@+id/contactNumber"
    app:layout_constraintEnd_toEndOf="parent"
    app:layout_constraintStart_toStartOf="parent"
    app:layout_constraintTop_toTopOf="parent"
    tools:text="@tools:sample/full_names" />

<TextView
    android:id="@+id/contactNumber"
    android:layout_width="match_parent"
    android:layout_height="wrap_content"
    android:gravity="center_horizontal"
    android:padding="5dp"
    android:textAppearance="?android:textAppearanceSmall"
    app:layout_constraintBottom_toTopOf="@+id/email"
    app:layout_constraintEnd_toEndOf="parent"
    app:layout_constraintStart_toStartOf="parent"
    app:layout_constraintTop_toBottomOf="@+id/name"
    tools:text="@tools:sample/cities" />

<TextView
    android:id="@+id/email"
    android:layout_width="match_parent"
    android:layout_height="wrap_content"
    android:gravity="center_horizontal"
    android:padding="5dp"
    android:textAppearance="?android:textAppearanceSmall"
    app:layout_constraintEnd_toEndOf="parent"
    app:layout_constraintStart_toStartOf="parent"
    app:layout_constraintTop_toBottomOf="@+id/contactNumber"
    tools:text="@tools:sample/cities" />


</android.support.constraint.ConstraintLayout>
```

Here, we have a TextView of name, contactNumber, and email.

After that, we'll create the adapter, named `UserListAdapter.kt`, as follows:

```
class UserListAdapter(context: Context,
                      private val userList: List<UserModel>?) :
BaseAdapter() {
    private val inflater: LayoutInflater =
context.getSystemService(Context.LAYOUT_INFLATER_SERVICE)
            as LayoutInflater
    override fun getView(position: Int, convertView: View?, parent:
ViewGroup?): View {
        val rowView = inflater.inflate(R.layout.user_list_item, parent,
false)
        val name = rowView.findViewById(R.id.name) as TextView
        val email = rowView.findViewById(R.id.email) as TextView
        val contactNumber = rowView.findViewById(R.id.contactNumber) as
TextView
        val userDetails = getItem(position) as UserModel
        name.text = userDetails.name
        email.text = userDetails.email
        contactNumber.text = userDetails.contactNumber
        return rowView
    }
    override fun getItem(position: Int): Any {
        return userList!![position]
    }
    override fun getItemId(position: Int): Long {
        return position.toLong()
    }
    override fun getCount(): Int {
        return userList!!.size
    }
}
```

This class extends `BaseAdapter()`, which will add several inherited functions.

Then you need to add `LayoutInflater`, which converts the XML layout into corresponding `ViewGroups` and Widgets:

- `getView()` creates a view for a row of the list. Here, you'll define all the UI-based information.
- `getItem()` returns the position of the list that's obtained from the server.
- `getItemId()` defines a unique ID for each row in the list.
- `getCount()` returns the size of the list.

Now, in `getView()`, you'll add the element of the layout, as follows:

```
val name = rowView.findViewById(R.id.name) as TextView
        val email = rowView.findViewById(R.id.email) as TextView
        val contactNumber = rowView.findViewById(R.id.contactNumber) as
    TextView
```

You should never perform long-running tasks on the main thread. This will result in an Application Not Responding (ANR).

Mobile applications

Once we've completed our code, it's time to see the output. Run your basic authentication Spring project and then run your app. Here's the output of your app, where we can see the user details:

In the following screenshot, the left side is the server API, where we have the user details, and on the right we have the client output of the Android application:

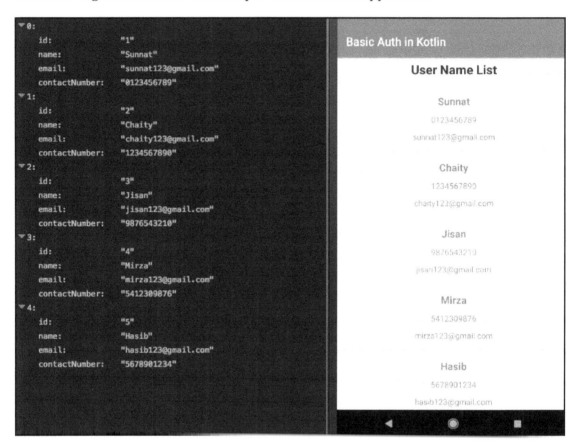

We've created a client application that will fetch the data of a basic authentication Spring-Security-based REST API.

Securing REST with Spring Security OAuth2

In the last section, we learned how to make a basic authorization project. This provides solid security for a project, but it doesn't have the dimension of security required for a complex or enterprise-level project. Since this security can be broken or hacked, we require a more grounded security framework to handle these sorts of hacking. OAuth is one of the best security frameworks – it's exceedingly utilized by Google, Facebook, Twitter, and many other popular platforms. Now we'll learn about OAuth2 and its use.

What is OAuth2?

OAuth is a safe authorization convention, and **OAuth2** is the second form of the OAuth protocol. This protocol is called a **framework**. OAuth2 enables a third-party application to provide limited access to an HTTP service, such as Google, GitHub, or Twitter. This access is either intended for the benefit of the proprietor or to enable the third-party application to get access to the user account. This creates an authorization stream between web and desktop or mobile devices. It has some important roles that control the users' access limitation.

OAuth2 Roles

There are four roles in OAuth2:

- **Resource Owner**: Normally, this is you.
- **Resource Server**: The server host's protected data. For example, Google, Github, or Twitter hosts your personal and professional information.
- **Client**: An application that requests a resource server to access data. The client can be a website, a desktop application, or even a mobile application.
- **Authorization Server**: This server will issue an access token to the client. This token will be the key to accessing the information and it's mainly used to request the resource server for the client.

Here's a diagram of the general workflow of the OAuth protocol (the flow isn't fixed for every protocol; it's based on the type of authorization granted):

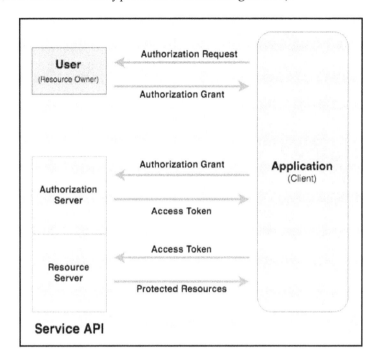

Here are the steps of the workflow:

1. To access the service resources, the **Application** sends the **Authorization Request** to the **User**.
2. The **Application** receives an **Authorization Grant** if the **User** authorizes the request.
3. The **Application** sends the grant to the **Authorization Server** for an **Access Token**.
4. If the **Authorization Grant** is valid and the **Application** is authenticated, the **Authorization Server** creates an **Access Token**.
5. The **Application** gets the **Access Token** from the **Authorization Server**.
6. The application sends a request to the **Resource Server** for resources from the server as well as authentication.
7. Using the token, the **Resource Server** provides the requested recourses to the **Application**.

OAuth2 grant types

There are four kinds of OAuth2 Grants:

- **Authorization Code:** This is used in a server-side application and allows the client to get a long-lasting access token. However, this token will be invalidated if the client asks the server for a new token.
- **Implicit:** For the most part, this is utilized with mobile or web applications.
- **Resource Owner Password Credentials:** In this grant, the credentials are first sent to the customer. Then they're sent to the authorization server.
- **Client Credentials:** This is used when the client itself is the resource owner. There's no authorization to get from the client's end.

So, that's a brief summary of the OAuth protocol. Now let's create a project using the Spring Security OAuth2 modules.

Creating a project

We'll create a simple Spring Security OAuth2-based project. To do so, go to `https://start.spring.io/` and modify the given field with your requirement.

Here, we're using the **Maven** Project and selecting the language as **Kotlin**. The Spring Boot version is **2.1.1 (SNAPSHOT)**.

After you select **Generate Project**, you'll get the project as a ZIP file. Unzip and open this project with your IDE.

Maven dependencies

Our main dependencies are `Web`, `Security`, `Cloud Security`, `Cloud OAuth2`, `JPA`, `H2`, `Lombok`, and `Thymeleaf`.

Here are the mentioned Maven dependencies in `pom.xml`:

```
----
----
  <dependencies>
---
---
<!--spring security-->
<dependency>
    <groupId>org.springframework.security</groupId>
```

```
    <artifactId>spring-security-config</artifactId>
    <version>5.2.0.BUILD-SNAPSHOT</version>
</dependency>
<dependency>
    <groupId>org.springframework.boot</groupId>
    <artifactId>spring-boot-starter-security</artifactId>
</dependency>

<!--spring cloud security-->
<dependency>
    <groupId>org.springframework.cloud</groupId>
    <artifactId>spring-cloud-starter-oauth2</artifactId>
</dependency>
<dependency>
    <groupId>org.springframework.cloud</groupId>
    <artifactId>spring-cloud-starter-security</artifactId>
</dependency>

----
----

<!--database-->
<dependency>
    <groupId>org.springframework.boot</groupId>
    <artifactId>spring-boot-starter-data-jpa</artifactId>
</dependency>
<dependency>
    <groupId>com.h2database</groupId>
    <artifactId>h2</artifactId>
    <scope>runtime</scope>
</dependency>
----
----
```

Configuring the resource server

A resource server will have all the protected resources, and these are protected by the OAuth2 token. It's time to learn about this resource server with the help of the code. Create a resource server named ResourceServerConfig.kt.

Here is the code of our ResourceServerConfig.kt:

```
@Configuration
@EnableResourceServer
class ResourceServerConfig: ResourceServerConfigurerAdapter(){
```

```
@Throws(Exception::class)
override fun configure(http: HttpSecurity?) {
    http!!
            .authorizeRequests()
            .antMatchers("/open_for_all").permitAll() // anyone can
enter
            .antMatchers("/private").authenticated() // only authorized
user can enter
    }
}
```

To enable the features of the OAuth 2.0 resource-server mechanism, you need to add an annotation named `@EnableResourceServer`, and although it's a configuration class, you need to add the `@Configuration` annotation.

This class extends `ResourceServerConfigurerAdapter`, this then extends `ResourceServerConfigurer`, which will make it possible to override and configure `ResourceServerConfigurer`.

We override `configure(http: HttpSecurity?)`, where we mention which URL paths are protected and which are not protected.

`authorizeRequests()` permits confining access dependent on the utilization of `HttpServletRequest`.

`antMatchers()` refers to the implementation of the Ant-style path patterns in mappings.

We use `.antMatchers("/").permitAll()`, which allows all users to access this URL path, `"/"`. In addition, we use `.antMatchers("/private").authenticated()`, which means a user needs a token to access this `/private` path.

Configuring the authorization server

An authorization server is a configuration class. In this class, we'll create a grant-type environment. A grant type helps a client get an access token from the end user. This server's configuration is designed to implement the client details' service and token service. It's also responsible for enabling or disabling certain components of the mechanism globally. Now, create an authorization server class named `AuthorizationServerConfig.kt`.

Here's the code for `AuthorizationServerConfig.kt`:

```
@Configuration
@EnableAuthorizationServer
```

```
class AuthorizationServerConfig: AuthorizationServerConfigurerAdapter() {

    @Autowired
    lateinit var authenticationManager: AuthenticationManager

    @Autowired
    lateinit var passwordEncoder: BCryptPasswordEncoder

    @Throws(Exception::class)
    override fun configure(security:
AuthorizationServerSecurityConfigurer?) {
        security!!.checkTokenAccess("isAuthenticated()")
    }

    @Throws(Exception::class)
    override fun configure(clients: ClientDetailsServiceConfigurer?) {
        clients!!
                .inMemory()
                .withClient("client")
                .secret(passwordEncoder.encode("secret"))
                .authorizedGrantTypes("password")
                .authorities("ROLE_CLIENT", "ROLE_TRUSTED_CLIENT")
                .scopes("read", "write", "trust")
                .resourceIds("oauth2-resource")
                .accessTokenValiditySeconds(5000) // token validity time
duration 5 minuets

    }

    @Throws(Exception::class)
    override fun configure(endpoints:
AuthorizationServerEndpointsConfigurer?) {
        endpoints!!.authenticationManager(authenticationManager)
    }
}
```

The @EnableAuthorizationServer annotation enables the features of the OAuth 2.0 authorization server mechanism. You need to add the @Configuration annotation to make it the configuration class.

This class extends `AuthorizationServerConfigurerAdapter`, which then extends `ResourceServerConfigurer`. It will make it possible to override and configure `AuthorizationServerConfigurer`. There are three types of `configure()` functions:

- `ClientDetailsServiceConfigurer`: This defines the details service of a client.
- `AuthorizationServerSecurityConfigurer`: This defines the security constraints on the token endpoint.
- `AuthorizationServerEndpointsConfigurer`: This defines the authorization and token endpoints and the token services.

According to our code, in `configure(security: AuthorizationServerSecurityConfigurer?)`, we define whether or not to check the token endpoint which is authenticated.

In `configure(clients: ClientDetailsServiceConfigurer?)`, we define the `ClientDetails` service. In this project, we didn't use a database, so we use an in-memory implementation of the `ClientDetails` service. Here are the important attributes of the client:

- `withClient()`: This is required and this is where we define the client ID, `"client"`.
- `secret()`: This is required for trusted clients and is where we define the secret, `"secret"`, but we have to encode the password. Here, we inject `BCryptPasswordEncoder` to encode the password or secret key.
- `authorizedGrantTypes()`: We have used the `"password"` grant type that's authorized for the client to use.
- `scope()`: The scope is used to limit the access for the resources of a client. If the scope is undefined or empty, that means the client isn't limited by scope. Here, we use `"read"`, `"write"`, and `"trust"`.
- `authorities()`: This is used to grant the client.
- `resourceId()`: This optional ID is used for the resource.
- `accessTokenValiditySeconds()`: This refers to the token validity time duration.

In `configure(endpoints: AuthorizationServerEndpointsConfigurer?)`, we've configured `AuthorizationEndpoint`, which supports the grant type. We inject `AuthenticationManager` and configure it via `AuthorizationServerEndpointsConfigurer`.

Creating the security config

This is a Java configuration class for Spring Security that enables users to configure Spring Security easily without the use of XML. Create a secure config file named SecurityConfiguration.kt. Here's the code for the class:

```kotlin
@Configuration
@EnableWebSecurity
class SecurityConfiguration: WebSecurityConfigurerAdapter() {

    @Throws(Exception::class)
    override fun configure(auth: AuthenticationManagerBuilder?) {
        auth!!
                .inMemoryAuthentication()
                .passwordEncoder(passwordEncoder())
            // user1 as USER
                .withUser("sunnat")
                .password(passwordEncoder().encode("password"))
                .roles("USER")
                .and()

                // user2 as ADMIN
                .withUser("admin")
                .password(passwordEncoder().encode("password"))
                .roles("ADMIN")
    }

    @Throws(Exception::class)
    override fun configure(http: HttpSecurity?) {
        http!!
                .antMatcher("/**").authorizeRequests()
                .anyRequest().authenticated()
                .and()
                .formLogin()
                .and()
                .httpBasic()
    }

    @Bean(name = [BeanIds.AUTHENTICATION_MANAGER])
    @Throws(Exception::class)
    override fun authenticationManagerBean(): AuthenticationManager {
        return super.authenticationManagerBean()
    }


    @Bean
    fun passwordEncoder(): BCryptPasswordEncoder {
        return BCryptPasswordEncoder(16)
```

```
        }
    }
```

This is a configuration class, so you need to add the `@Configuration` annotation.

This class extends `WebSecurityConfigurerAdapter`, and the `@EnableWebSecurity` annotation provides the web-based security mechanism.

According to this code, we use two `@Bean` annotations in the required functions. We inject `AuthenticationManager` and configure it via `AuthorizationServerEndpointsConfigurer`. The `BCryptPasswordEncoder` instance is used to encode the passwords.

In `configure(http: HttpSecurity?)`, note the following:

- `antMatcher("/**").authorizeRequests()` means that this `HttpSecurity` will only be applicable to URLs that start with `/**`.
- `anyRequest().authenticated()` utilization guarantees that any request to our application requires the client to be confirmed.
- `formLogin()` allows users to authenticate with form-based logins.
- `httpBasic()` means the user is validated with HTTP Basic authentication.

In `configure(auth: AuthenticationManagerBuilder?)`, note the following:

- `inMemoryAuthentication()` includes memory confirmation to `AuthenticationManagerBuilder` and restores `InMemoryUserDetailsManagerConfigurer` to permit customization of the in-memory validation.
- `passwordEncoder(passwordEncoder())` means that the password will be an encoded password.
- `withUser("user")` and `withUser("admin")` is the name of the user.
- `password(passwordEncoder().encode("password"))` is the encoded password.
- `roles("USER")` and `roles("ADMIN")` is the role of a user.

Creating the controller class

Create a controller class named `UserController.kt`, as follows:

```
@RestController
@RequestMapping("/")
```

```
class UserController{

//    This is for all means there is no security issue for this URL path
    @GetMapping(value = ["/open_for_all", ""])
    fun home(): String{
        return "This area can be accessed by all."
    }

    //    Yu have to use token to get this URL path
    @GetMapping("/private")
    fun securedArea(): String{
        return "You used an access token to enter this area."
    }
}
```

Here, we've annotated this class as @RestController, which handles all the web requests. @RequestMapping("/") means that the default URL path is "/".

The @GetMapping implemented functions are home(), which can be accessed by everyone, and securedArea(), which can be accessed only by those who have the *access token*. We configured these in the ResourceServerConfig class.

Creating the application class

Lastly, create the application class, named SpringSecurityOAuth2Application.kt, which will convert your application into a SpringBoot application:

```
@SpringBootApplication
class SpringSecurityOAuth2Application

fun main(args: Array<String>) {
    runApplication<SpringSecurityOAuth2Application>(*args)
}
```

Application properties

This step is optional, particularly in this project. Here, we just change the port number for this project. To change it, modify application.properties under the resources folder:

```
#this project server port
server.port=8081
```

Here, we change the port number to 8081.

Checking the output

If you're reading this section, that means you've configured everything correctly. After finishing the project, you'll have these files:

After completing the setup, run the project. If there are no errors, you can find the run window. The following screenshot shows that there are no errors and the application is ready to use:

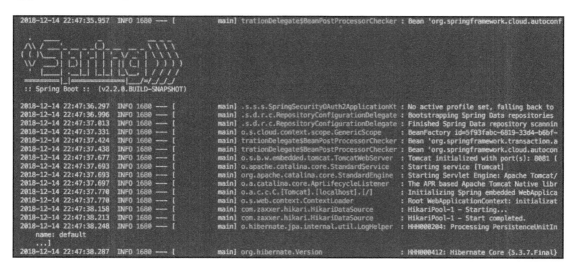

Checking unprotected URLs

Now, open the *Insomnia* application.

Create a GET request from the top inbox and use the `http://localhost:8081/open_for_all` URL.

Your result will look like the following screenshot:

In the `ResourceServerConfig` class, we configured that `"/open_for_all"` can be accessed by everyone.

Getting access tokens

Create a `POST` request from the top inbox and put down the `http://localhost:8081/oauth/token` URL. This is the default `POST` *URL* to get the token.

Add three parameters—`username=sunnat`, `password=password`, and `grant_type=password`—in the **Multipart** window:

You can find the information of `username` and `password` in the `SecurityConfiguration` class, and `grant_type` will be found in `AuthorizationServerConfig`. Here, we're using the **password** grant type.

Go to the **Basic** window and input the **username** and **password**. You can find this information in the `AuthorizationServerConfig` class, where the username is mentioned in `withClient()` and the password is `secret()`.

We added an image of the Insomnia tool where we wrote down the **username** and **password**. Now click the send button. If there are no errors, you'll get the following `access_token`:

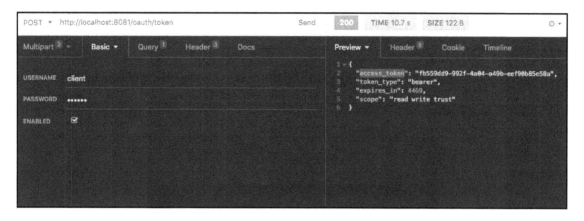

You can see the access_token that will be used to access the protected resources. expires_in means that after 4469 seconds the token will expire. "scope": "read write trust" means you can read, write, and modify the resources.

Accessing the protected URL

We found the access_token and now we'll use it. To do this, create another GET request and insert http://localhost:8081/private.

As a parameter, use access_token with the value of the given token key, and click **Send**:

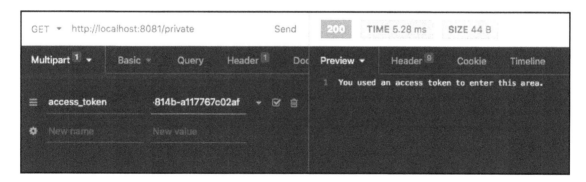

Once that's done, you can access the /private URL, which is protected and configured in the ResourceServerConfig class.

We're now ready to use the OAuth2 Spring Security in our project.

Common mistakes and errors

During this project, you may encounter some common errors.

For example, you might get some errors during building and running the project. To solve this, check that all versions of the dependencies are the latest. In addition, check whether every dependency is present. If you use the database, make sure you have the correct database and scheme name in `application.properties`.

In the `POST` request, sometimes you can find the following error message:

```
1 ▾ {
2       "error": "invalid_request",
3       "error_description": "Missing grant type"
4   }
```

The previous screenshot indicates that you entered an incorrect `grant_type`. Please check the parameter, as well as the `AuthorizationServerConfig` class where you mention the `grant_type`:

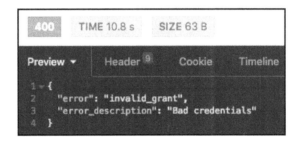

Please check the `SecurityConfiguration` class and match the system `username-password` with the given `username` and `password` parameters. The following screenshot means you entered an incorrect client or secret value in the `Basic Auth` tab:

```
401   TIME 5.33 s    SIZE 127 B

Preview ▾    Header 10    Cookie    Timeline

1 ▾ {
2       "timestamp": "2018-12-14T17:34:15.355+0000",
3       "status": 401,
4       "error": "Unauthorized",
5       "message": "Unauthorized",
6       "path": "/oauth/token"
7   }
```

The preceding screenshot means you entered an incorrect `client` or `secret` value in the **Basic** Auth tab. Please match the `client` and `secret` value from `AuthorizationServerConfig` and the `Basic Auth` tab's value:

The preceding screenshot means your token key has expired. You need to refresh a new access token to solve this error.

You may face some other errors. To see the solutions, you can always search StackOverflow (`https://stackoverflow.com/`).

Summary

In this chapter, you learned how to use Spring Security with confidence. First, we covered what Spring Security is as well as its architecture. We also learned about the advantage of using Spring Security, looking at its features and modules. Now, we're able to implement Spring Security in any project. We learned what the basic authentication is and, using an example, we saw how to implement the basic authentication in a project as well as how to secure the resources in a server. We also learned how to create a secured REST API. Then we learned how to create a client application in Android to fetch and use the protected resources from the REST API. We also learned how to implement a username and password to get access to the basic authentication-based secured server. In addition, we familiarized ourselves with how to use a custom adapter in a listview in the client application. In the last section, we explored a better-secured protocol: OAuth2. We learned the role and workflow of this protocol. With a simple project, we learned how to configure the OAuth2 authorization and resource servers. Finally, we saw how to retrieve the REST API using a third-party HTTP client.

In the next chapter, we'll learn about the database, which is very important, as it's the main place to store and handle your data.

Questions

1. What does Spring Security target?
2. What are the fundamental classes of Spring Security?
3. Which filter class is required for Spring Security?
4. Is password hashing supported in Spring Security?
5. What are the OAuth 2.0 Grant Types?

Further reading

Here is a list of information you can refer to:

- *Spring Security - Third Edition* (`https://www.packtpub.com/application-development/spring-security-third-edition`) by Mick Knutson, Robert Winch, Peter Mularien
- *Hands-On Spring Security 5 for Reactive Applications* (`https://www.packtpub.com/application-development/hands-spring-security-5-reactive-applications`) by Tomcy John
- *OAuth 2.0 Cookbook* (`https://www.packtpub.com/virtualization-and-cloud/oauth-20-cookbook`) by Adolfo Eloy Nascimento

Accessing the Database

6

In this chapter, we will learn about the database in the Spring Framework. The database is a collection of data that is stored in the server in an organized way, so that an application can retrieve the data in the way that the user requests. In this chapter, you will learn how to use the database on both the client and server side. In addition to this, we will explore the usage of JDBC, JPA, Hibernate, and MySQL from the server side, and we will look at the room persistence library from the client side.

This chapter covers the following topics:

- What is a database?
- What is a database management system?
- Data access in Spring.
- Data access with JDBC in Spring.
- Creating a sample project using JDBC.
- Data access with JPA and Hibernate in Spring.
- Creating a sample project using JPA + Hibernate.
- What is the room persistence library?
- Creating an Android application using the room persistence library.

Technical requirements

We have previously demonstrated how to set up the environment and what tools, software, and IDE are needed in order to develop Spring. To create your project, visit this link: `https://start.spring.io/`. The following options will be available here:

- Maven project
- Language – Kotlin

- Spring Boot version – 2.1.1 (SNAPSHOT)
- When you create the project, you need to provide some information, such as—**Group**, **Artifact**, **Name**, **Description**, **Package Name**, **Packaging**, and **Java Version**.

We will use MySQL in upcoming projects. Consequently, you need to download the tools for MySQL from `https://dev.mysql.com/downloads/workbench/` and install it. Please try to configure the MySQL database with the given information to make your project easier:

```
Host -- localhost
Port -- 3306
Username -- root
Password -- 12345678
```

The source code with an example for this chapter is available on GitHub at the following link: `https://github.com/PacktPublishing/Learn-Spring-for-Android-Application-Development/tree/master/Chapter06`.

Database

A **database** is a collection of information that is stored in the server in an organized way. A user can fetch and use this data from the server in various systems. In the database, a user can add, delete, update, get, or manage the data. Normally, data is assembled into tables, columns, and rows, making it easier to find relevant data. A computer database contains aggregations of data records or files. A company's data can include their statistics or client information, or it can be top secret documents. A database manager provides the client or the user with the ability to control read and/or write access, analyze the data, and so on. We will now look at various types of database and their uses.

Types of database

Databases are used for a variety of purposes, such as to store personal or company information. There are several databases available on the market, as described in the following sections.

Personal database

A personal database is designed for data stored on a personal computer. This database is small and very easy to manage, and it is normally used by a small group of people or a small organization.

Relational database

The relational database is created on a set of tables that fit into a pre-defined category. These databases are sorted by an arrangement of tables where information gets fit into a pre-characterized class. The table is comprised of rows and columns. The column has a passage for information for an explicit classification. On the other side, rows contain a case for that information characterized by the classification. The relational database has a standard user and application program interface named **Structured Query Language** (**SQL**).

Distributed database

A distributed database is stored in multiple physical locations and distributed at various sites of an organization. The sites are connected with the help of communication links, so the user can access the distributed data easily. There are two kinds of distributed database—homogeneous and heterogeneous. In a homogenous distributed database, the physical locations have the same hardware and run in the same OS and database applications. However, in the heterogeneous distributed database, the hardware, OS, or database applications can be found in a different location.

Object-oriented database

In an object-oriented database, items are created by using object-oriented programming such as Java and C++, which are stored in relational databases. But for those items, an object-oriented database is well-suited. An object-oriented database is sorted out around objects as opposed to activities, and information instead of rationale.

NoSQL database

A NoSQL database is normally used for a large set of distributed data. This database is very effective for big data where an organization analyzes large chunks of unorganized data stored in multiple virtual servers in the cloud.

Graph database

A graph database is a type of NoSQL database that uses graph theory to store, map, and query the relationships of the data. It is a collection of lots of nodes and edges. The nodes represent the entity and the edges represent the connection between nodes. This database is used a lot in social media platforms such as Facebook.

Cloud database

A cloud database is mainly built for a virtualized environment. The virtualized environment can be a hybrid cloud, public cloud, or private cloud. These databases provide various benefits, such as the ability to pay for storage capacity and per-user basis bandwidth. As a software-as-a-server, it provides support to enterprise business applications.

Database management system

A **database management system** (**DBMS**) is system software that is made for creating and managing databases. With the help of the **DBMS**, a user or a developer can create, get, update, and manage data in a systemic way. This system is kind of an interface between a user and a database. It also ensures that data is consistently organized and easily accessible.

Here is a diagram regarding the use of a **DBMS**:

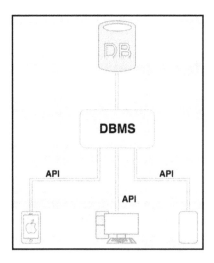

There are three important features of a **DBMS**, and these are the data, the database engine, and the database schema. The data is a collection of information, the database engine allows data to be locked, accessed, and modified, and the database schema defines the logical structure of the database.

The **DBMS** provides a general view of how data can be accessed by multiple users from multiple locations in a controlled manner. It also limits a user's access to user data. The database schema provides the logic of how a user can view the data. The **DBMS** handles all the requests and executes them on the database.

Both logical and physical data independence is offered by the **DBMS**. This means that an application can use APIs to utilize the data from the database. In addition, clients and applications don't need to worry about the locations of the stored data and changes to the physical structure of the data, such as storage and hardware.

Popular database models and their management systems include the following:

- **Relational database management system (RDMS)**
- NoSQL DBMS
- **In-memory database management system (IMDBMS)**
- **Columnar database management system (CDBMS)**
- Cloud-based data management system

Data access in the Spring

Data access is responsible for authorizing access to data repositories. It helps to distinguish the *role* ability, like users or administrators in the application. It maintains the data access system, such as insert, retrieve, update, or delete based on the role. In Chapter 3, *Overview of Spring Framework,* we have learned about the architecture of Spring.

Here is a diagram of the Spring architecture, where **Data Access** is one of the layers:

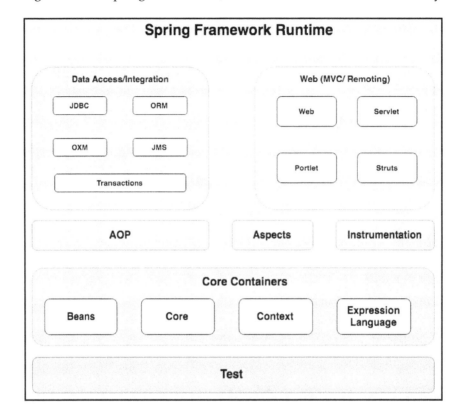

As you can see, **Data Access** is one of the layers of Spring architecture. This part is concerned with data access. **JDBC, ORM, OXM, JMS,** and **Transactions** modules are modules that are used in Spring. We have mentioned the details of this in Chapter 3, *Overview of Spring Framework*, under the Spring architecture topic. In this chapter, we will see the use of **JDBC** and **ORM** (**JPA, Hibernate**).

Java database connectivity in Spring

Java Database Connectivity (**JDBC**) is an API specification for connecting and moving data from the frontend to the backend. The classes and interfaces are written in Java. Nowadays, it also supports Kotlin. We will write in Kotlin throughout this chapter. This basically acts as an interface or bridge between the Java-based application and database. JDBC is very similar to the **Open Database Connectivity** (**ODBC**). Like ODBC, JDBC enables a JDBC application to access a collection of data.

In the Spring Framework, the JDBC is divided into the following four separate packages:

- **Core**: This is the JDBC's core functionality and `JdbcTemplate`, `SimpleJdbcInsert`, and `SimpleJdbcCall` are the important classes of this core part
- **DataSource**: This is used to access data sources
- **Object**: The JDBC can access in an object-oriented manner. As a business object, it executes queries and returns the results
- **Support**: Support classes work under core and object packages

Creating a sample project using JDBC

Let's learn JDBC using a project in which we will create REST APIs for users and show the list of user details. In this project, we will use JDBC, MySQL, and Spring Boot.

To create a project, go to this link: `https://start.spring.io` and create a Kotlin-based project. Here are the dependencies of JDBC:

- **JDBC**: this will implement all the features regarding JDBC
- **MySQL**: this will implement all the features of MySQL database

Maven dependencies

If you go to the `pom.xml` file, there you can see the dependencies for the JDBC, and we are using MySQL for the data. Here is a piece of code of the `pom.xml` file:

```xml
-----
-----
<!-- This is for JDBC use -->
<dependency>
    <groupId>org.springframework.boot</groupId>
    <artifactId>spring-boot-starter-jdbc</artifactId>
</dependency>
-----
-----

<!-- This is for use the MySQL -->
<dependency>
    <groupId>mysql</groupId>
    <artifactId>mysql-connector-java</artifactId>
    <scope>runtime</scope>
```

```
</dependency>
-----
-----
```

Creating DataSource

We configure the DataSource and connection pool in the `application.properties`. Spring Boot uses the `spring.datasource` interface as a prefix to configure DataSource. Our database schema name is `packtpub_dbtest_schema`. You can create this on your own and rename it. Here are the details of `application.properties`:

```
# Database Configuration

spring.datasource.url=jdbc:mysql://localhost:3306/packtpub_dbtest_schema
spring.datasource.username=root
spring.datasource.password=12345678
```

According to the previous code, `spring.datasource.url=jdbc:mysql://localhost:3306/packtpub_dbtest_schema` means the URL for the database schema called `packtpub_dbtest_schema` to access the data in the project. `spring.datasource.username=root` means the username of the database is `root`, and `spring.datasource.password=12345678` means the username of the database is `12345678`.

In our system, the MySQL details are as follows:

```
Host -- localhost                                // the host URL
Port -- 3306                                     // the host POST
number
Username -- root                                 // the username of the
database
Password -- 12345678                             // the password of the
database
Database Name - packtpub_dbtest                  // the Database name
Database Schema Name - packtpub_dbtest_schema    // the Database Schema
name
```

Creating a table in database

Go to the **MySQL Workbench** and select the **database**.

We have included some user details for the USERS table. You can copy and paste the following code to create a USERS table and insert some demo data:

```
create table users (id int not null auto_increment, name varchar(255),
email varchar(255), contact_number varchar(255)
, primary key (id)) engine=MyISAM;
INSERT INTO user (id, name, email, contact_number) values (1, 'Sunnat',
'sunnat629@gmail.com', '1234567890');
INSERT INTO user (id, name, email, contact_number) values (2, 'Chaity',
'chaity123@gmail.com', '9876543210');
INSERT INTO user (id, name, email, contact_number) values (3, 'Mirza',
'mirza123@gmail.com', '1234567800');
INSERT INTO user (id, name, email, contact_number) values (4, 'Hasib',
'hasib123@gmail.com', '1234500800');
INSERT INTO user (id, name, email, contact_number) values (4, 'Jisan',
'jisan123@gmail.com', '1004500800');
```

After inserting the user details in the user table, you can see the content in your users table, as in the following screenshot:

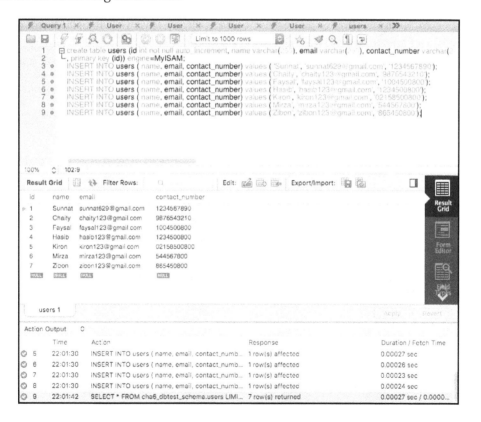

Creating a model

In this project, we will create a REST API to see the list of user details where we can get a username, email ID, and contact number. So let's create a model of a user; the class name is `UserModel.kt`.

Here is the code of the model class:

```
data class UserModel(val id: Int,
                     val name: String,
                     val email: String,
                     val contact_number: String)
```

We have created a class named `UserModel`, where we have initialized `id`, `name`, `email`, and `contact_number`.

Creating row mapper

`RowMapper` is an interface that is provided by the Spring JDBC. This is used to map a row with a Java object and to fetch data from the database. It uses the `query()` function of the `JdbcTemplate` class. Let's create a `RowMapper` interface named `UserRowMapper.kt`.

Here is the code of this interface:

```
class UserRowMapper : RowMapper<UserModel> {

    @Throws(SQLException::class)
    override fun mapRow(row: ResultSet, rowNumber: Int): UserModel? {
        return UserModel(row.getInt("id"),
                row.getString("name"),
                row.getString("email"),
                row.getString("contact_number"))
    }
}
```

In this code, we extended `RowMapper<UserModel>` and overrode the `mapRow` where we return the `UserModel`.

Creating an API interface

To get a REST API response, we need to create an interface where we will mention what we want to do with the data, such as getting the user list, creating a new user, and deleting or updating the user details. Let's create an interface named `UserInterface.kt`.

Here is the code of the interface:

```
interface UserInterface {
    fun getAllUserList(): List<UserModel>
    fun getUserByID(id: Int): UserModel?
    fun addNewUser(userModel: UserModel)
    fun updateUser(userModel: UserModel)
    fun deleteUser(id: Int)
}
```

We have used five functions, which are explained as follows:

- `getAllUserList()`: This will return a list of the details of all users
- `getUserByID(id: Int)`: This will return the details of a specific user
- `addNewUser(userModel: UserModel)`: This will add new user details
- `updateUser(userModel: UserModel)`: This will update an existing user's details
- `deleteUser(id: Int)`: This will delete a specific user

Creating a user repository

We will communicate with the database in this class. This is a repository class and so we annotate this class with `@Repository`. Let's create a repository class named `UserRepository.kt`, which implements the `UsersInterface`.

Here is the code of the repository class:

```
@Repository
class UserRepository: UsersInterface {

    override fun getAllUserList(): List<UserModel> {
    }

    override fun getUserByID(id: Int): UserModel? {
    }

    override fun addNewUser(userModel: UserModel) {
```

```
      }

      override fun updateUser(userModel: UserModel) {
      }

      override fun deleteUser(id: Int) {
      }
}
```

We have created a repository class named `UserRepository`, where we implement `UsersInterface`, and override all the functions of the interface. We use the `@Repository` annotation to make it a repository class.

Let's complete this class step by step in the following section.

JdbcTemplate implementation

`JdbcTemplate` is the heart of the JDBC. This is the center class of JDBC. SQL queries are executed by `JdbcTemplate`, which also fetches the results. To use this `JdbcTemplate`, we need to autowire the `JdbcTemplate` in this repository class. Here is the piece of code of this repository class:

```
@Repository
class UserRepository: UserInterface {

    @Autowired
    private lateinit var jdbcTemplate: JdbcTemplate
    ----
    ----
}
```

Creating HTTP methods for RESTful APIs

For this project, we will create **create, read, update, and delete (CRUD)** operations.

Create

Find the code snippet pertaining to the create operation, where we will insert the user details:

```
override fun addNewUser(userModel: UserModel) {
    val addQuery = "INSERT INTO users (name, email, contact_number) values
(?,?,?)"
    jdbcTemplate.update(addQuery,userModel.name,userModel.email,userModel.conta
ct_number)
    }
```

The `addQuery = "INSERT INTO users (name, email, contact_number) values (?,?,?)"` is the query to insert the user in the USER table.

The `jdbcTemplate.update()` is the function where we use the query and user details as the parameters to insert in the database.

READ

Find the code snippet pertaining to the read operation. The following function will return a list of all the user's details:

```
override fun getAllUserList(): List<UserModel> {
    val selectAllSql = "SELECT * FROM users"
    return jdbcTemplate.query(selectAllSql, UserRowMapper())
}
```

`selectAllSql = "SELECT * FROM users"` is the query to fetch all the users from user the table. `jdbcTemplate.query()` will execute the query and fetch the data.

This following function will get a user's details based on `id`:

```
override fun getUserByID(id: Int): UserModel? {
    val selectAllSql = "SELECT * FROM users WHERE id = ?"
    return jdbcTemplate.queryForObject(selectAllSql, UserRowMapper(), id)
}
```

`selectAllSql = "SELECT * FROM users WHERE id = ?"` is the query to fetch a user from the user table by using the ID. `jdbcTemplate.queryForObjec()` will execute the query and fetch the data.

UPDATE

Find the code snippet for update operation:

```
override fun updateUser(userModel: UserModel) {
    val updateQuery = "UPDATE users SET name=?,email=?, contact_number=?
WHERE id=?"
    jdbcTemplate.update(updateQuery, userModel.name, userModel.email,
userModel.contact_number, userModel.id)
}
```

`updateQuery = "UPDATE users SET name=?,email=?, contact_number=? WHERE id=?"` is the query to update a user from the user table by using the ID. `jdbcTemplate.update()` will execute the query and update the data.

DELETE

Find the code snippet for delete operation:

```
override fun deleteUser(id: Int) {
    val deleteQuery = "DELETE FROM users WHERE id=?"
    jdbcTemplate.update(deleteQuery, id)
}
```

`deleteQuery = "DELETE FROM users WHERE id=?"` is the query to update a user from user table by using the ID. `jdbcTemplate.update()` will execute the query and delete the specific data.

With these functions, we have finished our repository class.

Creating service

After creating the repository class, let's create the service class where we will autowire the repository class using the `@autowired` annotation. Let's create a service class named `UserService.kt` with the `@Service` annotation that implements the `UserInterface` and overrides all functions.

Here is the piece of code for the `UserService.kt`:

```
@Service
class UserService: UsersInterface {

    @Autowired
    private lateinit var userRepository: UserRepository
```

```
    ------
    ------
}
```

Let's override and modify the functions with the help of `UserRepository`. Here is the full code of the `UserService` class:

```
@Service
class UserService: UsersInterface {
    @Autowired
    private lateinit var userRepository: UserRepository

    override fun getAllUserList(): List<UserModel> {
        return userRepository.getAllUserList()
    }

    override fun getUserByID(id: Int): UserModel? {
        return userRepository.getUserByID(id)
    }

    override fun addNewUser(userModel: UserModel) {
        userRepository.addNewUser(userModel)
    }

    override fun updateUser(userModel: UserModel, id: Int) {
        userRepository.updateUser(userModel, id)
    }

    override fun deleteUser(id: Int) {
        userRepository.deleteUser(id)
    }
}
```

- `getAllUserList()`: This function will fetch all the users
- `getUserByID(id: Int)`: This function will fetch a user by ID
- `addNewUser(userModel: UserModel)`: This function will insert a new user
- `updateUser(userModel: UserModel, id: Int)`: This function will update a user by ID
- `deleteUser(id: Int)`: This function will delete a user by ID

Creating controller

If your model, repository, and service classes are complete, then you are ready to create the controller class, where we will create `GetMapping`, `PostMapping`, `PutMapping`, and `DeleteMapping` to create RESTful API URL paths. Let's create a controller class named `UserController.kt` using the `@RestController` annotation to create the controller class:

```
@RestController
class UserController {
    ----
    ----
}
```

Autowired service

Let's autowire the `UserService` using the `@Autowired` annotation. Here is the piece of code for this `UserController` class:

```
@Autowired
private lateinit var userService: UserService
```

Getting the user list

Find the code snippet for the `getAllUsers()` operation:

```
//    Getting the User List
@GetMapping(path = ["/users"])
fun getAllUsers(): ResponseEntity<List<UserModel>> {
    return ResponseEntity(userService.getAllUserList(),
            HttpStatus.OK)
}
```

The `@GetMapping(path = ["/users"])` annotation is the URL path of `/users` and it is a `GET` request function. Here, we will get a list of the users from the database.

Getting one user by ID

Find the code snippet for the `getAllUserByID()` operation:

```
//    Getting one User by ID
@GetMapping(path = ["/user/{id}"])
fun getAllUserByID(@PathVariable("id") id: Int): ResponseEntity<UserModel>
```

```
    {
        return ResponseEntity(userService.getUserByID(id),
            HttpStatus.OK)
    }
```

The `@GetMapping(path = ["/user/{id}"])` annotation is the URL path of `"/user/{id}"`, and it is a `GET` request with a specific ID. Here, we will get the specific user details from the database.

Inserting a new user

Find the code snippet for `addNewUser()` operation:

```
    //     Inserting new User
    @PostMapping(path = ["/user/new"])
    fun addNewUser(@RequestBody userModel: UserModel): String {
        ResponseEntity(userService.addNewUser(userModel), HttpStatus.CREATED)
        return "${userModel.name} has been added to database"
    }
```

The `@PostMapping(path = ["/user/new"])` annotation is the URL path of `"/user/new"`, and it is a `POST` request. Here, we can insert user details into the database.

Here, `@RequestBody` is an annotation of the Spring MVC framework. This is used in a controller to implement object serialization and deserialization. It helps you to avoid boilerplate codes by extracting the logic. The `@RequestBody` annotated function returns a value that is bound to the HTTP web response body. Here, the object is `UserModel`.

Updating a user

Find the code snippet for `updateUser()` operation:

```
    //     Updating a User
    @PutMapping(path = ["/user/{id}"])
    fun updateUser(@RequestBody userModel: UserModel, @PathVariable("id") id:
    Int): ResponseEntity<UserModel> {
        userService.updateUser(userModel, id)
        return ResponseEntity(userModel, HttpStatus.OK)
    }
```

The `@PutMapping(path = ["/user/{id}"])` annotation is the URL path of `"/user/{id}"`, and it is a `PUT` request with a specific ID. Here, we will update the specific user details in the database.

Deleting a user

Find the code snippet for `deleteUser()` operation:

```
//    Deleting a User
@DeleteMapping(path = ["/user/{id}"])
fun deleteUser(@PathVariable("id") id: Int): String {
    userService.deleteUser(id)
    return "$id User has been deleted."
}
```

The `@DeleteMapping(path = ["/user/{id}"])` annotation is the URL path of `"/user/{id}"`, and it is a delete request with a specific ID. Here, we will delete the specific user details from the database.

If you finish this controller class, then you are ready to run this application and test the REST API using Insomnia.

Testing the output

Let's *run* the project. If the project doesn't experience an error, then you'll be able to see the **RUN** tab of the IDE, as demonstrated in the following screenshot:

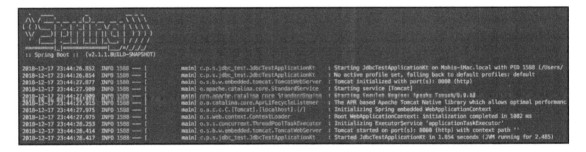

Now, open the Insomnia app. Let's apply the REST API request in this app.

Getting the user list

Use this `GET` request with this URL: `http://localhost:8080/users`, and hit **Send**. The user details will be fetched from the database and you can see the return JSON value, as the following screenshot:

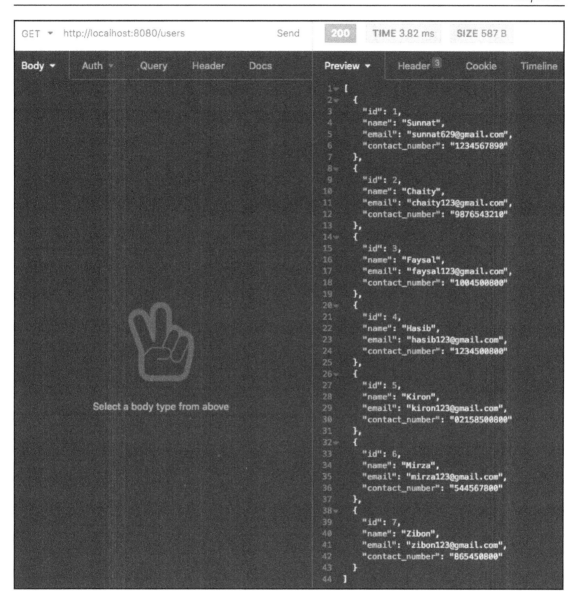

Getting one user by ID

Create a GET function with this URL: `http://localhost:8080/user/1`, and hit **Send**. The user details will be fetched from the database and you can see the return JSON value of a user whose id is 1, as in the following screenshot:

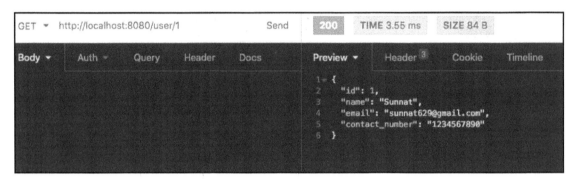

Inserting a new user

Create a POST function with this URL: `http://localhost:8080/user/new` a and hit **Send**. This will insert a user in the database and show the new user details, as in the following screenshot:

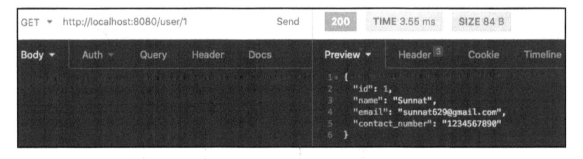

If you use the /users GET request URL path, you can check the user list containing the new user:

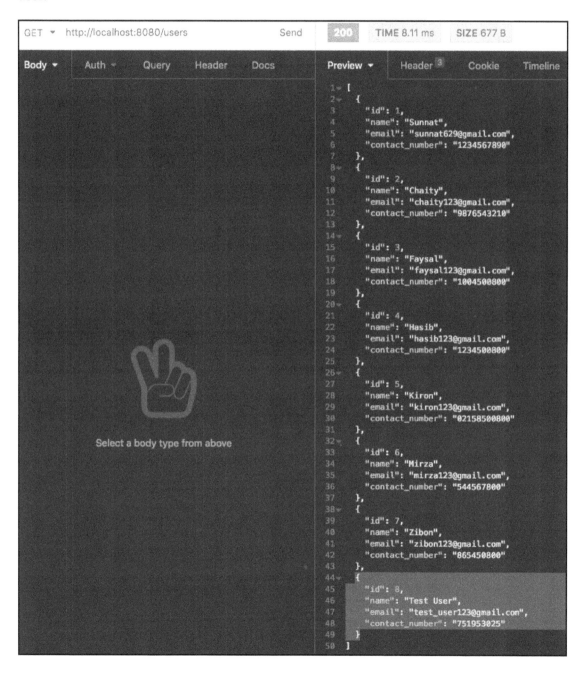

Updating a user

Create an UPDATE function with this URL: http://localhost:8080/user/8, and hit **Send**. It will update the user who has the ID number eight in the database and shows the updated user information, as in the following screenshot:

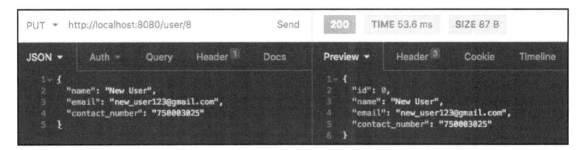

If you use the http://localhost:8080/user/8 GET request URL path, you can check the new user with the new details like the following screenshot:

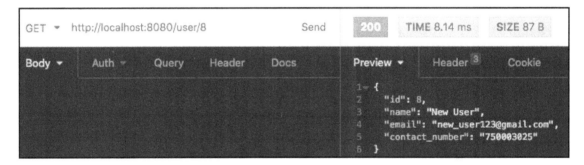

Deleting a user

Create a `DELETE` function with this URL: `http://localhost:8080/users`, and hit **Send**. This will delete the specific user from the database, as shown in the following screenshot:

If you check all the users, then you will see that there are only seven.

Finally, we have created an application that is using JDBC, and we have also created a REST API. You can check out our GitHub project for the latest update if there is any. I also add a SQL file with the MySQL code.

Java Persistence API

The **Java Persistence API** (**JPA**) is an approach to **object-relational mapping** (ORM). ORM is a system that maps Java objects to databases, tables, and vice-versa. JPA can be used in both Java enterprise and standard edition-based applications. Hibernate, TopLink, EclipseLink, and Apache OpenJPA are the implementations of the JPA. Among these, Hibernate is the most advanced and widely used.

JPA helps the developer to work directly with the objects, and therefore, there is no need to worry about the SQL statements. With the help of the JPA, they can map, store, update, and fetch the data from a relational database to a Java object or vice versa.

JPA metadata is mainly defined by the annotation in a class. However, it also supports XML, which means it can be defined by XML. We will use the annotation to define the JPA metadata throughout this book. Now, we will see the architecture of JPA, and its uses.

Architecture of JPA

The following diagram shows the class-level architecture of JPA:

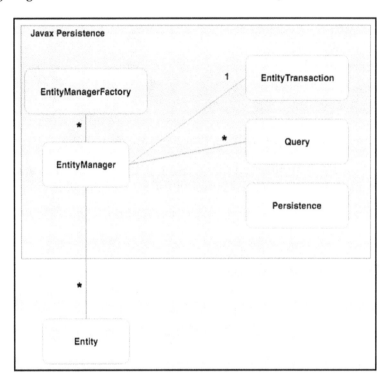

Let's describe the diagram:

- EntityManagerFactory: A factory class of EntityManager that creates and manages multiple EntityManager instances.
- EntityManager: This is an interface that manages the persistence operations on objects.
- Entity: This is a persistence object that is stored as records in the database
- EntityTransaction: This has a one-to-one relationship with EntityManager. For each EntityManager, operations are maintained by the EntityTransaction class.
- Query: This is an interface that is implemented by each JPA vendor to obtain relational objects with the criteria.
- Persistence: This is a class. To obtain an EntityManagerFactory instance, it contains static methods.

If you look at the diagram again, you may notice that there is some relation between the classes and interfaces that belong to the `javax.presistence` package:

- Between `EntityManagerFactory` and `EntityManager`, there is a one-to-many relationship
- Between `EntityManager` and `EntityTransaction`, there is a one-to-one relationship
- Between `EntityManager` and `Query`, there is a one-to-many relationship
- Between `EntityManager` and `Entity`, there is a one-to-many relationship

Creating a project using JPA

Let's create a simple project using Spring Boot with JPA, as well as Hibernate and MySQL. We will build a RESTful CRUD API of a user list.

To create a project, go to this link: `https://start.spring.io` and create a Kotlin-based project.

Maven dependencies

If you go to the `pom.xml` file, you can see the dependencies for the JDBC there. We are using MySQL for the database:

```
-----
-----
<dependency>
    <groupId>org.springframework.boot</groupId>
    <artifactId>spring-boot-starter-data-jpa</artifactId>
</dependency>

<dependency>
    <groupId>org.springframework.boot</groupId>
    <artifactId>spring-boot-starter-web</artifactId>
</dependency>

<dependency>
    <groupId>com.h2database</groupId>
    <artifactId>h2</artifactId>
    <scope>runtime</scope>
</dependency>

<dependency>
```

```
    <groupId>mysql</groupId>
    <artifactId>mysql-connector-java</artifactId>
    <scope>runtime</scope>
</dependency>
-----
-----
```

According to this code, here are the dependencies:

- Web
- JPA
- MySQL
- H2

Here, we have seen a new dependency named h2. This is one of the well known, in-memory databases. Spring Boot and H2 have a great combination between one another.

Creating the DataSource

We configure the *DataSource* and *connection pool* in the `application.properties`. Spring boot uses the `spring.datasource` interface as a prefix to configure DataSource. Our database schema name is `cha6_dbtest_schema`. You can create this on your own and rename it. Here are the details of `application.properties`:

```
## Spring DATASOURCE (DataSourceAutoConfiguration & DataSourceProperties)
spring.datasource.url =
jdbc:mysql://localhost:3306/cha6_dbtest_schema?useSSL=false
spring.datasource.username = root
spring.datasource.password = 12345678


## Hibernate Properties
# The SQL dialect makes Hibernate generate better SQL for the chosen
database
spring.jpa.properties.hibernate.dialect =
org.hibernate.dialect.MySQL5Dialect

# Hibernate ddl auto (create, create-drop, validate, update)
spring.jpa.hibernate.ddl-auto = update
```

In our system, the MySQL details are as follows:

- Host -- localhost
- Port -- 3306

- Username -- rootPassword -- 12345678
- Database Name – packtpub_dbtest
- Database Schema Name – packtpub_dbtest_schema

Creating a model

In this project, we will create a REST API to see the list of user details where we can get a username, email ID, and contact number. So let's create a model of a user where the class name is UserModel.kt.

Here is the code of the model class:

```
@Entity
@Table(name="user_jpa")
@EntityListeners(AuditingEntityListener::class)
data class UserModel(
    @Id
    @GeneratedValue(strategy = GenerationType.IDENTITY)
    @Column(name = "id")
    var id: Long = 0,

    @NotBlank
    @Column(name = "name")
    var name: String ?= null,

    @NotBlank
    @Column(name = "email")
    var email: String ?= null,

    @NotBlank
    @Column(name = "contact_number")
    var contact_number: String ?= null
)
```

Here, our UserModel class has the following fields:

- id: Primary key with auto increment
- name: (NOT NULL field)
- email: (NOT NULL field)
- contact_number: (NOT NULL field)

Unlike JDBC, you don't need to create any table manually in your database. JPA will create a table using the `UserModel`. Let's look at how to create a table in our database using this `UserModel` object:

- `@Entity`: All your domain models must be annotated with this annotation. This annotation is used to mark the class as a persistent Java class.
- `@Table`: This annotation is used to provide the details of the table. The entity will be mapped by it.
- `@Id`: This is used to define the primary key.
- `@GeneratedValue`: This annotation is used to define the primary key generation strategy. In the preceding case, we have declared the primary key as an auto increment field.
- `@NotBlank`: This is used to verify that the annotated field is not null or empty.
- `@Column`: This is used to verify the properties of the column that will be mapped to the annotated field.

Creating a user repository

We will communicate with the database in this repository class. This is a `Repository` class, and so we annotate it with `@Repository`. Let's create a `Repository` class named `UserRepository.kt`, which extends the `JpaRepository`. By extending `JpaRepository`, this interface will get a set of generic CRUD functions to create, update, delete, and fetch the data.

Here is the code of the `Repository` class:

```
@Repository
interface UserRepository: JpaRepository<UserModel, Long>
```

Here are some functions we will get from this `JPARepository`:

- `List<T> findAll()`: To fetch all the data
- `List<T> findAll(Sort var1)` : To fetch all the data in sort
- `List<T> findAllById(Iterable<ID> var1)`: To fetch data by ID
- `<S extends T> List<S> saveAll(Iterable<S> var1)`: To insert data using the list of a data

Creating controller

If your model and repository classes are complete, then you are ready to create the controller class where we will create the GetMapping, PostMapping, PutMapping, and DeleteMapping to create *RESTful API URL* paths. Let's create a controller class named UserController.kt using the @RestController annotation to create the controller class:

```
@RestController
class UserController {
    ----
    ----
}
```

Autowired repository

Let's autowire the UserRepository using the @Autowired annotation. Here is the piece of code of this class:

```
@RestController
class UserController {

    @Autowired
    private lateinit var userRepository: UserRepository

    ----
    ----
}
```

Getting the user list

Find the code snippet for getAllUsers() operation:

```
// to get all the users details
    @GetMapping("/users")
    fun getAllUsers(): List<UserModel>{
        return userRepository.findAll()
    }
```

The @GetMapping(path = ["/users"]) annotation means it is used to GET a request. Here, we will get a list of the users from the database using findAll() of the UserRepository interface, which implemented JpaRepository. Consequently, we don't need to create a *custom interface*, unlike *JDBC*.

Getting one user by ID

Find the code snippet `getAllUserByID()` operation as follows:

```
// to get one specific user details
@GetMapping("/user/{id}")
fun getUser(@PathVariable(name = "id") id: Long): UserModel {
    return userRepository.findById(id).get()
}
```

The `@GetMapping(path = ["/user/{id}"])` annotation is the URL path of `"/user/{id}"`, and it is a `GET` request with a specific ID. Here, we return `findById(id).get()` to get the specific user details from the database.

Inserting new user

Find the code snippet for `addNewUser()` operation as follows:

```
// to add a user
@PostMapping("/users")
fun addUser(@Valid @RequestBody userModel: UserModel): UserModel {
    return userRepository.save(userModel)
}
```

The `@PostMapping(path = ["/user/"])` annotation is the URL path of `"/user/"`, and it is a `POST` request. Here, we enter the details of a user to insert the user data in the database.

To bind the request body with a method parameter, we are using the `@RequestBody` annotation.

The `@Valid` annotation makes sure that the request body is valid and not null.

Here, we return `save(userModel)` to insert new user details into the database.

Updating a user

Find the code snippet for the `updateUser()` operation:

```
// to update a user
@PutMapping("/user/{id}")
fun updateUser(@PathVariable(name = "id")id: Long, @Valid @RequestBody
userDetails: UserModel): UserModel {
    val currentUser: UserModel = userRepository.findById(id).get()
```

```
        currentUser.name = userDetails.name
        currentUser.email = userDetails.email
        currentUser.contact_number = userDetails.contact_number

        return userRepository.save(currentUser)
    }
```

The @PutMapping("/user/{id}") annotation is the URL path of "/user/{id}", and it is a PUT request with a specific ID. Here, we will update the specific user details in the database.

Deleting a user

Find the code snippet for deleteUser() operation as follows:

```
// to delete a user
    @DeleteMapping("/user/{id}")
    fun deleteUser(@PathVariable(name = "id")id: Long): ResponseEntity<*>{
        userRepository.delete(userRepository.findById(id).get())
        return ResponseEntity.ok().build<Any>()
    }
```

The @DeleteMapping("/user/{id}") annotation is the URL path of "/user/{id}" and it is a DELETE request with a specific ID. Here we will delete the specific user details from the database.

If you finish this controller class, then you are ready to run this application and test the *REST API* using *Insomnia*.

Seeing the output

Before running the project, go to the MySQL Workbench app, the cha6_dbtest table, and cha6_dbtest_schema. There you will notice that there will be no table named user_jpa, which was mentioned in the UserModel class as a table name.

Here is the screenshot of the schema where we have no table:

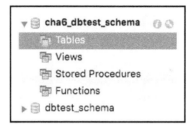

Let's run the application, check the database again, and *refresh* the schema. Notice that now there is a table as we mentioned in the @Table annotation of the UserModel. This has all the columns of that object, including—id, name, email, and contact_number.

Here is the screenshot of the updated database:

The testing system is the same as the JDBC. Please check this yourself, and if you are confused, then go to the Testing the Output of JDBC project.

Here is the REST API URL of this project:

- GET http://localhost:8080/users: To get a list of all users
- GET http://localhost:8080/user/1: To get a specific user details
- POST http://localhost:8080/user/new: To insert a new user
- PUT http://localhost:8080/user/1: To update a specific user details
- DELETE http://localhost:8080/user/2: To delete a specific user details

Database of client-side application

Up to this point, you have learned about databases for the server-side. Now we are going to understand databases for the client-side. The Android application will be our client-side application. The demand for Android is now rapidly increasing, and it has also surpassed the PC-based operating systems. Even nowadays, hardware is also more powerful than a PC or laptop.

The database is the essential part for a smart device, and it is the best way to store and manage the data on a device. This data can be handled in two ways. One way is online based, which means all the data is handled by a server-side or cloud and mobile communicates with them through the network. Without the internet connection, this system is almost useless. The second option is to store all the data in the local database. This means that it can be used offline and is also less dependent on the internet.

There are some criteria for the mobile-based database:

- Lightweight and fast
- Secured
- Independent from an online server
- Easy to handle using the code
- Can be shared publicly or privately
- Low power consumption and low memory

There are lots of mobile databases available on the market but very few databases have met these criteria. *SQLite*, *Realm* DB, and *ORMLite* are few of them.

We will use the SQLite database throughout this book. However, we are not going to use the raw SQLite. We will instead use a library called **room persistence library**, which is part of the architecture components. IT provides an abstraction layer over the SQLite. This allows database access that is more robust and helps with much less code.

Architecture components

The **architecture components** are one of the components of Android Jetpack. This is a guideline for application architecture. This component is built on some libraries to do common tasks in an easier way. With the help of this component, a developer can develop their project, which can be robust, maintainable, and testable.

Today we will create an Android offline application where we will use Android components.

Here is the diagram of this architecture:

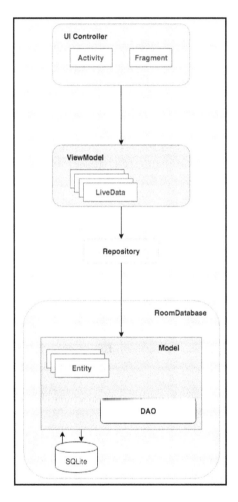

The following is a brief description of all the components:

- UI Controller: UI components like activities and fragments are under this component.
- ViewModel: This fetches data with the help of model and provides it to the UI.
- LiveData: This class holds the observable data. This is lifecycle-aware, unlike the regular observable.

- `Repository`: This manages multiple data sources.
- `Room Database`: This is a top database layer, which is from the SQLite database.
- `Entity`: This describes a database table.
- `DAO`: The full form is **a data access object** (**DAO**). It maps SQL queries.
- `SQLite database`: Data is stored using this in the device. It is created and maintained by the room.

Creating an Android app

Let's create a simple Android app that has a database. This will store the details of users (including name, contact number, and email ID) and show these details in a list using `RecyclerView`.

First of all, we need to create an app from Android Studio, write down your project, and the company domain. Don't forget to check **Include Kotlin support** to make it a Kotlin-based application. The following screenshot shows the **Create Android Project** window:

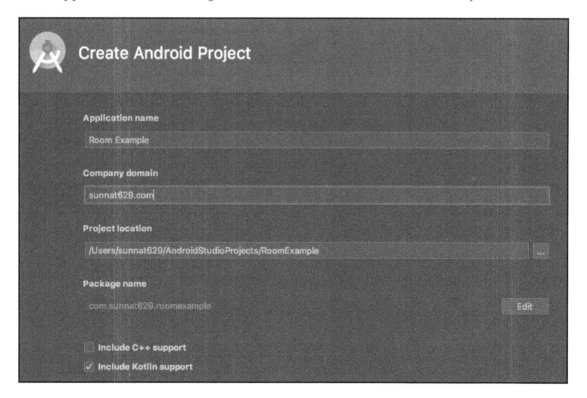

Now select the minimum API version from the **Phone and Tablet** option. There is no need to add other options for this project. After clicking **Next** in the **Add an Activity to Mobile**, you can select **Basic Activity** and then, after renaming the **Activity Name** and **layout**, click **Finish**. After building the project, you will be ready to start creating an Android app.

Here is the screenshot of the **Add an Activity to Mobile** window and here we select the **Basic Activity** template like the following screenshot:

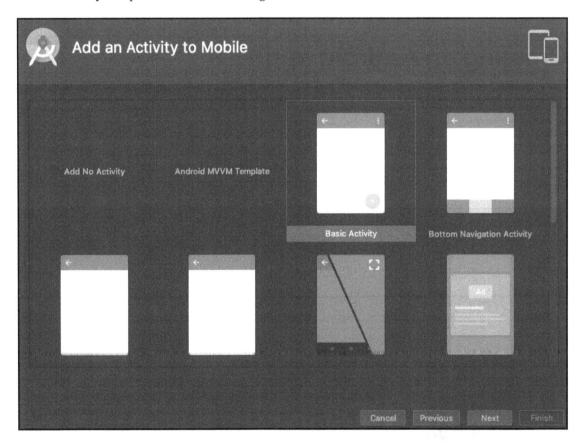

The final files of this project are shown in the following screenshot, where you can see all the files and resources after finishing this project:

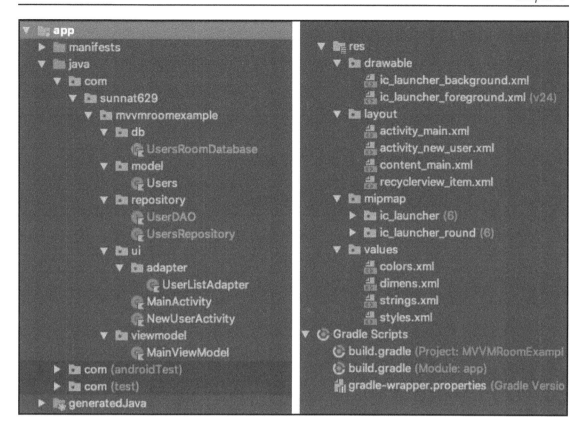

Gradle information

Here are the details of my Android Studio's Gradle file:

```
buildscript {
    -----
-----
    dependencies {
        classpath 'com.android.tools.build:gradle:3.2.1'
        classpath "org.jetbrains.kotlin:kotlin-gradle-plugin:1.3.10"

    }
}
-----
-----
```

This file injects the dependencies of the Gradle and Kotlin. In this project, the Gradle version is 3.2.1 and the Kotlin version is 1.3.10

Gradle dependencies

This Gradle file is for the application. It contains all the dependencies and other Android SDK versions.

Here is the following code in the dependencies block:

```
    // Room components
    implementation
"android.arch.persistence.room:runtime:$rootProject.roomVersion"
    kapt "android.arch.persistence.room:compiler:$rootProject.roomVersion"
    androidTestImplementation
"android.arch.persistence.room:testing:$rootProject.roomVersion"

    // Lifecycle components
    implementation
"android.arch.lifecycle:extensions:$rootProject.archLifecycleVersion"
    kapt
"android.arch.lifecycle:compiler:$rootProject.archLifecycleVersion"

    // Coroutines
    api "org.jetbrains.kotlinx:kotlinx-coroutines-
core:$rootProject.coroutines"
    api "org.jetbrains.kotlinx:kotlinx-coroutines-
android:$rootProject.coroutines"
```

To enable the coroutines features, add the following code end of the app's `build.gradle` file:

```
kotlin {
    experimental {
        coroutines "enable"
    }
}
```

Creating entity

Let's create a class of user named `UserModel.kt` with the `@Entity` annotation so that each user is an entity. All variables columns shouldn't be private and so that `Room` will able to instantiate your objects:

```
@Entity(tableName = "users")
class Users(): Parcelable {
    @PrimaryKey(autoGenerate = true)
    @NonNull
    @ColumnInfo(name = "userId")
```

```
    var userId: Int = 0

    @NonNull
    @ColumnInfo(name = "username")
    lateinit var username: String

    @NonNull
    @ColumnInfo(name = "email")
    lateinit var email: String

    @NonNull
    @ColumnInfo(name = "contactNumber")
    lateinit var contactNumber: String

    @NonNull
    @ColumnInfo(name = "address")
    lateinit var address: String

    constructor(username: String, email: String, contactNumber: String,
address: String):this(){
        this.username = username
        this.email = email
        this.contactNumber = contactNumber
        this.address = address
    }

    override fun toString(): String {
        return "Users(username='$username', email='$email',
contactNumber='$contactNumber', address='$address')"
    }
}
```

Let's see what is in this class:

- `@Entity(tableName = "users")`: An entity class represents a table, and our table name is `users`
- `@ColumnInfo(name = "**")`: This specifies a name in the table
- `@PrimaryKey(autoGenerate = true)`: This means the ID is our primary key and it will automatically increase the value
- `@NonNull`: This means there will be no null or empty value in the columns

To pass this object from one activity to another, we need to convert this class into a `Parcelable` class. So let's extend this class. In the traditional way, it will need lots of code like the following:

```kotlin
@Entity(tableName = "users")
class Users(): Parcelable {
    ----
    ----
    constructor(parcel: Parcel) : this() {
        userId = parcel.readInt()
        username = parcel.readString()!!
        email = parcel.readString()!!
        contactNumber = parcel.readString()!!
        address = parcel.readString()!!
    }
    ----
    ----
    override fun writeToParcel(parcel: Parcel, flags: Int) {
        parcel.writeInt(userId)
        parcel.writeString(username)
        parcel.writeString(email)
        parcel.writeString(contactNumber)
        parcel.writeString(address)
    }

    override fun describeContents(): Int {
        return 0
    }

    companion object CREATOR : Parcelable.Creator<Users> {
        override fun createFromParcel(parcel: Parcel): Users {
            return Users(parcel)
        }

    override fun newArray(size: Int): Array<Users?> {
            return arrayOfNulls(size)
        }
    }
}
```

So, it's really complex to understand and handle, though we don't need to modify the override functions and constructors. However, if you omit these lines, then, of course, you will be happy, and your code will look nice. To do this, we need to apply the lazy coder's way.

We just need an annotation named @Parcelize on top of the model class. Here is the full code for this:

```kotlin
@Parcelize
@Entity(tableName = "users")
class Users(): Parcelable {
    @PrimaryKey(autoGenerate = true)
    @NonNull
    @ColumnInfo(name = "userId")
    var userId: Int = 0

    @NonNull
    @ColumnInfo(name = "username")
    lateinit var username: String

    @NonNull
    @ColumnInfo(name = "email")
    lateinit var email: String

    @NonNull
    @ColumnInfo(name = "contactNumber")
    lateinit var contactNumber: String

    @NonNull
    @ColumnInfo(name = "address")
    lateinit var address: String

    constructor(username: String, email: String, contactNumber: String,
    address: String):this(){
        this.username = username
        this.email = email
        this.contactNumber = contactNumber
        this.address = address
    }

    override fun toString(): String {
        return "Users(username='$username', email='$email',
contactNumber='$contactNumber', address='$address')"
    }
}
```

So there is no more extra code. To enable this, you need to add the following code in the android block of the build.gradle (Module: app) file:

```gradle
android {
    ----
    ----
    androidExtensions {
```

```
            experimental = true
        }
    }
    dependencies {
        ----
        ----
    }
```

Creating the DAO

Let's create an interface named `UserDAO.kt`, and annotated with `@DAO` annotation. This will help `Room` to identify the `DAO` class. Here is the code for the `DAO` interface:

```
@Dao
interface UserDAO
```

In this interface, we will create functions that will be responsible for inserting, deleting, and getting the user details:

```
@Insert
fun addNewUser(users: Users)
```

In the preceding code, `@Insert` is used to insert a user:

```
@Query("DELETE FROM USERS")
fun deleteAllUsers()
```

In the previous code, `@Query("DELETE FROM USERS")` is used to delete all the users from the `USERS` table:

```
@Query("SELECT * FROM USERS")
fun getAllUsers():  List<Users>
```

In this code, `@Query("SELECT * FROM USERS")` is used to get all the users as a list from the `USERS` table.

Creating the LiveData class

Data always changes dynamically and so we have to keep it updated and show the latest result to users. For this reason, we need to observe the data. `LiveData` is a lifecycle library class that can observe the data and react.

Let's wrap the `getAllUsers()` function of `UserDao.kt` with the `LiveData`:

```
@Query("SELECT * FROM USERS")
fun getAllUsers():  LiveData<List<Users>>
```

The `@Query("SELECT * FROM USERS")` is to get all the information from the `USERS` table

So here is the full code of the DAO interface:

```
@Dao
interface UserDAO {

    @Insert(onConflict = OnConflictStrategy.REPLACE)
    fun addNewUser(users: Users)

    @Query("DELETE FROM USERS")
    fun deleteAllUsers()

    @Query("SELECT * FROM USERS")
    fun getAllUsers():  LiveData<List<Users>>
}
```

In the `MainActivity`, we will see how to create an `Observer` of the data and override the observer's `onChanged()` function.

Creating a Room database

`Room` is not a database but a layer of the `SQLite` database. It mainly uses `DAO` and the queries to make it easier to fetch the database for the clients. It doesn't use the main thread, but runs asynchronously on a background thread and so the UI performance doesn't fall.

Let's create an abstract class named `UsersRoomDatabase` and extend `RoomDatabase`. Use the `@Database` annotation with an entity of `Users` class and add the version number. Lastly, initialize an abstract function of the `UserDao` class:

```
@Database(entities = [Users::class], version = 1)
abstract class UsersRoomDatabase : RoomDatabase() {
    abstract fun userDAO(): UserDAO
    ----
    ----
}
```

Let's create a singleton. This will handle multiple instances of the database when it opens at the same time.

Initialize the `UsersRoomDatabase` object.

The name of the `UsersRoomDatabase` is `"user_database"`.

Here is the piece of code for this object:

```
// static members
companion object {
    @Volatile
    private var INSTANCE: UsersRoomDatabase? = null

    fun getDatabase(context: Context, scope: CoroutineScope):
UsersRoomDatabase {
        val tempInstance = INSTANCE
        if (tempInstance != null) {
            return tempInstance
        }
        synchronized(this) {
            val instance = Room.databaseBuilder(
                context.applicationContext,
                UsersRoomDatabase::class.java,
                "user_database"
            ).addCallback(UserDatabaseCallback(scope))
                .build()
            INSTANCE = instance
            return instance
        }
    }
}
```

Populating the database

To store data in the database, we can input some demo data by using the code for the users. The rest of the data will be stored by using the `NewUserActivity.kt` class.

For the demo data, we are creating a simple function where we insert two demo user details and it will show after running the app.

To do this, let's create an inner callback named `UserDatabaseCallback()` with the `CoroutineScope` parameter and extend `RoomDatabase.Callback()`. Lastly, we will override the `onOpen(db: SupportSQLiteDatabase)` and there we can add two random user objects:

```
fun populateDatabase(userDao: UserDAO) {
        userDao.addNewUser(
```

```
                    Users(
                        "Sunnat", "sunnat629@gmail.com",
                        "1234567890", "Dhaka"
                    )
                )
                userDao.addNewUser(
                    Users(
                        "Chaity", "chaity123@gmail.com",
                        "54321987", "Dhaka"
                    )
                )
            }
```

Here we have created the user details using the `userDao.addNewUser()`. These user details will show in the listview if we run the application.

Lastly, we need to add the callback to the database and call `build()` to finish this callback like this code shows:

```
fun getDatabase(context: Context, scope: CoroutineScope): UsersRoomDatabase
{
    val tempInstance = INSTANCE
    if (tempInstance != null) {
        return tempInstance
    }
    synchronized(this) {
        val instance = Room.databaseBuilder(
            context.applicationContext,
            UsersRoomDatabase::class.java,
            "user_database"
        ).addCallback(UserDatabaseCallback(scope))
            .build()
        INSTANCE = instance
        return instance
    }
}

private class UserDatabaseCallback(
    private val scope: CoroutineScope
) : RoomDatabase.Callback() {

    override fun onOpen(db: SupportSQLiteDatabase) {
        super.onOpen(db)
        INSTANCE?.let { database ->
            scope.launch(Dispatchers.IO) {
                populateDatabase(database.userDAO())
            }
        }
```

```
    }
    ----
    ----
    }
```

In the preceding code, we created a callback class named `UserDatabaseCallback` where we populate the database using the `DAO` function named `userDAO()`.

Then we add this callback in the `instance` of `getDatabase()` function using `addCallback()`.

Implementing the repository

Repository class is the bridge between the `Room` database and the `ViewModel`. This provides data from multiple data sources and isolates the data layer.

We can separate this repository into two sections; one is DAO, which is mainly used for the local database and to connect the local database with the application. Another section is the network, which is mainly used for handling and communicating between the cloud and application.

Now create a repository class named `UsersRepository.kt` and declare `UserDAO` as the constructor of this class.

Here is the code of `UsersRepository.kt`:

```
class UsersRepository(private val mUserDAO: UserDAO) {

    val mAllUsers: LiveData<List<Users>> = mUserDAO.getAllUsers()

    @WorkerThread
    suspend fun insert(user: Users){
        mUserDAO.addNewUser(user)
    }
}
```

Here, we have initialized the user list. Now the `Room` will execute all queries. The queries will be done in a different thread.

`LiveData` will notify the callback function if there are any changes in the database. The `insert(user: Users)` is the function that is used to wrap the `addNewUser()`. This insert function has to run on a non-UI thread or the application will crash. To avoid this, we need to use `@WorkerThread` annotation, which helps to execute this function on a non-UI thread.

Creating the ViewModel

Now create a ViewModel class named MainViewModel.kt.

Here is the MainViewModel.kt class:

```
open class MainViewModel(application: Application) :
AndroidViewModel(application) {
    private val mRepository: UsersRepository
    private val mAllUsers: LiveData<List<Users>>

    private var  parentJob = Job()
    private val coroutineContext: CoroutineContext
        get() = parentJob + Dispatchers.Main

    private val scope = CoroutineScope(coroutineContext)

    init {
        val userDao = UsersRoomDatabase.getDatabase(application,
scope).userDAO()
        mRepository = UsersRepository(userDao)
        mAllUsers = mRepository.mAllUsers
    }

    fun getAllUsers(): LiveData<List<Users>>{
        return mAllUsers
    }

    fun insert(users: Users) = scope.launch(Dispatchers.IO){
        mRepository.insert(users)
    }

    override fun onCleared() {
        super.onCleared()
        parentJob.cancel()
    }
}
```

This class gets the Application as a parameter and extends the AndroidViewModel.

Initialize a private variable of WordRepository and a LiveData, which will cache the list of the users.

In the init block, add a UserDAO reference from the UsersRoomDatabase. Initialize the mAllUsers with the mRepository.mAllUsers.

Creating new activity

Now we need an activity where we will create a function to insert the user details and save into the database. Right-click on the app folder and create **Empty Activity** named `NewUserActivity.kt` like the following screenshot:

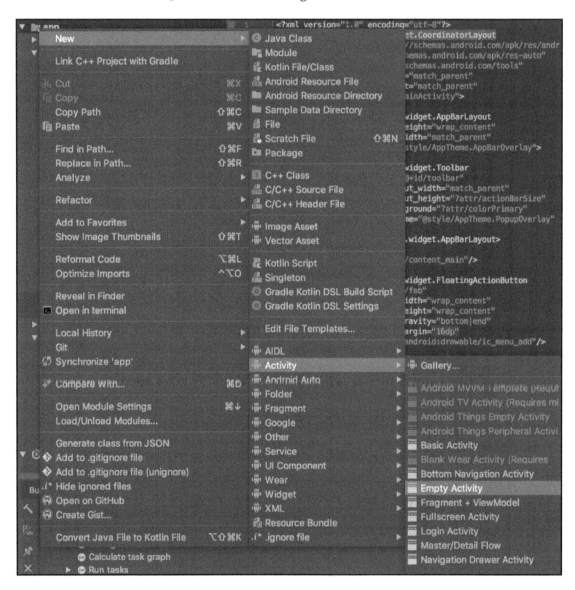

Here is the code of the layout of this class named `activity_new_user.xml`. (The entire code can be found at GitHub link):

```
----
----
    <EditText
            android:id="@+id/editEmail"
            android:layout_width="match_parent"
            android:layout_height="wrap_content"
            android:hint="@string/hint_email"
            android:inputType="textEmailAddress"
            android:padding="5dp"
            android:textSize="18sp" android:layout_marginTop="8dp"
            app:layout_constraintTop_toBottomOf="@+id/editUsername"
app:layout_constraintStart_toStartOf="parent"
            app:layout_constraintEnd_toEndOf="parent"/>

    <EditText
            android:id="@+id/editContactID"
            android:layout_width="match_parent"
            android:layout_height="wrap_content"
            android:hint="@string/hint_contact"
            android:inputType="phone"
            android:padding="5dp"
            android:textSize="18sp" android:layout_marginTop="8dp"
            app:layout_constraintTop_toBottomOf="@+id/editEmail"
app:layout_constraintStart_toStartOf="parent"
            app:layout_constraintEnd_toEndOf="parent"
    />
----
---
    <Button
            android:id="@+id/buttonSave"
            android:layout_width="match_parent"
            android:layout_height="wrap_content"
            android:background="@color/colorPrimary"
            android:text="@string/button_save"
            android:textColor="@android:color/white"
            android:layout_marginBottom="8dp"
            app:layout_constraintBottom_toBottomOf="parent"
app:layout_constraintStart_toStartOf="parent"
            app:layout_constraintEnd_toEndOf="parent"
android:layout_marginTop="8dp"
            app:layout_constraintTop_toBottomOf="@+id/editAddress"
app:layout_constraintVertical_bias="1.0"/>
    </android.support.constraint.ConstraintLayout>
```

Here we have added four `EditText` where we can input—`username`, `contactNumber`, `email`, `address`, and a button named `buttonSave` to save this information into the database.

Here is the code of the `NewUserActivity.kt` class:

```kotlin
class NewUserActivity : AppCompatActivity(), View.OnClickListener {

    override fun onCreate(savedInstanceState: Bundle?) {
        super.onCreate(savedInstanceState)
        setContentView(R.layout.activity_new_user)
        buttonSave.setOnClickListener(this)
    }

    override fun onClick(view: View?) {
        if (view!!.id == R.id.buttonSave){
            val intent = Intent()
            if (isTextFieldEmpty()){
                Snackbar.make(view, "Empty Field", Snackbar.LENGTH_LONG)
                    .setAction("Action", null).show()
                setResult(Activity.RESULT_CANCELED, intent)
            } else {
                val users = Users(editUsername.text.toString(),
                    editEmail.text.toString(),
                    editContactID.text.toString(),
                    editAddress.text.toString())

                Log.wtf("CRAY", editUsername.text.toString()+" "+
                        editEmail.text.toString()+" "+
                        editContactID.text.toString()+" "+
                        editAddress.text.toString())

                Log.wtf("CRAY", users.toString())
                // If an instance of this Activity already exists, then it
will be moved to the front.
                // If an instance does NOT exist, a new instance will be
created.
                intent.addFlags(Intent.FLAG_ACTIVITY_REORDER_TO_FRONT)
                intent.putExtra(getString(R.string.result_replay), users)
                setResult(Activity.RESULT_OK, intent)
            }
            finish()
        }
    }

    private fun isTextFieldEmpty(): Boolean {
        return TextUtils.isEmpty(editUsername.text) ||
                TextUtils.isEmpty(editEmail.text) ||
```

```
                    TextUtils.isEmpty(editContactID.text) ||
                    TextUtils.isEmpty(editAddress.text)
        }
    }
```

According to the preceding code:

- Implement the `View.OnClickListener` and override the `onClick(view: View?)`.
- In the `onCreate()`, `setOnClickListener()` for the `buttonSave`, and override the `onClick(view: View?)` that we want to execute with the button. Lastly, we call an `Intent`, which will change the activity from the `UserModel` to the `MainActivity` class.
- The `isTextFieldEmpty()` is designed to check whether the `EditText` fields are empty or not.
- Then we get all the text, make a `UserObject`, and pass this *Parcelable user object* to the `MainActivity` using `intent.putExtra(getString(R.string.result_replay), users)`.

Creating custom RecyclerView adapter

To show all the user list, we will use the `RecyclerView`. For our project, we need to customize the `RecyclerView` adapter in our own way. In this adapter, we mainly pass the user model. This will show the username, email, and contact number. Let's create an adapter named `UserListAdapter.kt` and extend `RecyclerView.Adapter<UserListAdapter.UserViewHolder>()`. Here is the code for the `UserListAdapter.kt`:

```
class UserListAdapter internal constructor(context: Context) :
    RecyclerView.Adapter<UserListAdapter.UserViewHolder>() {

    private val mLayoutInflater: LayoutInflater =
LayoutInflater.from(context)!!
    private var mUsers: List<Users> = emptyList() // Cached copy of users


    inner class UserViewHolder(itemView: View) :
RecyclerView.ViewHolder(itemView) {
        val rowName: TextView = itemView.name
        val rowEmail: TextView = itemView.email
        val rowContactNumber: TextView = itemView.contactNumber
        val rowAddress: TextView = itemView.contactNumber
```

```
    }

    override fun onCreateViewHolder(parent: ViewGroup, viewType: Int):
UserViewHolder {
        val itemView: View =
mLayoutInflater.inflate(R.layout.recyclerview_item, parent, false)
        return UserViewHolder(itemView)
    }

    override fun onBindViewHolder(holder: UserViewHolder, position: Int) {
        holder.rowName.text = mUsers[position].username
        holder.rowEmail.text = mUsers[position].email
        holder.rowContactNumber.text = mUsers[position].contactNumber
        holder.rowAddress.text = mUsers[position].address
    }

    override fun getItemCount(): Int {
        return mUsers.size
    }

    internal fun setNewUser(users: List<Users>) {
        mUsers = users
        notifyDataSetChanged()
    }
}
```

According to the code:

```
onCreateViewHolder()
onBindViewHolder()
UserViewHolder()
```

Here we initialize four attributes of the `activity_new_user.xml` in the `UserViewHolder` inner class :

```
val rowName: TextView = itemView.name
val rowEmail: TextView = itemView.email
val rowContactNumber: TextView = itemView.contactNumber
val rowAddress: TextView = itemView.contactNumber
```

We have set the **userModel**'s value in these four attributes in `onBindViewHolder()` function as follows:

```
holder.rowName.text = mUsers[position].username
holder.rowEmail.text = mUsers[position].email
holder.rowContactNumber.text = mUsers[position].contactNumber
holder.rowAddress.text = mUsers[position].address
```

Implementing RecyclerView

`RecyclerView` is a list where we can see all the user list. `RecyclerView` is a part of design material that helps to make the list smoother and faster to load the data.

In the `MainActivity`, we set `RecycleView` in the `onCreate()` function as shown by this code:

```
val userListAdapter = UserListAdapter(this)
recyclerview.adapter = userListAdapter
recyclerview.layoutManager =  LinearLayoutManager(this)
```

Modifying main activity

Let's modify this `MainActivity` class to complete our project. Let's start by connecting the UI to the database. We will use the `RecyclerView` to show the list of data from the database.

Let's create a variable of `ViewModel` as shown by the following code:

```
private lateinit var mMainViewModel: MainViewModel
```

Use `ViewModelProviders` to connect the `MainViewModel` with `MainActivity`. In `onCreate()`, we will get the `ViewModel` from the `ViewModelProvider` as shown by the following code:

```
mMainViewModel = ViewModelProviders.of(this).get(MainViewModel::class.java)
```

To add the `LiveData` observer let's add this `observe()` for `getAllUsers()` as shown by the following code:

```
mMainViewModel.getAllUsers().observe(this,
    Observer {
            userList -> userListAdapter.setNewUser(userList!!)
    })
```

Getting data from another activity

We mentioned in the *Creating new activity* section that we have passed the *Parcelable* user object to the `MainActivity`. To get this object, we need to create a request code. Let's create a request code like the following:

```
private val requestCode: Int = 1
```

Now override the `onActivityResult()` function, where we will retrieve the passed object of the `NewUserActivity`.

Here is the code of `onActivityResult()` function:

```
override fun onActivityResult(requestCode: Int, resultCode: Int, data:
Intent?) {
    super.onActivityResult(requestCode, resultCode, data)
    if (requestCode == this.requestCode && resultCode ==
Activity.RESULT_OK){
        data?.let {
        val users: Users =
it.getParcelableExtra(getString(R.string.result_replay)) as Users
        mMainViewModel.insert(users)
        }
    }
}
```

The `getParcelableExtra()` is used to retrieve a `Parcelable` object. After then, we call the `mMainViewModel.insert(users)` to insert the returned `User` into the database.

Adding XML layouts

In the `content_main.xml`, we add the `RecyclerView`. Here is the code of this layout:

```
<?xml version="1.0" encoding="utf-8"?>
<android.support.constraint.ConstraintLayout
        xmlns:android="http://schemas.android.com/apk/res/android"
        xmlns:tools="http://schemas.android.com/tools"
```

```
        xmlns:app="http://schemas.android.com/apk/res-auto"
        android:layout_width="match_parent"
        android:layout_height="match_parent"
        app:layout_behavior="@string/appbar_scrolling_view_behavior"
        tools:showIn="@layout/activity_main"
        tools:context=".ui.MainActivity">
    <android.support.v7.widget.RecyclerView
            android:id="@+id/recyclerview"
            android:background="@android:color/darker_gray"
            tools:listitem="@layout/recyclerview_item"
            app:layout_constraintBottom_toBottomOf="parent"
            app:layout_constraintStart_toStartOf="parent"
            app:layout_constraintEnd_toEndOf="parent"
            app:layout_constraintTop_toTopOf="parent"
            android:layout_height="0dp" android:layout_width="0dp"/>
</android.support.constraint.ConstraintLayout>
```

Switching another activity

In the `activity_main.xml`, we have added a `FloatingActionButton`, which we will use to go to `NewUserActivity`. To complete this task, use the following code in the `onCreate()` with the mentioned request code:

```
fab.setOnClickListener {
    val intent = Intent(this@MainActivity, NewUserActivity::class.java)
    startActivityForResult(intent, requestCode)

    /*Snackbar.make(view, "Replace with your own action",
Snackbar.LENGTH_LONG)
        .setAction("Action", null).show()*/
}
```

So, here is the complete code of `MainAcivity.kt`:

```
class MainActivity : AppCompatActivity() {

    private val requestCode: Int = 1

    private lateinit var mMainViewModel: MainViewModel

    override fun onCreate(savedInstanceState: Bundle?) {
        super.onCreate(savedInstanceState)
        setContentView(R.layout.activity_main)
        setSupportActionBar(toolbar)

        val userListAdapter = UserListAdapter(this)
```

```
        recyclerview.adapter = userListAdapter
        recyclerview.layoutManager =  LinearLayoutManager(this)

        mMainViewModel =
ViewModelProviders.of(this).get(MainViewModel::class.java)
        mMainViewModel.getAllUsers().observe(this,
            Observer {
                    userList -> userListAdapter.setNewUser(userList!!)
            })


        fab.setOnClickListener {
            val intent = Intent(this@MainActivity,
NewUserActivity::class.java)
            startActivityForResult(intent, requestCode)
        }
    }

    override fun onActivityResult(requestCode: Int, resultCode: Int, data:
Intent?) {
        super.onActivityResult(requestCode, resultCode, data)
        if (requestCode == this.requestCode && resultCode ==
Activity.RESULT_OK){
            data?.let {
            val users: Users =
it.getParcelableExtra(getString(R.string.result_replay)) as Users
            mMainViewModel.insert(users)
            }
        }
    }
}
```

Now that we have completed the project, *run* the application. We will explore this in the next section.

Run the app

After running the app on your Android device or emulator, you will see this screen:

We can see our pre-added user details here. Now click the **float** button and go to the new user activity where you can write down the information of a user as shown by this screenshot:

Lastly, click the **Save** button. You can now see the new username, which is displayed as **Naruto** in this image:

So, in this way we have learned how to use Room for the local database. In the next chapter, you will see more use of this library in an Android application.

Summary

The database itself is a large platform and we have covered those parts that are relevant to our Spring and Android projects and contents. In this chapter, we have learned what the database is, as well as looking at the various types of it. We have seen a brief description of the DBMs. After that, we have learned about the JDBC, which is an API specification for connecting and moving data from frontend to backend. Then we have developed a project using JDBC where we created, read, updated, and deleted data from the databases. After this topic, we have learned another API called JPA, which is an approach to ORM and a system that maps Java objects to database tables and vice-versa. Then we have learned more about the JPA and its use with the help of a project. There, we have also learned about CRUD-based REST API. Lastly, we have learned about the latest technology of Android called architecture components. Also, we looked at one of the components called Room, which is a wrap of the top level of the SQLite database. Finally, I want to reiterate that this database chapter has not explained everything. If you want to learn more about the database, you can read our recommended books, and we have mentioned the links with the names of the books and authors under the *Further reading* section. In the next chapter, you can learn about the concurrency, which means the ability of different units of a program, algorithm, or problem.

Questions

1. What is the H2 in the Spring Boot?
2. What is a resource in REST API?
3. What is the full meaning of CRUD?
4. What is the difference between the DAO and repository?
5. What is SQLite?
6. What datatypes does SQLite support?
7. What are the standard SQLite commands?
8. What are the disadvantages of SQLite?

Further reading

- *Spring Persistence with Hibernate* (`https://www.packtpub.com/application-development/spring-persistence-hibernate`) by Ahmad Seddighi
- *Hands-On Full Stack Development with Spring Boot 2.0 and React* (`https://www.packtpub.com/application-development/hands-full-stack-development-spring-boot-20-and-react`) by Juha Hinkula
- *Working with Data and Cloud in Spring 5.0 [Video]* (`https://www.packtpub.com/application-development/working-data-and-cloud-spring-50-video`) by Ranga Rao Karanam
- *Android Database Programming* (`https://www.packtpub.com/application-development/android-database-programming`) by Jason Wei

7
Concurrency

Concurrency is the ability of a program or algorithm to be divided into parts that can be executed out of order without affecting the results. This approach allows for parallel execution in a multi-core environment, which can significantly improve the performance. It's important to understand the difference between *concurrency* and *parallelism*. Parallelism assumes that a program is implemented in a concurrent way, but concurrency doesn't mean that the program is executed in parallel.

This chapter will cover the following topics:

- Coroutines
- Sequential operations
- Callback hell
- Thread pools

Technical requirements

To run the code in this chapter, you will need to integrate the `coroutines-core` library. To do this, you should add the following line to the `repositories` block of the `build.gradle` file:

```
jcenter()
```

You should also add the following line to the `dependencies` block:

```
implementation 'org.jetbrains.kotlinx:kotlinx-coroutines-core:0.30.2'
```

Add the following line to integrate the `kotlinx-coroutines-android` library:

```
implementation 'org.jetbrains.kotlinx:kotlinx-coroutines-android:0.30.2'
```

If you are using a Kotlin version lower than 1.3, you should also add the following lines to the `build.gradle` file:

```
kotlin {
    experimental {
        coroutines "enable"
    }
}
```

To integrate Spring for the Android library, you should add the following lines:

```
implementation 'org.springframework.android:spring-android-rest-
template:2.0.0.M3'
implementation group: 'com.fasterxml.jackson.core', name: 'jackson-
databind', version: '2.8.6'
```

You should also add the `repositories` block, as follows:

```
repositories {
    maven {
        url 'https://repo.spring.io/libs-milestone'
    }
}
```

This chapter will also work with the JSON to Kotlin Class plugin. To install this plugin, open the **Preferences** window and select the **Plugins** section.

Press the **Install** button and restart Android Studio.

The source code for this chapter, with examples, is available on GitHub, at the following link: https://github.com/PacktPublishing/Learn-Spring-for-Android-Application-Development/tree/master/Chapter07.

Coroutines

A **coroutine** is a powerful feature of the Kotlin programming language. Its main objective is to allow for suspending a function while it waits for the result of another function that invokes a long-term operation. This feature allows us to write asynchronous code without callbacks in a sequential way.

This section will cover the following topics:

- Coroutine basics
- Call stacks
- Coroutine testing
- Coroutine scope

Coroutine basics

If you are familiar with the concept of threads, you will know that each thread has its own call stack. We will cover the thread's call stack topic in the next section. The creation of a new thread is a complex operation that takes about two megabytes of memory. Coroutines use a thread pool under the hood, and only require the creation of several additional methods and classes. That is why you can consider coroutines as lightweight threads.

Let's imagine that we have a long-term operation, as shown in the following code:

```
class Image

fun loadImage() : Image {
    Thread.sleep(3000)
    return Image()
}
```

The `loadImage` function takes three seconds and returns an instance of the `Image` class. We also have the `showImages` function that takes three instances of the `Image` class, and looks as follows:

```
fun showImages(image1: Image, image2: Image, image3: Image) {
    // .......
}
```

So, we have three independent tasks that can be executed in parallel. We can create three coroutines here, each of which will execute the `loadImage` function. To create a new coroutine, we can use one of the functions called a **coroutine builder**, such as `async` or `launch`:

```
val subTask1 = GlobalScope.async { loadImage() }
val subTask2 = GlobalScope.async { loadImage() }
val subTask3 = GlobalScope.async { loadImage() }
```

The `async` function returns an instance of `Deferred`. This class encapsulates a task that will return the result in the future. A `caller` function suspends when it invokes the `await` function of an instance of the `Deferred` class. This means that a thread that has a call stack with this function is not blocked, but is just suspended. The following snippet shows how this may look:

```
showImages(subTask1.await(), subTask2.await(), subTask3.await())
```

When we call the `await` function, we suspend invoking the current function. In addition, the `showImages` function will be called when all of the subtasks return the result.

The following diagram shows how these functions can be executed:

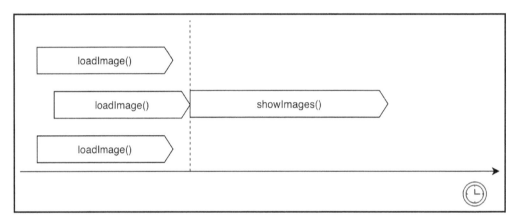

This diagram shows that three tasks can be executed almost in parallel, depending on whether the distribution of the load between cores and the `showImages` function is invoked when all three of the images are loaded.

Call stacks

Each coroutine and thread has its own call stack. This means that a coroutine or a thread is created along with its call stack. A **call stack** contains something like blocks for each function that is invoked using a context of this thread or coroutine. This block represents a memory space that contains metadata, primitive local variables, and local references to objects in the heap. You can consider a call stack a part of the memory that is allocated for a thread or coroutine.

The following diagram shows how a **Call stack** looks when a thread or coroutine is created:

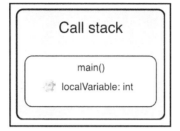

If the `main()` function invokes another function, a new block is added to the call stack. This looks as follows:

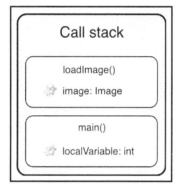

When the `loadImage` function returns a value to the `main` function, the block of the `loadImage` function is removed from the stack.

Coroutine testing

The `runBlocking` coroutine builder can be used for testing. This creates a coroutine that uses a current thread. The test within the JUnit framework may look as follows:

```
class ExampleUnitTest {

    @Test
    fun comicLoading() = runBlocking {
        val image = async { loadImage() }.await()
        assertNotNull(image)
    }
}
```

This snippet loads an image using the `async` coroutine builder, and checks that the `image` is not null. The source code of the `runBlocking` function looks as follows:

```
@Throws(InterruptedException::class)
public fun <T> runBlocking(context: CoroutineContext =
EmptyCoroutineContext, block: suspend CoroutineScope.() -> T): T {
    val currentThread = Thread.currentThread()
    val contextInterceptor = context[ContinuationInterceptor]
    val privateEventLoop = contextInterceptor == null // create private
event loop if no dispatcher is specified
    val eventLoop = if (privateEventLoop) BlockingEventLoop(currentThread)
else contextInterceptor as? EventLoop
    val newContext = GlobalScope.newCoroutineContext(
        if (privateEventLoop) context + (eventLoop as
ContinuationInterceptor) else context
    )
    val coroutine = BlockingCoroutine<T>(newContext, currentThread,
eventLoop, privateEventLoop)
    coroutine.start(CoroutineStart.DEFAULT, coroutine, block)
    return coroutine.joinBlocking()
}
```

As you can see, the `runBlocking` coroutine builder uses the `currentThread` function to obtain an instance of the `Thread` class. When you run this test, you will see the following window:

This window shows that the test has passed successfully.

Coroutine scope

With the release of version 0.26.0 of coroutines, a new, important feature was introduced—coroutine scope. All of the coroutine builders from the `coroutines-core` library are extension functions of the `CoroutineScope` interface.

The `CoroutineScope` interface looks as follows:

```
public interface CoroutineScope {
    @Deprecated(level = DeprecationLevel.HIDDEN, message = "Deprecated in
favor of top-level extension property")
    public val isActive: Boolean
        get() = coroutineContext[Job]?.isActive ?: true

    public val coroutineContext: CoroutineContext
}
```

We need the coroutine scope to provide a proper cancellation mechanism for the coroutines that we launch in our application. Modern frameworks, such as Android SDK or React Native, are built in such a way that all components, and the application itself, have a life cycle. In Android SDK, this can be an activity or a fragment, and in React Native, it can be a component.

The coroutine scope represents a scope of an object that has a life cycle, such as an activity or a component. The `coroutines-core` library provides a scope for an entire application, and we can use it if we want to launch a coroutine that works as long as an application runs. The scope of the entire application is represented by the `GlobalScope` object, and looks as follows:

```
object GlobalScope : CoroutineScope {
    @Deprecated(level = DeprecationLevel.HIDDEN, message = "Deprecated in
favor of top-level extension property")
    override val isActive: Boolean
        get() = true

    override val coroutineContext: CoroutineContext
        get() = EmptyCoroutineContext
}
```

Let's create a new activity with its own coroutine scope. The easiest way to do this is to call the context menu of a package and choose the **New** section, which looks as follows:

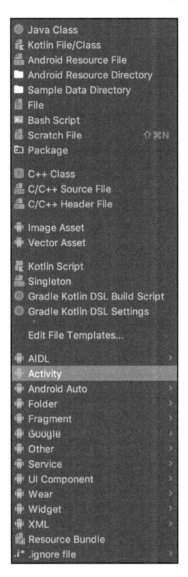

Then, choose the **Empty Activity** option in the **Activity** subsection, as follows:

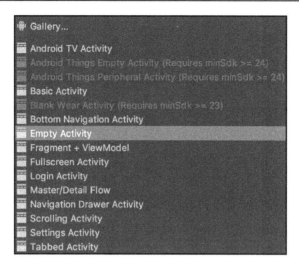

Android Studio will open the **Configure Activity** window, where you can change a configuration of **Activity** and press the **Finish** button:

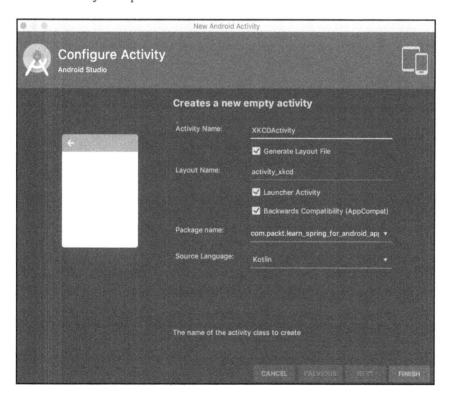

A newly created XKCDActivity class will look as follows:

```
class XKCDActivity : AppCompatActivity() {

    override fun onCreate(savedInstanceState: Bundle?) {
        super.onCreate(savedInstanceState)
        setContentView(R.layout.activity_xkcd)
    }
}
```

If we want to launch a life cycle aware coroutine from this class, we should implement the CoroutineScope interface, as follows:

```
class XKCDActivity : AppCompatActivity(), CoroutineScope {
    override val coroutineContext: CoroutineContext
        get() = Dispatchers.Main

    override fun onCreate(savedInstanceState: Bundle?) {
        super.onCreate(savedInstanceState)
        setContentView(R.layout.activity_xkcd)
    }
}
```

The CoroutineScope interface looks as follows:

```
public interface CoroutineScope {
    @Deprecated(level = DeprecationLevel.HIDDEN, message = "Deprecated in
favor of top-level extension property")
    public val isActive: Boolean
        get() = coroutineContext[Job]?.isActive ?: true

    public val coroutineContext: CoroutineContext
}
```

The XKCDActivity class implements the CoroutineScope interface and overrides the coroutineContext property. The overridden coroutineContext property contains a getter that returns Dispatchers.Main.

The Dispatchers is an object from the coroutines-core library, which contains the following dispatchers:

- Default is used by all standard coroutine builders, such as launch or async
- Main is used to run a coroutine on the main thread
- Unconfident invokes a coroutine immediately, on the first available thread
- IO is used to run coroutines that perform input/output operations

Since a getter of the overridden `coroutineContext` property returns the `Main` dispatcher, all coroutine builders from this class will launch coroutines that work on the main thread.

The `XKCDActivity` has its own coroutine scope, but it is not life cycle aware. This means that a coroutine launched in a scope of this activity will not be destroyed if the activity is destroyed. We can fix this in the following way:

```
class XKCDActivity : AppCompatActivity(), CoroutineScope {
    private lateinit var lifecycleAwareJob: Job
    override val coroutineContext: CoroutineContext
        get() = Dispatchers.Main + lifecycleAwareJob

    override fun onCreate(savedInstanceState: Bundle?) {
        super.onCreate(savedInstanceState)
        setContentView(R.layout.activity_xkcd)
        lifecycleAwareJob = Job()
    }

    override fun onDestroy() {
        super.onDestroy()
        lifecycleAwareJob.cancel()
    }
}
```

The `lifecycleAwareJob` will be used as a parent for all coroutines, and will cancel all child coroutines when an activity is destroyed. The following example code shows how to use this approach:

```
override fun onCreate(savedInstanceState: Bundle?) {
    super.onCreate(savedInstanceState)
    setContentView(R.layout.activity_xkcd)
    lifecycleAwareJob = Job()
    launch {
        val image = async(Dispatchers.IO) { loadImage() }.await()
        showImage(image)
    }
}
```

The launch coroutine builder creates a coroutine that works on the main thread, and the async coroutine builder creates a coroutine that works on the input/output thread. When the `image` is ready, it will be shown on the main thread of the application. If we press the **back** button, the coroutines will be destroyed, along with `XKCDActivity`.

Channels

The `async` function returns an instance of the `Deferred` class that allows us to compute a single value. If we need to transfer a sequence of values between coroutines, we can use channels.

A channel is an interface that looks as follows:

```
public interface Channel<E> : SendChannel<E>, ReceiveChannel<E> {
    //.....
}
```

The `SendChannel` interface looks as follows:

```
public interface SendChannel<in E> {
    @ExperimentalCoroutinesApi
    public val isClosedForSend: Boolean
    @ExperimentalCoroutinesApi
    public val isFull: Boolean
    public suspend fun send(element: E)
    public val onSend: SelectClause2<E, SendChannel<E>>
    public fun offer(element: E): Boolean
    public fun close(cause: Throwable? = null): Boolean
    @ExperimentalCoroutinesApi
    public fun invokeOnClose(handler: (cause: Throwable?) -> Unit)
}
```

The `SendChannel` interface contains the `send` method that takes a parameter and adds it to this channel. The `isFull` property is `true` if this channel already contains a value. In this case, the `send` function suspends the caller until the contained value is not consumed.

A channel can be closed by invoking the `close` method. In this case, the `isClosedForSend` property is `true`, and the `send` method throws an exception.

While the `SendChannel` interface allows us to put a value into a channel, the `ReceiveChannel` interface allows us to get the value from the channel. The `ReceiveChannel` interface looks as follows:

```
public interface ReceiveChannel<out E> {

    @ExperimentalCoroutinesApi
    public val isClosedForReceive: Boolean
    @ExperimentalCoroutinesApi
    public val isEmpty: Boolean
    public suspend fun receive(): E
    public val onReceive: SelectClause1<E>
```

```
@ExperimentalCoroutinesApi
public suspend fun receiveOrNull(): E?

@ExperimentalCoroutinesApi
public val onReceiveOrNull: SelectClause1<E?>
public fun poll(): E?
public operator fun iterator(): ChannelIterator<E>
public fun cancel(): Boolean
@ExperimentalCoroutinesApi
public fun cancel(cause: Throwable? = null): Boolean
}
```

The receiveOrNull() method returns and removes an element from this channel, or returns null if the isClosedForReceive property is true. The ReceiveChannel contains the iterator method, and can be used in the for loop.

Let's look at the following example code:

```
fun channelBasics() = runBlocking<Unit> {
    val channel = Channel<Int>()
    launch {
        println("send 0 ${Date().toGMTString()}")
        channel.send(0)
        delay(1000)
        println("send 1 ${Date().toGMTString()}")
        channel.send(1)
    }
    delay(3000)
    val theFirstElement = channel.receive()
    println("receive $theFirstElement ${Date().toGMTString()}")
    delay(4000)
    val theSecondElement = channel.receive()
    println("receive $theSecondElement ${Date().toGMTString()}")
}
```

In the preceding example, we sent two values by a channel and received those values. We also used the delay function to show that an operation takes some time.

The output looks as follows:

```
send 0 21 Oct 2018 13:30:12 GMT
 receive 0 21 Oct 2018 13:30:15 GMT
send 1 21 Oct 2018 13:30:16 GMT
 receive 1 21 Oct 2018 13:30:19 GMT
```

This output shows that the send function suspends a coroutine until a value is consumed.

We can use the `for` loop to receive values from a channel, as follows:

```
fun channelIterator() = runBlocking<Unit> {
    val channel = Channel<Int>()
    launch {
        (0..5).forEach {
            channel.send(it)
        }
    }
    for (value in channel) {
        println(value)
    }
}
```

The output looks as follows:

```
0
1
2
3
4
5
```

The producer function

The `producer` function is called a **channel builder**, and it returns an instance of the `ReceiveChannel` class. This function looks as follows:

```
@ExperimentalCoroutinesApi
public fun <E> CoroutineScope.produce(
    context: CoroutineContext = EmptyCoroutineContext,
    capacity: Int = 0,
    block: suspend ProducerScope<E>.() -> Unit
): ReceiveChannel<E> {
    val channel = Channel<E>(capacity)
    val newContext = newCoroutineContext(context)
    val coroutine = ProducerCoroutine(newContext, channel)
    coroutine.start(CoroutineStart.DEFAULT, coroutine, block)
    return coroutine
}
```

As you can see in the preceding snippet, the `produce` function contains a receiver parameter of the `ProducerScope` type. The `ProducerScope` interface looks as follows:

```
public interface ProducerScope<in E> : CoroutineScope, SendChannel<E> {
    val channel: SendChannel<E>
}
```

As you can see, the `ProducerScope` interface extends the `SendChannel` interface. This means that we can use the `send` method inside a lambda that we pass to the `producer` function.

An example of using the `producer` function may look as follows:

```
suspend fun numbersProduce(): ReceiveChannel<Int> = GlobalScope.produce {
    launch {
        (0..10).forEach {
            send(it)
        }
    }
}
```

We can use the `numbersProduce` function in the following way:

```
fun producerExample() = runBlocking<Unit> {
    val numbers = numbersProduce()
    for (value in numbers) {
        println(value)
    }
}
```

The actor function

The `actor` function contains a receiver parameter of the `ActorScope` type. The source code of the `actor` function looks as follows:

```
public fun <E> CoroutineScope.actor(
    context: CoroutineContext = EmptyCoroutineContext,
    capacity: Int = 0,
    start: CoroutineStart = CoroutineStart.DEFAULT,
    onCompletion: CompletionHandler? = null,
    block: suspend ActorScope<E>.() -> Unit
): SendChannel<E> {
    val newContext = newCoroutineContext(context)
    val channel = Channel<E>(capacity)
    val coroutine = if (start.isLazy)
        LazyActorCoroutine(newContext, channel, block) else
        ActorCoroutine(newContext, channel, active = true)
    if (onCompletion != null) coroutine.invokeOnCompletion(handler =
onCompletion)
    coroutine.start(start, coroutine, block)
    return coroutine
}
```

The `ActorScope` interface looks similar to the `ProducerScope` interface, but implements the `ReceiveChannel` interface:

```
public interface ActorScope<E> : CoroutineScope, ReceiveChannel<E> {
    val channel: Channel<E>
}
```

As you probably know, it is not a good idea to access mutable data from different coroutines. To deal with this, we can use channels and the `actor` function, in the following way:

```
suspend fun numberConsumer() = GlobalScope.actor<Int> {
    var counter = 0
    for (value in channel) {
        counter += value
        println(counter)
    }
}
```

The preceding snippet contains a mutable variable named `counter`. We change the value of the `counter` variable when a channel receives a new value. Since a channel suspends the caller until a consumer finishes processing the current value, we can be sure that the `counter` variable will be modified in the right way.

The `numbersCounter` function can be used as follows:

```
@Test
fun actorExample() = runBlocking<Unit> {
    val actor = numberConsumer()
    (0..10).forEach {
        launch {
            actor.send(it)
        }
    }
}
```

The preceding snippet launches ten coroutines that send a value to an actor in parallel.

The output looks as follows:

```
0
1
3
6
10
15
21
```

```
28
36
45
55
```

The output shows that the `counter` variable is modified in the right way.

Sequential operations

One of the most important benefits of the coroutines approach is a guarantee that functions are invoked in the same order in which they are written. The order of the operations is a very important nuance when we execute concurrent code in a multithreaded environment.

Let's imagine that we have to load a user's details, using the following function:

```
suspend fun loadUserDetails(): User {
    delay(3000)
    return User(0, "avatar")
}
```

The `loadUserDetails` function invokes the `delay` function from the `coroutines-core` library and returns an instance of the `User` class. The `delay` function suspends the invocation of the current coroutine. When a user is ready, we have to pass a value of the `avatar` property to the `loadImage` function:

```
suspend fun loadImage(avatar: String): Image {
    delay(3000)
    return Image()
}
```

The `loadImage` function also invokes the `delay` function, and returns an instance of the `Image` class. We should then pass the received instance of the `Image` class to the `showImage` function.

The following code shows how to execute these functions sequentially, using coroutines:

```
fun main(args: Array<String>) = runBlocking {
    val user = async { loadUserDetails() }.await()
    val image = async { loadImage(user.avatar) }.await()
    showImage(image)
}
```

The preceding snippet invokes all three functions that use different coroutines, sequentially. The following diagram shows a sequence of functions invoking:

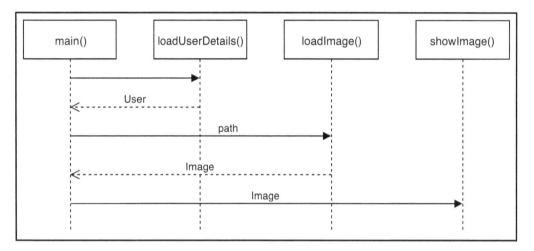

Callback hell

One of the main reasons that you should use coroutines is to avoid callback hell.

This section will cover the following topics:

- What is a callback?
- Wrapping callbacks

What is a callback?

A **callback** is a pattern that is used to retrieve the results of an asynchronous task. This approach assumes that we pass a reference to a function that should be invoked when an asynchronous operation is done.

 By *synchronous operations*, we mean that the tasks are executed one after another. The asynchronous approach assumes that several tasks can be performed in parallel.

The `loadImage` function in the following example code uses a callback to return the result:

```
fun loadImage(callback: (Image) -> Unit) {
    executor.submit {
        Thread.sleep(3000)
        callback(Image())
    }
}
```

The preceding code snippet shows the simplest example of how to create an asynchronous function that returns the results using the callback. In our case, the callback is a lambda that takes an instance of the `Image` class and returns `Unit`. The following diagram shows how this sequence works:

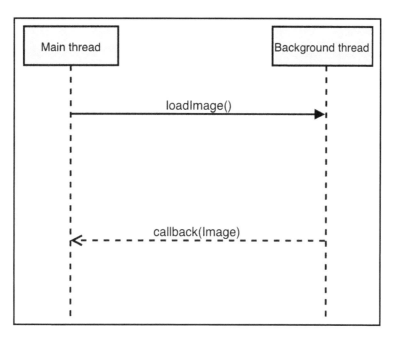

This function can be used as follows:

```
fun main(args: Array<String>) {
    loadImage { image ->
        showImage(image)
    }
}
```

The preceding snippet shows that it is easy to use a callback to deal with asynchronous code. We just implement and pass a lambda that is invoked when an image is ready.

The following diagram shows how to implement this approach:

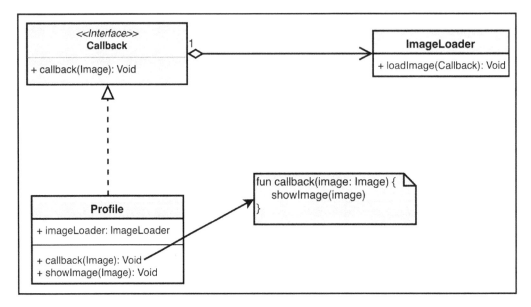

Let's imagine that we are requesting a list of users from the server. After that, we send another request to get detailed information about a user, and then, we load an avatar. In code, this may look as follows:

```
fun loadListOfFriends(callback: (List<ShortUser>) -> Unit) {
    executor.submit {
        Thread.sleep(3000)
        callback(listOf(ShortUser(0), ShortUser(1)))
    }
}
```

The `loadListOfFriends` function takes a lambda that takes a list of instances of the `ShortUser` class, as follows:

```
fun loadUserDetails(id: Int, callback: (User) -> Unit) {
    executor.submit {
        Thread.sleep(3000)
        callback(User(id, "avatar"))
    }
}
```

The `loadUserDetails` function takes a lambda and an identifier of a user, as follows:

```
fun loadImage(avatar: String, callback: (Image) -> Unit) {
    executor.submit {
        Thread.sleep(3000)
        callback(Image())
    }
}
```

The `loadImage` function takes a path to the avatar and lambda. The following example code demonstrates the most common problem that occurs when we use an approach with callbacks. We encounter the problem of code complexity and readability when concurrent tasks have to pass data to each other:

```
fun main(args: Array<String>) {
    loadListOfFriends {users ->
        loadUserDetails(users.first().id) {user ->
            loadImage(user.avatar) {image ->
                showImage(image)
            }
        }
    }
}
```

The preceding snippet demonstrates what callback hell is. We have a lot of nested functions, and it is hard to maintain this code.

Thread pools

The creation of a new thread is a complex operation that takes up a lot of resources. In the *Call stacks* section, we covered how memory is allocated for a new thread. When the lower block of a function is removed from a stack, the thread is destroyed. To avoid constantly creating new threads, we can use thread pools. There is no logic in creating a new thread for invoking each short-term operation, because this operation and switching the program flow to a created context can take more time than executing the task itself. The thread-pool pattern assumes a class that contains a set of threads that are waiting for a new task, and a queue that holds the tasks.

The following diagram shows how this works:

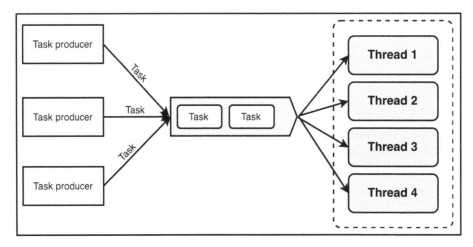

The preceding diagram shows that a pool contains a queue that holds tasks submitted by producers. The threads from the pool take tasks from the queue and execute them.

Coroutines use thread pools under the hood. The `java.util.concurrent` package provides the functionality to create your own thread pools. The `Executers` class contains a lot of static factory functions to create a pool, as shown in the following screenshot:

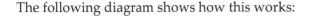

The following example code demonstrates how to create and use a single-threaded executor:

```
fun main(args: Array<String>) {
    val executor = Executors.newSingleThreadExecutor()
    executor.submit { loadImage() }
    executor.submit { loadImage() }
}
```

In the preceding snippet, we instantiated the `executor` variable and used the `submit` method to add a task to the queue.

Summary

In this chapter, we looked at concurrency and the problems that can arise in a multithreaded environment. We introduced and looked at the most common examples of coroutine usage. We also familiarized ourselves with patterns, such as thread pools and callbacks, and how to use them. Furthermore, we covered synchronous and asynchronous programming, and the problems related to these topics.

In the next chapter, we will look at an overview of reactive programming, which is useful when we want to process asynchronous actions.

Questions

- What is a call stack?
- What is a thread pool?
- What is a callback?
- Why are coroutines called lightweight threads?

Further reading

Mastering High Performance with Kotlin (`https://www.packtpub.com/application-development/mastering-high-performance-kotlin`) by Igor Kucherenko, published by Packt Publishing.

8
Reactive Programming

Reactive programming is an asynchronous approach to event handling. We encounter asynchronous events, such as user interactions with the interface or the delivery of long-term operation results, all the time. There are also libraries, such as `RxJava` and `Reactor`, that allow us to write reactive code in Kotlin or Java.

In this chapter, you will learn about the Observer pattern, and how to transform asynchronous events from one type to another. You will also learn how to use the Mono, Single, Observable, and Flux classes that implement the reactive programming concepts.

This chapter will cover the following topics:

- Reactive programming with Spring Reactor
- Blocking and non-blocking
- RxJava
- RxJava in Android

By the end of this chapter, you will be able to apply reactive programming to your applications, using the RxJava and Reactor libraries.

Technical requirements

You can find the examples from this chapter on GitHub, at the following link: `https://github.com/PacktPublishing/Learn-Spring-for-Android-Application-Development/tree/master/app/src/main/java/com/packt/learn_spring_for_android_application_development/chapter8`.

To integrate the Reactor library into your project, add the following line to the repositories section of the `build.gradle` file:

```
maven { url 'https://repo.spring.io/libs-milestone' }
```

Add the following line to the dependencies section:

```
implementation "io.projectreactor:reactor-core:3.2.2.RELEASE"
```

The Reactor library works with a version of the **Java Development Kit** (JDK), 8 or above. So, we should add the following line to the Android section:

```
compileOptions {
    sourceCompatibility JavaVersion.VERSION_1_8
    targetCompatibility JavaVersion.VERSION_1_8
}
```

To integrate the RxJava library, add the following line to the dependencies section:

```
implementation "io.reactivex.rxjava2:rxjava:2.2.3"
```

To integrate the RxAndroid library, add the following line to the dependencies section:

```
implementation 'io.reactivex.rxjava2:rxandroid:2.1.0'
```

To integrate the RxBinding library, you should add the following line to the dependencies section:

```
implementation 'com.jakewharton.rxbinding3:rxbinding:3.0.0-alpha1'
```

Reactive programming with Spring Reactor

Reactor is a library that implements reactive programming concepts for the JVM. This approach is based on the Observer pattern, and it provides types that can emit *zero*, *one*, or a sequence of values.

In this section, you will learn the following:

- How to implement the Observer pattern
- How to use the Flux publisher
- How to use the Mono publisher

The Observer pattern

The *Observer pattern* assumes that there is an object that sends a message, and another object that receives it. The following diagram shows how a class hierarchy can be organized to implement this approach:

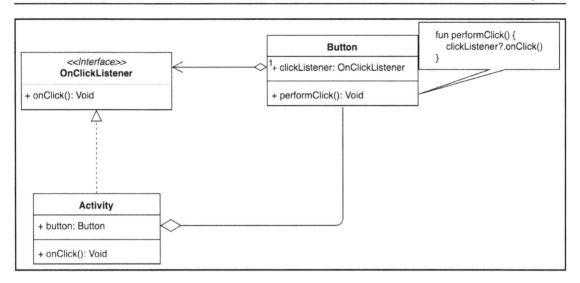

The `Activity` class implements the `OnClickListener` interface and contains an instance of the `Button` class, while the `Button` class contains the `performClick` method that invokes the `onClick` method of an instance of the `OnClickListener` class, if it is not null. The `onClick` method of the activity will then be invoked. In this way, an instance of the `Activity` class will be notified when a user clicks on the button.

The following example code shows how this approach works.

The `ObserverActivity` contains an instance of the `Button` class and invokes the `setOnClickListener` method:

```
class ObserverActivity : AppCompatActivity() {

    override fun onCreate(savedInstanceState: Bundle?) {
        super.onCreate(savedInstanceState)
        setContentView(R.layout.activity_observer)
        findViewById<Button>(R.id.button).setOnClickListener {
            Toast.makeText(this, "Clicked!", Toast.LENGTH_LONG).show()
        }
    }
}
```

The `setOnClickListener` method looks as follows:

```
public void setOnClickListener(@Nullable OnClickListener l) {
    if (!isClickable()) {
        setClickable(true);
    }
    getListenerInfo().mOnClickListener = l;
}
```

The `performClick` method invokes the `onClick` function, as follows:

```
public boolean performClick() {
    ////......
    final boolean result;
    final ObserverInfo li = mObserverInfo;
    if (li != null && li.mOnClickObserver != null) {
    playSoundEffect(SoundEffectConstants.CLICK);
    li.mOnClickObserver.onClick(this);
    result = true;
    } else {
    result = false;
    }
    ///........
    return result;
}
```

This shows that the `performClick` method invokes the `onClick` method if a reference of the `OnClickObserver` type is not `null`.

The Flux publisher

The `Flux` class represents a stream of values. This means that an instance of the Flux type can emit values, and a subscriber can receive them. This class contains a lot of functions that can be divided into two groups:

- Static factories that allow us to create a new instance of the Flux type from different sources, such as callbacks or arrays.
- Operators that allow us to process emitted values

The following example code shows how this works:

```
fun fluxTest() {
    Flux.fromArray(arrayOf(1, 2, 3))
            .map { it * it }
            .subscribe { println(it) }
}
```

The `fromArray` function creates a new instance of the Flux type that emits values from passed arrays, one by one. The `map` method allows us to modify a value from the upstream, and the `subscribe` method is needed to pass an Observer that takes the resulting values.

The output of this example looks as follows:

```
1
4
9
```

The `Flux` provides a lot of operators that can be used to process the emitted values. The following example code demonstrates this:

```
Flux.fromArray(arrayOf(1, 2, 3))
        .filter { it % 2 == 1 }
        .map { it * it }
        .reduce { sum, item -> sum + item }
        .subscribe { println(it) }
```

The `.filter`, `.map`, `.reduce`, and `.subscribe` operators are provided by the flux. We will look at each one of them in detail in just a bit.

From the operator point of view, a stream is divided into **upstream** and **downstream**. An **operator** takes a value from the **upstream**, modifies it, and passes the result to the **downstream**. The following diagram shows how operators work:

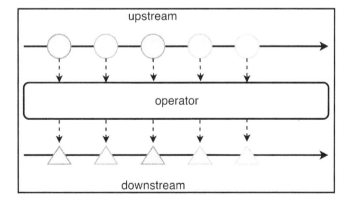

From the `map` operator point of view, the values emitted from the `filter` function belong to the **upstream,** and the items that are taken by `reduce` belong to the **downstream**.

The result of the preceding example looks as follows:

```
1
9
```

The output shows that after all of the transformations, an instance of the `Flux` class emits only two numbers.

The filter operator

The `filter` method takes a predicate, and if a value from the upstream doesn't meet a condition of the predicate, it isn't passed to the downstream.

 A predicate is a function that takes parameters and returns a Boolean value.

The following diagram shows how the `filter` method works in the previous example:

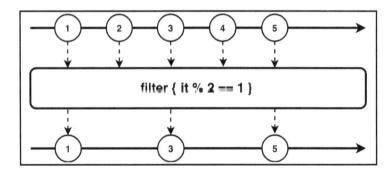

In this example, the `filter` operator is only used to receive odd numbers.

The map operator

The map operator takes a lambda that applies a transformation for each value from the upstream. The map function can be used to change the values of the primitive values, or to transform an instance from one type to another.

The following diagram shows how this works:

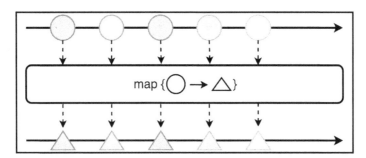

The map function takes another function that describes how an element from the upstream should be transformed.

The flatMap operator

The flatMap operator works in a similar way to the map, but works *asynchronously*. This means that it should return an instance that can return a value in the future, such as Flux or Mono. The following example code shows how it can be used:

```
Flux.fromArray(arrayOf(1, 2, 3))
        .flatMap { Mono.just(it).delayElement(Duration.ofSeconds(1)) }
        .subscribe { println(it) }
```

The output of this example looks as follows:

```
1
2
3
```

Mono is similar to Flux, but it can emit one or zero elements. In this example, we use the delayElement function, which is why each element is received by a subscriber with a one-second delay.

The following diagram shows how it works:

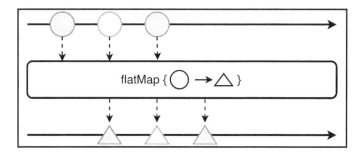

This shows that each `flatMap` operator passes each value to the downstream asynchronously, with a one-second delay.

The reduce operator

The `reduce` function takes an instance of the `BiFunction` type, which contains the `apply` function, taking two values and returning a single one. The `this` operator can be used to combine all items from the upstream into a single value, as follows:

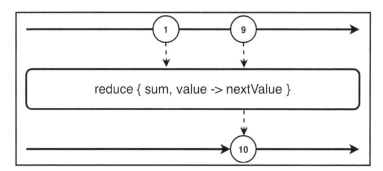

The preceding diagram shows that the upstream contains two values, and the `reduce` function passes a sum of them to the downstream.

The from static method

The `fromArray` function is one of many static factory methods that are provided by the `Flux` class. If we want to create our own source of events, we can use the `from` function. Let's create an instance of the `Flux` class that emits the `Unit` object when a user clicks on the button.

We can implement this case as follows:

```
Flux.from<Unit> { subscriber ->
    findViewById<Button>(R.id.button).setOnClickListener {
        subscriber.onNext(Unit)
    }
}.subscribe {
    Toast.makeText(this, "Clicked!", Toast.LENGTH_LONG).show()
}
```

The preceding snippet shows how to wrap an Observer into an instance of the `Flux` class. This example illustrates using the `from` function to create a new instance of the `Flux` class.

Let's run an application and press the **THE OBSERVER PATTERN** button:

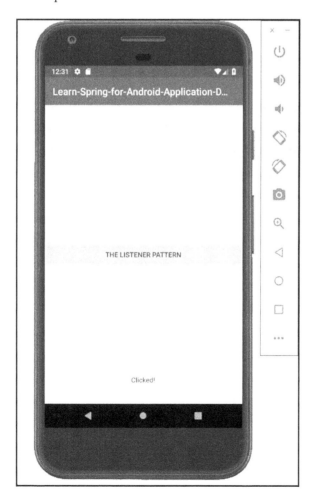

The preceding screenshot shows how an example works. When a user clicks the button, the onNext method is invoked and the Observable emits a value. The lambda that we passed to the subscribe method is invoked, and it shows a message.

Cancellation

Instances of the Activity or Fragment class have life cycles that are represented by methods, such as onCreate and onDestroy. We should clean all resources by using the onDestroy method, in order to avoid memory leaks.

The subscribe method returns an instance of the Disposable type, as follows:

```
public final Disposable subscribe(Consumer<? super T> consumer) {
    Objects.requireNonNull(consumer, "consumer");
    return subscribe(consumer, null, null);
}
```

The Disposable interface contains two methods, as follows:

- dispose cancels a publisher
- isDisposed returns true if a publisher has already been cancelled

The following example code shows how to cancel a publisher when the onDestroy method is invoked:

```
class ObserverActivity : AppCompatActivity() {
    private var disposable: Disposable? = null

    override fun onCreate(savedInstanceState: Bundle?) {
        super.onCreate(savedInstanceState)
        setContentView(R.layout.activity_observer)
        disposable = Flux.from<Unit> { subscriber ->
            findViewById<Button>(R.id.button).setOnClickListener {
                subscriber.onNext(Unit)
            }
        }.subscribe {
            Toast.makeText(this, "Clicked!", Toast.LENGTH_LONG).show()
        }
    }

    override fun onDestroy() {
        super.onDestroy()
        disposable?.dispose()
    }
}
```

As you can see, the `onDestroy` method invokes the `dispose` method to unsubscribe from an instance of the `Flux` class.

The Mono publisher

The *Mono* publisher works in a similar way to Flux, but can only emit no values or a single value. We can use this to perform a request to a server and return the result.

The following example code makes a request and receives an instance of the `Comic` class, loading an instance of the `Bitmap` class and displaying the retrieved image:

```
Mono.fromDirect<Comic> { subscriber -> subscriber.onNext(loadComic()) }
        .map { comic -> comic.img }
        .flatMap { path -> Mono.fromDirect<Bitmap> { subscriber ->
subscriber.onNext(loadBitmap(path)) } }
        .subscribeOn(Schedulers.single())
        .subscribe { bitmap ->
            Handler(Looper.getMainLooper()).post {
findViewById<ImageView>(R.id.imageView).setImageBitmap(bitmap)
            }
        }
```

The `subscribeOn` method is used to specify a scheduler for long-term tasks. Let's run this example, as follows:

The preceding snippet retrieves an instance of the `Comic` class, transforms it to a path to an image, loads the image, and then shows a downloaded image.

Blocking and non-blocking

When we work with Android, we should remember that we have a main thread that is responsible for a user interface. First, it is not a good idea to invoke long-term operations in the main thread, because in that case, a user interface freezes. Secondly, when we invoke a synchronous method, this blocks a thread. Our user interface is unresponsive until a function that is invoked from the main thread returns the result. That is why we should invoke a long-term operation asynchronously, and reactive programming can help us to do just that.

The `Mono` and `Flux` classes contain the `publishOn` and `subscribeOn` methods that can switch threads when operators are invoked. The `subscribeOn` method is used to specify a scheduler that produces emitted values, and the `publishOn` is used to specify a thread scheduler for the downstream of an `observable`.

Scheduler is an abstraction over thread pool. The following example code creates our own scheduler that uses the main thread:

```
val UIScheduler = Schedulers.fromExecutor { runnable ->
Handler(Looper.getMainLooper()).post(runnable)
}
```

Now, we can rewrite an example from the Mono publisher section, in the following way:

```
Mono.fromDirect<Comic> { subscriber -> subscriber.onNext(loadComic()) }
        .map { comic -> comic.img }
        .flatMap { path -> Mono.fromDirect<Bitmap> { subscriber ->
subscriber.onNext(loadBitmap(path)) } }
        .subscribeOn(Schedulers.single())
        .publishOn(UIScheduler)
        .subscribe { bitmap ->
findViewById<ImageView>(R.id.imageView).setImageBitmap(bitmap) }
```

The single function of the `Schedulers` class returns an instance of the `Scheduler` type that creates and uses a single thread under the hood. The `subscribeOn` method specifies that all operators from the upstream have to use a scheduler that is returned by the `single()` function.

We pass our own scheduler that uses **the main thread** under the hood. For this reason, the lambda that is passed to the `subscribe` method is performed on **the main thread**.

The following diagram shows how this works:

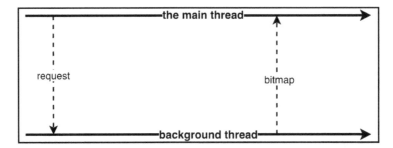

The diagram shows that **the main thread** is not blocked, and runs with a background, in parallel.

RxJava

RxJava is another popular library that implements the concept of reactive programming. It also provides types, such as Observable or Single, that emit values. All of these classes also provide static factories and operators.

In this section, we will cover the following:

- How to use the Flowable class
- How to use the Observable class
- How to use the Single class
- How to use the Maybe class
- How to use the Completable class

Flowable

The `Flowable` class was introduced in the second version of the RxJava library. This class represents a stream of events, such as Flux from Reactor.

You should consider using `Flowable` when you read data from a file, database, or network. The following example code shows how to create and use `Flowable`:

```
Flowable.fromIterable(listOf(1, 2, 3))
        .subscribe { println(it) }
```

This shows how to create an instance of the `Flowable` class that emits values.

Observable

The `Observable` class is similar to `Flowable`, but it can throw
a `MissingBackpressureException`.

 Backpressure is a case when an observable produces values faster than a subscriber can consume them. In this case, a `MissingBackpressureException` is thrown.

An example use case is as follows:

```
Observable.fromIterable(listOf(1, 2, 3))
        .subscribe { println(it) }
```

The preceding snippet shows how to create an instance of the `Observable` class that emits values.

It is worth mentioning that `Observable` has lower overhead than `Flowable`. You should consider using `Observable` when you handle user interface events.

There are operators that can help you to deal with backpressure, such as *debounce* or *throttle*. Let's take a look at each one of them.

The debounce operator

The `debounce` method takes a duration and returns an instance of the `Observable` class that only emits a value if a time frame that is equal to the passed time from the moment when the previous value was emitted. The following diagram explains how this works:

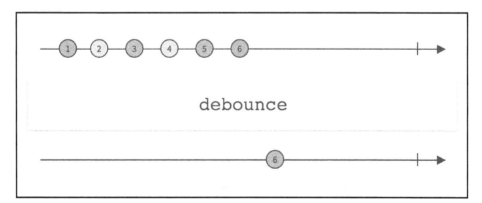

The preceding diagram shows how the debounce method reduces events. The debounce method takes a time frame and returns a new instance of the Observable type that only emits the last value that was produced during this timeframe.

The throttle operator

The throttle operator returns an instance of the Observable that only emits one item from the upstream during the sequential time window that has passed. The throttle is a family of methods, such as throttleFirst or throttleLast.

The following diagram shows how the throttleFirst method works:

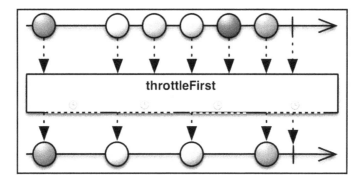

The throttleLast method works as follows:

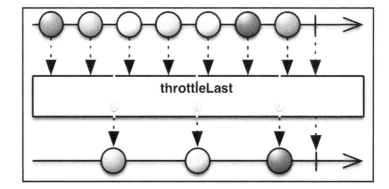

The preceding diagrams shows that the throttleFirst and throttleLast methods can be used to reduce the emitted values.

Single

The `Single` class works in a similar way to `Mono` from the Reactor library. This can also be used to perform a request to a server. We should consider using `Flowable` when a source returns only one item.

The following example code shows how `Single` can be used:

```
Single.just(1).subscribe(Consumer<Int> { println(it) })
```

This snippet contains an instance of the `Single` class that emits one value.

Maybe

An instance of the `Maybe` type can emit no value, or a single value. The following example code shows how to use `Maybe` and the `test` method:

```
Maybe.just(1)
        .map { item -> item + 1 }
        .filter { item -> item == 1 }
        .defaultIfEmpty(4)
        .test()
        .assertResult(4)
```

The `test` method returns an instance of the `TestObservable` that is used for testing and contains methods such as `assertResult`. The `defaultIfEmpty` method of the `Maybe` class allows us to specify a default value that can be emitted if an instance of the `Maybe` class is empty.

Completable

An instance of the `Completable` class doesn't emit a value at all. It can be used to notify the user of task completion. In addition, it can be used when we delete an item from a database, for instance.

The following example code shows a case of deleting an item from a database:

```
Completable.fromAction { Database.delete() }
        .test()
        .assertComplete()
```

The `test` method returns an instance of the `TestObservable` class.

RxJava in Android

RxJava is a very popular library for Android development, and there are a lot of other libraries that are based on RxJava, such as RxAndroid and RxBinding.

This section will cover the following topics:

- The RxAndroid library
- The RxBinding library

The RxAndroid library

The RxAndroid library provides a scheduler that uses the main thread. The following example code shows how to use this scheduler:

```
Flowable.fromIterable(listOf(1, 2, 3))
        .subscribeOn(Schedulers.computation())
        .observeOn(AndroidSchedulers.mainThread())
        .subscribe { println(it) }
```

The preceding snippet shows how to use the `observeOn` method to handle emitted values on the main thread.

The RxBinding library

The RxBinding library provides a reactive application programming interface. Let's imagine that we want to observe an input of `EditText` and display this text in `TextView`.

The RxBinding library provides extension functions for user interface components, such as `textChanges`:

```
fun TextView.textChanges(): InitialValueObservable<CharSequence> {
    return TextViewTextChangesObservable(this)
}
```

We can implement our example by using the `textChanges` function, as follows:

```
class RxActivity : AppCompatActivity() {

    private val editText by lazy(LazyThreadSafetyMode.NONE) {
        findViewById<EditText>(R.id.editText)
    }

    private val textView by lazy(LazyThreadSafetyMode.NONE) {
        findViewById<TextView>(R.id.textView)
    }

    override fun onCreate(savedInstanceState: Bundle?) {
        super.onCreate(savedInstanceState)
        setContentView(R.layout.activity_rx)
        editText
                .textChanges()
                .subscribe { textView.text = it }

    }
}
```

In the preceding snippet, we invoked the `textChanges` function and subscribed to a retrieved subscriber. The `textChanges` method returns an instance of the `Observable` class that emits the text from the input.

The result looks as follows, and shows that the text from the input immediately appears on the screen:

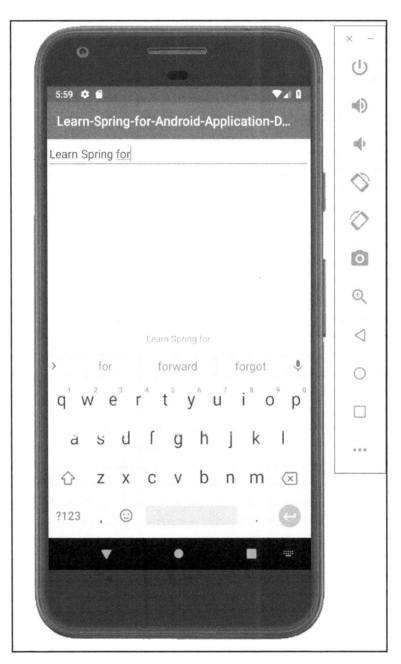

The RxBinding library also contains the `clicks` extension function, which looks as follows:

```
fun View.clicks(): Observable<Unit> {
    return ViewClickObservable(this)
}
```

The `clicks` extension function returns an instance of the `ViewClickObservable` class.

Furthermore, the `ViewClickObservable` looks as follows:

```
private class ViewClickObservable(
        private val view: View
) : Observable<Unit>() {

    override fun subscribeActual(observer: Observer<in Unit>) {
        if (!checkMainThread(observer)) {
            return
        }
        val observer = Observer(view, observer)
        observer.onSubscribe(observer)
        view.setOnClickListener(observer)
    }
}
```

It uses the `subscribeActual` method to pass an instance of the `Observer` class to the `setOnClickListener` of an instance of the `View` class.
The `ViewClickObservable` class inherits from the `Observable` class and overrides the `subscribeActual` method.
Finally, the `Observer` class looks as follows:

```
private class Observer(
        private val view: View,
        private val observer: Observer<in Unit>
    ) : MainThreadDisposable(), OnClickObserver {

    override fun onClick(v: View) {
        if (!isDisposed) {
            observer.onNext(Unit)
        }
    }

    override fun onDispose() {
        view.setOnClickListerner(null)
    }
}
```

The preceding snippet invokes the `onNext` method when the `onClick` method is invoked.

Summary

In this chapter, we looked at reactive programming and how it can help us to handle asynchronous events. We also introduced the React and RxJava libraries that provide classes such as `Mono`, `Flux`, `Single`, and `Observable`, which follow reactive programming concepts.

Reactive programming allows us to use different thread schedulers to process and transform events with multithreading. The Blocking and Non-Blocking section showed us how to work with thread schedulers. You also learned that reactive programming is based on the Observer pattern.

Modern Android applications handle a lot of different asynchronous events, such as user interactions and push notifications. Learning about Reactive programming is important, because it can help us to better manage our resources through asynchronous processing, allowing us to build more complex applications that are capable of multitasking.

In the next chapter, you will learn how to create the `Application` class.

Questions

- What is reactive programming?
- What is the Mono class?
- What is the Observable class?
- What is a scheduler?

Further reading

- To gain more comprehensive knowledge about applying reactive programming with Reactor, I recommend reading *Hands-On Reactive Programming with Reactor* (`https://www.packtpub.com/application-development/hands-reactive-programming-reactor`), by Rahul Sharma.

9
Creating an Application

So far, we have prepared you to become a professional Spring-based developer. You have learned what Spring is, as well as the functions of its architecture, components, security features, database, and so on. We have also shown you how to develop an Android app and handle HTTP requests and use the database.

As you know, we developed all the example projects in Kotlin, and nowadays, this language is very famous among developers for its conciseness and interoperability. In this chapter, we will implement all the features of the previous chapters to develop a project that will have a server and a client side.

This chapter covers the following topics:

- Project idea
- Creating the design
- Server side:
    - Developing a database model
    - Creating a project and Maven dependency
    - Creating entities, repositories, and a controller
    - Implementing security
    - Modified application.properties
- Client side:
    - Creating models
    - Creating HTTP requests
    - Creating API services
    - Modifying activities
    - Fetching REST APIs
    - Creating an adapter and XML layouts
    - Checking the output

Technical requirements

You will need almost all the dependencies, such as security, MySQL, JPA, Hibernate, and JDBC, from the previous chapters.

The source code with an example for this chapter is available on GitHub at the following link: `https://github.com/PacktPublishing/Learn-Spring-for-Android-Application-Development/tree/master/Chapter09`.

You will find two projects—`social_network` is the server side, which has been developed with the help of the Spring Framework, and `ClientSide` is the client side, which has been developed for the Android platform.

Project idea

The project idea is the most important part. You need to generate this idea very carefully and have to identify the facts behind your project. You need to keep in mind how this project could be effective on the market, how the users will accept your project, why they will use it, why they should choose your app instead of others, what features will make it different from other existing similar projects, and so on. After generating an idea, you need to create a draft in your mind of how will it look. Then you need to put it down on paper, design the workflow of the project, and then develop the project's code. Lastly, you need to test the project for its smoothness, check that it's bug/error free, and prepare it for the market.

In this chapter, we will create a small project that is like a social network. We will name it `Packt Network`. This project will have two parts. One is a server and one is a client, and both sides will be written in Kotlin. First of all, we create a Spring project where we will build our server and REST API. The data will be stored in a MySQL database, and we will handle the database using JDBC, JPA, and Hibernate. This data will be protected by the basic authentication of Spring Security.

In our second project, we will create an Android application and handle the created REST APIs of the server. We will use Retrofit to handle the REST APIs and the network. Then we will create a registration and login page to create and login as a user, using a username and password. After this, the user can post a status and see a list of all the other user's statuses. A comment can be also posted in a status.

Now we will start to design and develop our server-side project using Spring.

Server side

On the server side, we are using the Spring Framework. We will handle all the data with a MySQL database and protect the resources with basic authentication.

First of all, we will design the project's backend logic. Then we will plan for the REST API. We will create a data model using MySQL Workbench. Then we will create the project using `http://start.spring.io`. Then we will create the database entity using JPA and Hibernate, and we will check that the REST API is working. To check this, we will use an HTTP client software tool named Insomnia. Then we will implement basic authentication with Spring Security to protect our resources. Lastly, we will give you a task to complete, on upgrading the project, and becoming a contributor to this project on GitHub.

Creating the design

As we mentioned before, this project will be like a social media platform; the users can post their statuses and others can see them in the timeline and can like it, add comments, and so on. For this project, there won't be a UI for the server side. We will create a backend server. To create this server, we will have to create a REST API that can be used by the client application. To do this, we need to create a database based on our REST API.

First of all, we split our database table names, the HTTP function requests, and the URL path.

There will be four tables:

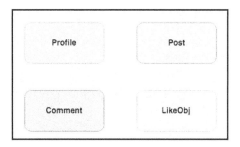

Let's have a look at each of them:

- One is for the users. All their information will be stored in a table named `Profile`.
- There will be another table named `Post`, where all the posted statuses of all the users will be stored.

- Another table named `Comment` will store all the comments of all the posted statuses.
- Another table named `LikeObj` will store all the likes of all the posted statuses, but we won't provide this feature for the comments.

Now we will create the URL path of the REST API using an HTTP function request, and all the output will be designed for JSON. We are using JSON because it is very easy to handle and understand for all developers.

Regarding the `Profile` table, here are the URL paths of the HTTP requests:

- `POST http://localhost:8080/user/new`: This request will create a user profile with all the information the user has posted on their profile
- `GET http://localhost:8080/user/{id}`: This request will get the details of the given `id` holder
- `PUT http://localhost:8080/user/{id}`: This request will update the user details of the given `id` holder
- `DELETE http://localhost:8080/user/{id}`: This request will delete the user details of the given `id` holder, including all the posts, comments, and likes from this user

Regarding the `Post` table, here are the URL paths of the HTTP requests:

- `POST http://localhost:8080/post/{id}/new`: This request will create a post from the `id` holder
- `GET http://localhost:8080/posts`: This request will get all the post's details
- `GET http://localhost:8080/post/{id}`: This request will get the post details of the given `id` holder
- `DELETE http://localhost:8080/post/{id}`: This request will delete the post details of the given `id` holder, including all the comments

Regarding the `Comment` table, here are the URL paths of the HTTP requests:

- `POST HTTP://localhost:8080/comment/{post_id}`: This request will create a comment on the `post_id` holder
- `DELETE HTTP://localhost:8080/comment/{post_id}`: This request will delete the comment of the given `post_id` holder

Regarding the `LikeObj` table, here are the URL paths of the HTTP requests:

- `POST http://localhost:8080/like/new`: This request will like a post of the `post_id` holder
- `DELETE ttp://localhost:8080/like/new`: This request will unlike a post of the `post_id` holder

Developing a database model

We will use JPA, and one of the most noticeable points is that creating a database is not recommended, because as we know, JPA will automatically create database tables with fields using the entity class of the project. But still, we need to create a demo database and draw an EER diagram. You can create your EER on paper or you can create one digitally using MySQL Workbench. Here, we will use MySQL Workbench, which has a free version. This is one of the best tools for developing a database or creating a model for a database:

1. You need to download this software from `https://dev.mysql.com/downloads/workbench/`, if you don't have it. Then install and run it. As we mentioned before, we have some default values:

   ```
   Host -- localhost // our hosting URL
   Port -- 3306 // our hosting port
   Username -- root // username of the MySQL
   Password -- 12345678 // password of the MySQL
   ```

2. Open this application and select the **Models** option, as shown in the following screenshot:

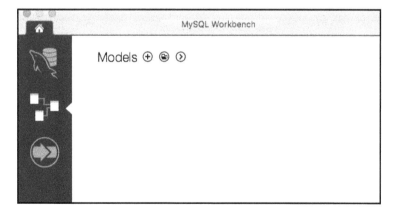

3. Click the plus (+) sign to create a new model for our application. In the new window, you will find all the necessary features to create a model. Save this model as `my_app`:

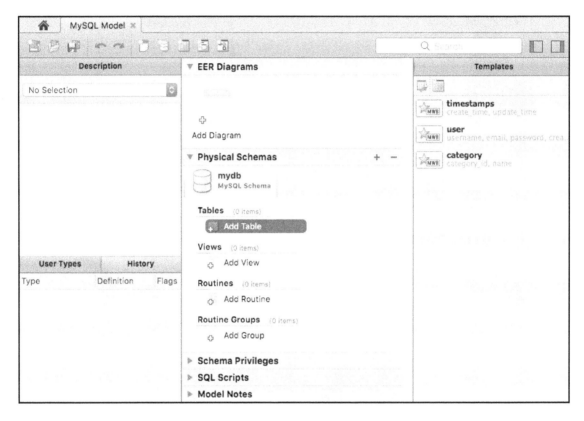

4. Create a table called `Profile`. The columns will be `id (primary key)`, `username`, `password`, `email`, `first_name`, `last_name`, `acc_created_time`, `contact_number`, `dob`, `city`, and `country`.

5. A table called `Post`. The columns will be `id (primary key)` and `text`.

6. Create another table called `Comment`. The columns will be `id (primary key)` and `text`.

7. Lastly, create a table called `Like`. The column will be `id (primary key)`.

But there are some relationships between the tables:

- Between `Profile` and `Post`: There is a many-to-one relation for `Post` because a user can post multiple statuses, and each post has only one user.
- Between `Profile` and `Comment`: There is a many-to-one relation for `Comment` because a user can post multiple comments, and each comment has only one user.
- Between `Profile` and `Like`: There is a many-to-one relation for `Like` because a user can like multiple posts, and each like has only one user.
- Between `Post` and `Comment`: There is a one-to-many relation for `Post` because a post may have multiple comments, but a comment is for only one specific post.
- Between `Post` and `Like`: There is a one-to-many relation for `Post` because a post may have multiple likes, but each like is for only one specific post:

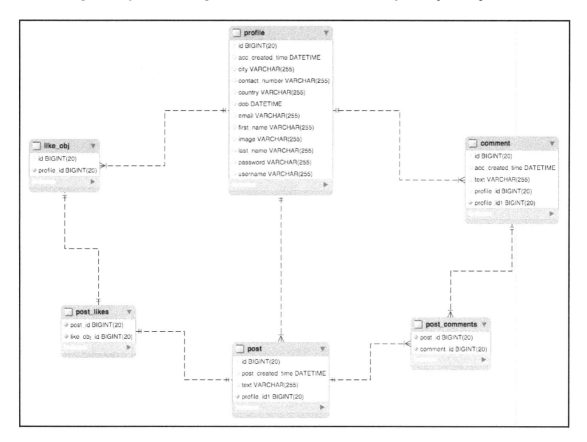

So after all the relations, we can see the table names of the database, as shown in the following screenshot:

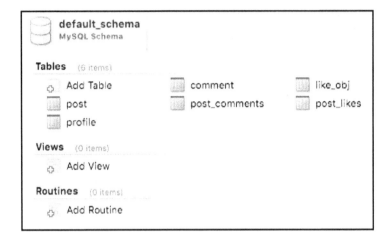

Finally, you can create the EER diagram by clicking on the EER Diagram icon, as shown in the following screenshot:

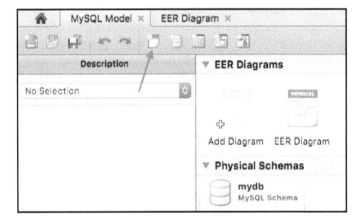

This is the EER diagram model of our project. You may find two extra tables, named post_likes and post_comments. It generates these using JPA and Hibernate. We will discuss this later.

So, our database modeling is done. Now you can export it as SQL and create the database for the project. But we recommend you not to do this because we need to do some modification.

Now create the project.

Creating a project

To create a project, go to `https://start.spring.io` and create a Kotlin-based project. Here are the dependencies of the project:

- Web
- JDBC
- MySQL
- DevTools
- JPA
- H2

You can find these in the `pom.xml` file. There you can update, add, or remove the dependencies.

To enable JPA auditing, you need to annotate `@EnableJpaAuditing` annotation on the `SocialNetworkApplication.kt` class. It will enable the use of JPA functionalities.

Here is the code for this class:

```
@SpringBootApplication
@EnableJpaAuditing
class SocialNetworkApplication

fun main(args: Array<String>) {
    runApplication<SocialNetworkApplication>(*args)
}
```

Creating entities

First of all, we need to create four as the table details of the database. The four entities are `Profile`, `Post`, `Comment`, and `LikeObj`. In the following sections, you'll learn how to create the entity classes.

Creating a Profile entity

Create a `Profile` entity named `Profile.kt` with the `@Entity` annotation to convert this class into an entity class. Here is the code of this model class (the entire code can be found at the provided GitHub Link):

```
@Entity
class Profile : Serializable {

    constructor(id: Long) {
        this.id = id
    }

    constructor(name: String) {
        this.username = name
    }
    -----

    -----
@JsonProperty("contactNumber")
var contactNumber: String? = null

@JsonProperty("dob")
var dOB: Date? = null

@JsonProperty("city")
var city: String? = null

@JsonProperty("country")
var country: String? = null
}
```

In this class, we have 11 elements, which contain all the user's details. We have four constructors to use this model according to our tasks. Here are the constructors:

```
constructor(id: Long) {
    ----

    ----
}

constructor(name: String) {
    ----

    ----
}

constructor(id: Long, name: String, password: String) {
    ----

    ----
}
```

```
constructor(username: String, password: String, email: String,
accCreatedTime: Instant,
 firstName: String?, lastName: String?, contactNumber: String?, dOB: Date?,
 city: String?, country: String?) {
   ----
   ----
}
```

Now let's discuss the annotations that are used in this class:

```
@Id
@GeneratedValue
var id: Long? = 0
```

According to the previous code, we used `@Id` annotation on the `id`, which means that `id` is the primary key of the `Profile` entity. The `@GeneratedValue` annotation means it increments the value of `id`.

Here is a snippet of the code for the `password` object:

```
@JsonIgnore
@JsonProperty("password")
var password: String = ""
```

According to this code, `@JsonIgnore` uses variables or functions. If you use it, then the requested JSON won't show this variable. Here, we used it on the `password`, and that means no-one can fetch the password.

`@JsonProperty` defines that during the serialization and deserialization of JSON, it changes the visibility of the logical property of its element.

Creating a Post entity

Create a `Post` entity named `Post.kt` with the `@Entity` annotation to convert this class into an entity class. Here is the code of this model class:

```
@Entity
class Post(text: String, postedBy: Profile) : Serializable {

    @Id
    @GeneratedValue
    var id: Long? = 0

    var text: String? = text

    @ManyToOne(fetch = FetchType.LAZY)
```

```
        @JoinColumn(name = "profile_id")
        @JsonIgnoreProperties("username","password",
"email","accCreatedTime","firstName","lastName",
                "contactNumber","dob","city","country")
        var postedBy: Profile? = postedBy

        @JsonIgnore
        @JsonProperty("postCreatedTime")
        var postCreatedTime: Instant? = Instant.now()

        @OneToMany(cascade = [CascadeType.ALL], fetch = FetchType.LAZY,
orphanRemoval=true)
        val comments = mutableListOf<Comment>()


        @OneToMany(cascade = [CascadeType.ALL], orphanRemoval = true)
        var likes: List<LikeObj>? = mutableListOf<Comment>()
    }
```

Here we have two elements and one constructor. Here is the constructor:

```
@Entity
class Post(text: String, postedBy: Profile) : Serializable {
    -----
    -----
}
```

It's time now to discuss some new annotations that have been used in this class:

```
@ManyToOne(fetch = FetchType.LAZY)
@JoinColumn(name = "profile_id")
@JsonIgnoreProperties("username","password",
"email","accCreatedTime","firstName","lastName",
            "contactNumber","dob","city","country")
    var postedBy: Profile? = postedBy
```

@ManyToOne on the Profile variable means that this will indicate which user posted that specific status.

@JoinColumn means its access element Profile is connected with the foreign key using profile_id.

@JsonIgnoreProperties(......) ignores the JSON properties during deserialization. In this project, when you get the post's JSON, in the profile attribute you will only find the id. Here is a simple example of a JSON:

```
1 ▾ {
2       "text": "this is status",
3 ▾     "postedBy": {
4           "id": 1
5       },
6       "id": 0,
7       "postCreatedTime": "2019-01-13T17:51:32.239Z",
8       "comments": [],
9       "likes": []
10    }
```

You can see `"id":0`, which is the `id` of the post.

Now create a mutable list of the `Comment` and annotate it with `@OneToMany`, as follows:

```
@OneToMany(cascade = [CascadeType.ALL], fetch = FetchType.LAZY,
orphanRemoval=true)
    val comments = mutableListOf<Comment>()
```

`@OneToMany(....)` means a post can be many comments and likes.

`cascade = [CascadeType.ALL]` attribute is a feature of Hibernate. It means you can apply all primary cascade types.

`fetch = FetchType.LAZY` means it fetches the data lazily during the first access.

`orphanRemoval=true` means if the post has been deleted, then all the comments and likes on this post will be deleted automatically.

Creating a Comment entity

Create a `Comment` entity named `Comment.kt` with the `@Entity` annotation to convert this class into an entity class. Here is the code of this model class:

```
@Entity
class Comment(text: String, postedBy: Profile) : Serializable {

    @Id
    @GeneratedValue
    var id: Long? = 0

    var text: String? = text

    @JsonIgnore
```

```
    @JsonProperty("accCreatedTime")
    var accCreatedTime: Instant? = Instant.now()

    @ManyToOne
    @JoinColumn(name = "profile_id")
@JsonIgnoreProperties("username","password","email","accCreatedTime","first
Name","lastName"        , "contactNumber","dob","city","country")
    var postedBy: Profile? = postedBy
}
```

Here we have three elements and one constructor. Here is the constructor:

```
@Entity
class Comment(text: String, postedBy: Profile) : Serializable {
    -----
    -----
}
```

Creating like entity

Create a like entity named `LikeObj.kt` with the `@Entity` annotation to convert this class into an entity class. Here is the code of this model class:

```
@Entity
class LikeObj(mProfile: Profile) : Serializable {

    @Id
    @GeneratedValue
    var id: Long? = 0

    @ManyToOne
    @JoinColumn(name = "profile_id")
@JsonIgnoreProperties("username","password","email","accCreatedTime","first
Name","lastName",
            "contactNumber","dob","city","country")
    var profile: Profile? = mProfile
}
```

Here we have one element and one constructor. Here is the constructor:

```
@Entity
class LikeObj(profile: Profile) : Serializable {
    -----
    -----
}
```

Creating repositories

Create a repository for a profile named `ProfileRepository.kt` and implement the `JpaRepository` repository that has all the necessary CRUD request methods to fetch the database. Here is the code for this class:

```
@Repository
interface ProfileRepository : JpaRepository<Profile, Long>
```

Now create a repository for a post named `PostRepository.kt` and implement the `JpaRepository` repository that has all the necessary CRUD request methods to fetch the database. Here is the code for this class:

```
@Repository
interface PostRepository : JpaRepository<Post, Long>
```

Then create a repository for a comment named `CommentRepository.kt` and implement the `JpaRepository<>` repository that has all the necessary CRUD request methods to fetch the database. Here is the code for this class:

```
@Repository
interface CommentRepository : JpaRepository<Comment, Long>
```

Lastly, create a repository for the like model named `LikeRepository.kt` and implement the `JpaRepository<>` repository that has all the necessary CRUD request methods to fetch the database. Here is the code for this class:

```
@Repository
interface LikeRepository : JpaRepository<LikeObj, Long>
```

To delete all the data regarding the deleted post, we need to create a repository for the profile named `DeletePCLRepository.kt` and implement an interface named `DeletePCLByIDInterface.kt` with one function, which will delete all the data regarding the deleted user. Here is the code for the interface:

```
interface DeletePCLByIDInterface {
    fun deleteAllUsersInfoByUserID(userID: Long): Any
}
```

Here is the code for the `DeletePCLRepository.kt` class:

```
@Repository
class DeletePCLRepository : DeletePCLByIDInterface {

    @Autowired
    private lateinit var jdbcTemplate: JdbcTemplate
```

```
override fun deleteAllUsersInfoByUserID(userID: Long): Any {

    val deletePosts = "DELETE FROM post, comment WHERE profile_id = ?;"
    val deleteComments = "DELETE FROM comment WHERE profile_id = ?"
    val deleteLikes = "DELETE FROM like_obj WHERE profile_id = ?"

    jdbcTemplate.update(deletePosts, userID)
    jdbcTemplate.update(deleteComments, userID)
    jdbcTemplate.update(deleteLikes, userID)

    return "DONE"
    }
}
```

To check a registered user, create a repository named `UserExistRepository.kt` and implement an interface named `UserExistInterface.kt` with two functions.

Here is the code for the interface:

```
interface UserExistInterface{
    fun isUserExist(name: String): Boolean
}
```

In this interface, `isUserExist(username: String)` will search the `Profile` table of the database and return a `Boolean` based on the existing of the user.

Here is the code for the `UserExistRepository.kt` class:

```
@Repository
class UserExistRepository: UserExistInterface {
    @Autowired
    private lateinit var jdbcTemplate: JdbcTemplate

    override fun isUserExist(name: String): Boolean {
        val sql = "SELECT count(*) FROM PROFILE WHERE username = ?"
        val count = jdbcTemplate.queryForObject(sql, Int::class.java, name)
        return count != 0
    }
}
```

In this class, we add the `@Autowired` annotation to autowire the `JdbcTemplate` to utilize the JDBC database. We `override` the `issue exist(name: String)` function.

`"SELECT count(*) FROM PROFILE WHERE username = ?"` is an SQL query that is used to search the existing users from the `Profile` table of the database. If there is a user, then it will return `true`.

Creating a controller

Now, create a controller class named `AppController.kt` and annotate it
with `@RestController` to convert it into a controller class:

```
@RestController
class AppController {
    _____
    _____
}
```

Now autowire the repositories, as shown in the following code:

```
@Autowired
private lateinit var profileRepository: ProfileRepository

@Autowired
private lateinit var userExist: UserExistRepository

@Autowired
private lateinit var postRepository: PostRepository

@Autowired
private lateinit var commentRepository: CommentRepository

@Autowired
private lateinit var likeRepository: LikeRepository

@Autowired
private lateinit var deletePCLRepository : DeletePCLRepository
```

Then create HTTP function requests. We won't discuss this here because we have already
described the use of the HTTP requests in `Chapter 4`, *Spring Modules for Android*.

Creating a profile's HTTP requests

Now create HTTP function requests for the profiles.

Here is the function for creating a profile's `POST` request:

```
// New Profile registration
@PostMapping("/profile/new")
fun registerUser(@RequestBody profile: Profile): Any {
    if (!userExist.isUserExist(profile.username)) {
        profile.password = passwordEncoder.encode(profile.password)
        profileRepository.save(profile)
```

```
            return profile
    }
    return "{\"duplicate\": \"${profile.username} is taken. Try another\"}"
}
```

Here is the function for creating a profile's GET request:

```
// Get Profile by ID
@GetMapping("/profile/{id}")
fun getUserById(@PathVariable("id") id: Long): Any {
    return profileRepository.findById(id)
}
```

Here is the function for creating a profile's PUT request:

```
//    Update Profile by ID
@PutMapping("/profile/{id}")
fun updateUserById(@PathVariable("id") id: Long, @RequestBody mUser:
Profile): Any {
    val profile = profileRepository.getOne(id)
    if (mUser.firstName != null) profile.firstName = mUser.firstName
    if (mUser.lastName != null) profile.lastName = mUser.lastName
    if (mUser.contactNumber != null) profile.contactNumber =
mUser.contactNumber
    if (mUser.city != null) profile.city = mUser.city
    if (mUser.country != null) profile.country = mUser.country
    return profileRepository.save(profile)
}
```

Here is the function for creating a profile's DELETE request:

```
// Delete Profile by ID
@DeleteMapping("/profile/{userId}")
fun deleteUserById(@PathVariable("userId") userId: Long): Any {
    deletePCLRepository.deleteAllUsersInfoByUserID(userId)
    return profileRepository.deleteById(userId)
}
```

Creating a post's HTTP requests

Now create the HTTP request functions for the Post.

Here is the function for creating a post's POST request:

```
// Post status by Profile ID
@PostMapping("/post/{profile_id}/new")
fun submitPost(@PathVariable("profile_id") profile_id: Long, @RequestParam
```

```
text: String): Any {
        val mPost = Post(text, Profile(profile_id))
        postRepository.save(mPost)

        return mPost
    }
```

Here is the function for the creating a post's GET request to fetch all the posts:

```
// Get all posted status
@GetMapping("/posts")
fun getPostList(): Any {
    return postRepository.findAll()
}
```

Here is the function for creating a post's GET request to fetch one post:

```
// Get all posted status by Profile ID
@GetMapping("/post/{id}")
fun getPostById(@PathVariable("id") id: Long): Any {
    return postRepository.findById(id)
}
```

Here is the function for the creating a post's PUT request to update one post:

```
// Update all posted status by Profile ID
    @PutMapping("/post/{profile_id}")
    fun updatePostById(@PathVariable("profile_id") id: Long, @RequestParam
text: String): Any {
        val modifiedPost = postRepository.getOne(id)
        modifiedPost.text = text
        return postRepository.save(modifiedPost)
    }
```

Here is the function for creating a post's DELETE request:

```
// Delete a posted status by Profile ID
@DeleteMapping("/post/{id}")
fun deletePostByUserId(@PathVariable("id") id: Long): Any {
    return postRepository.deleteById(id)
}
```

Creating a comment's HTTP requests

Now create the HTTP request functions for the Comment.

Here is the function for creating a comment's POST request:

```
// Post comment in a post by Profile ID and Post ID
    @PostMapping("/comment/{post_id}")
    fun postCommentByPostId(@PathVariable("post_id") postId: Long,
@RequestParam id: Long, @RequestParam commentText: String): Any {
        val optionalPost: Optional<Post> = postRepository.findById(postId)
        return if (optionalPost.isPresent) {
            val myComment = Comment(commentText, Profile(id))
            val post = optionalPost.get()
            post.comments.add(myComment)
            postRepository.save(post)
            return post
        } else {
            "There is no post.."
        }
    }
```

First, we need to initialize an optionalPost object by finding the existing post. Then, if the post exists, we create a Comment model named myComment, then add the mutable list of Comment, and then save the post using postRepository.

Here is the function for creating a comment's GET request:

```
// get comment List of a post
@GetMapping("/comment/{id}")
fun getCommentListByPostId(@PathVariable("id") id: Long): Any {
    return commentRepository.findById(id)
}
```

Here is the function for creating a comment's PUT request:

```
// get comment List of a post
@GetMapping("/comment/{id}")
fun getCommentListByPostId(@PathVariable("id") id: Long, @RequestParam
text: String): Any {
    val modifiedComment = commentRepository.getOne(id)
    modifiedComment.text = text
    return commentRepository.save(modifiedComment)
}
```

Here is the function for creating a comment's DELETE request:

```
// delete comment List of a status
@DeleteMapping("/comment/{id}")
fun deleteCommentByPostId(@PathVariable("id") id: Long): Any {
    return commentRepository.findById(id)
}
```

Implementing security

We are implementing basic authentication security. It will be similar to what we covered in Chapter 5, *Securing Applications with Spring Security*. But there we used `inMemoryAuthentication()`, and here we will fetch the username and password from the database and implement them for the project using `UserDetailsService`:

1. Create a service class named `CustomUserDetailsService.kt`.

2. Implement the `UserDetailsService` and annotated by `@Service` to make it a service class. Here is the code for this service class:

```
@Service
class CustomUserDetailsService: UserDetailsService {

 @Autowired
 private lateinit var userByNameRepository: UserByNameRepository

 @Throws(UsernameNotFoundException::class)
 override fun loadUserByUsername(username: String): User {
 val profile = userByNameRepository.getUserByName(username)

 return
org.springframework.security.core.userdetails.User(username,
profile.password,
 AuthorityUtils.createAuthorityList("USER"))
 }
}
```

3. Here, we autowire the `UserByNameRepository.kt` repository and override `loadUserByUsername(username: String)`. We will fetch the `username` and `password` from the repository and match them with the `username` and `password` given by the client. Here is the code for `UserByNameRepository.kt`:

```
@Repository
class UserByNameRepository: UserByNameInterface {
 @Autowired
 private lateinit var jdbcTemplate: JdbcTemplate

 override fun getUserByName(username: String): Profile {
 val sql = "SELECT * FROM PROFILE WHERE username = ?"
 val profile = jdbcTemplate.queryForObject(sql, UserRowMapper(),
username)

 return profile!!
 }
```

```
override fun getUserByNamePassword(username: String, password:
String): Boolean {
 val sql = "SELECT * FROM PROFILE WHERE username = ?, password = ?"
 val profile = jdbcTemplate.queryForObject(sql, UserRowMapper(),
username, password)
 return profile != null
 }
}

interface UserByNameInterface {
 fun getUserByName(username: String): Profile
 fun getUserByNamePassword(username: String, password: String):
Boolean
 }
```

4. Now create the code for the RowMapper class of the user named UserRowMapper.kt to fetch the user details. Here is a piece of code from this class:

```
class UserRowMapper : RowMapper<Profile> {

    @Throws(SQLException::class)
    override fun mapRow(row: ResultSet, rowNumber: Int): Profile? {
        val profile = Profile(row.getLong("id"),
                row.getString("username"),
                row.getString("password"))
        return profile
    }
}
```

5. Let's create a WebSecurityConfigurerAdapter class named SecurityConfigurer.kt and annotate it with @Configuration and @EnableWebSecurity to make a configuration file and enable web security. Here is the code for the SecurityConfigurer.kt class:

```
@Configuration
@EnableWebSecurity
class SecurityConfigurer : WebSecurityConfigurerAdapter() {

 @Autowired
 private lateinit var authEntryPoint: AuthenticationEntryPoint

 @Autowired
 private lateinit var customUserDetailsService:
CustomUserDetailsService

 @Throws(Exception::class)
```

```
override fun configure(http: HttpSecurity) {
http.csrf().disable().authorizeRequests()
.antMatchers("/profile/new").permitAll()
.anyRequest()
.authenticated()
.and()
.formLogin()
.and()
.httpBasic()
.authenticationEntryPoint(authEntryPoint)
}

@Autowired
@Throws(Exception::class)
fun configureGlobal(auth: AuthenticationManagerBuilder) {
auth
.userDetailsService(customUserDetailsService)
.passwordEncoder(getPasswordEncoder())
}

@Bean
fun getPasswordEncoder(): PasswordEncoder {
return object : PasswordEncoder {
override fun encode(charSequence: CharSequence): String {
return charSequence.toString()
}

override fun matches(charSequence: CharSequence, s: String): Boolean {
return true
}
}
}
}
```

In the previous code, we've done the following:

- To use this registration URL path, "/profile/new", any user can access. It doesn't need a username and password.
- We use PasswordEncoder to encode the password.
- We autowired configureGlobal(auth: AuthenticationManagerBuilder) and passed CustomUserDetailsService via auth.userDetailsService(customUserDetailsService) to check and match the username.

Modified application.properties

The `application.properties` file is used to connect the database with the application and define how the database will behave. Here is the code for `application.properties`:

```
# ================================
# DATABASE
# ================================

spring.datasource.url=jdbc:mysql://localhost:3306/my_app_schema?useSSL=fals
e&allowPublicKeyRetrieval=true
spring.datasource.username=root
spring.datasource.password=12345678


# ================================
# JPA / HIBERNATE
# ================================
spring.jpa.show-sql=true

# Hibernate ddl auto (create, create-drop, validate, update)
spring.jpa.hibernate.ddl-auto = update

## Hibernate Properties
# The SQL dialect makes Hibernate generate better SQL for the chosen
database
spring.jpa.properties.hibernate.dialect=org.hibernate.dialect.MySQL5Dialect
```

Here we have used the database named `my_app`, and the schema is `my_app_schema`. We disable `useSSL` with `useSSL=false`, and to retrieve the public key we use `allowPublicKeyRetrieval=true`.

Here, we use `spring.jpa.hibernate.ddl-auto = update`, which means after restarting your server the data won't be lost.

Client side

After creating our backend, we need to create a client-based application to utilize the server. In this part, we will create an Android application as a client-based frontend application. To create the application, we need to make a design before starting coding. We will create an Android application and handle HTTP requests with the use of Retrofit.

First of all, we will design the workflow of the application.

Creating the design

To design our application, we have to keep in mind what the project is about and how the backend was designed. As we know, this is a mini-social-network-type app. So we have to create some model objects that are exactly the same as the server's model objects. In the application's workflow, we will have some layouts that will represent our applications.

The workflow is shown in the following diagram:

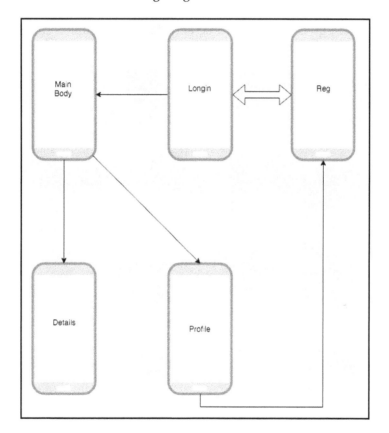

Here are the brief of the workflow according to this diagram:

- **Login page**: If you have a registered account, you can input the username and password to enter the application's main page. Or, if you are new, you need to go to the registration page and register an account.
- **Registration page**: This is for registering an account.
- **Home activity**: This is the main part of your application.

- **Profile**: You can see your details here.
- **Status details**: You can see the details of any post that you click on.

So far, this project is based on these layouts. Now we need to create an Android application.

Creating a project

To create a new project, go to Android Studio and click **New Project**. This time, select **Android for Mobile,** then select **Basic Activity**, as shown in the following screenshot:

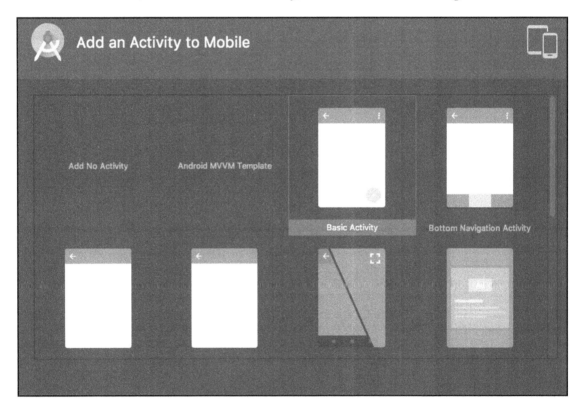

Implementing dependencies

After building the project, add these dependencies in the dependencies{} block of build.gradle (Module:app). These are for Material Design, Retrofit, and RxJava:

```
// Design
implementation 'com.android.support:design:28.0.0'
implementation 'com.android.support:recyclerview-v7:28.0.0'
implementation 'com.android.support:cardview-v7:28.0.0'

// Retrofit
implementation "com.squareup.retrofit2:retrofit:$retrofit_version"
implementation "com.squareup.retrofit2:converter-gson:$retrofit_version"
implementation "com.squareup.retrofit2:adapter-rxjava2:$retrofit_version"
implementation "com.squareup.retrofit2:retrofit-
converters:$retrofit_version"
implementation "com.squareup.retrofit2:retrofit-adapters:$retrofit_version"
implementation "com.squareup.okhttp3:logging-interceptor:$okhttp3_version"
implementation "com.google.code.gson:gson:$gson_version"

// Rx
implementation 'io.reactivex.rxjava2:rxandroid:2.0.2'
implementation 'io.reactivex.rxjava2:rxjava:2.2.0'
```

Creating HomeActivity

After creating the project, you will find MainActivity, but here we have renamed it as HomeActivity.kt, and the layout name is activity_home.

Now go to the activity, and here is the default code for this class:

```
class HomeActivity : AppCompatActivity() {

  override fun onCreate(savedInstanceState: Bundle?) {
        super.onCreate(savedInstanceState)
        setContentView(R.layout.activity_main2)
        setSupportActionBar(toolbar)

        fab.setOnClickListener { view ->
            Snackbar.make(view, "Replace with your own action",
Snackbar.LENGTH_LONG)
                .setAction("Action", null).show()
        }
    }
}
```

Modifying the layout

First, create a layout named home_content.xml, add FrameLayout, and add an id name. Here is the code for this XML file (you can see the full version on GitHub):

```xml
<?xml version="1.0" encoding="utf-8"?>
<android.support.design.widget.CoordinatorLayout
        xmlns:android="http://schemas.android.com/apk/res/android"
        xmlns:app="http://schemas.android.com/apk/res-auto"
        xmlns:tools="http://schemas.android.com/tools"
        android:layout_width="match_parent"
        android:layout_height="match_parent"
        tools:context=".ui.MainActivity">
    <android.support.constraint.ConstraintLayout
xmlns:android="http://schemas.android.com/apk/res/android"
xmlns:app="http://schemas.android.com/apk/res-auto"
xmlns:tools="http://schemas.android.com/tools"
android:layout_width="match_parent"
android:layout_height="match_parent"
tools:context=".ui.MainActivity">


        ----

----


        <android.support.v7.widget.RecyclerView
                android:id="@+id/displayList"
                android:layout_width="0dp"
                android:layout_height="0dp"
                app:layout_constraintEnd_toEndOf="parent"
                app:layout_constraintStart_toStartOf="parent"
                tools:listitem="@layout/post_item"
                app:layout_constraintBottom_toBottomOf="parent"
                app:layout_constraintHorizontal_bias="0.0"
android:layout_marginTop="8dp"
                app:layout_constraintTop_toBottomOf="@+id/appBarLayout"/>

    </android.support.constraint.ConstraintLayout>


    <android.support.design.widget.FloatingActionButton
            android:id="@+id/fabMain"
            android:layout_width="wrap_content"
            android:layout_height="wrap_content"
            android:layout_gravity="bottom|end"
            android:layout_margin="@dimen/fab_margin"
            app:srcCompat="@android:drawable/ic_dialog_email"/>
</android.support.design.widget.CoordinatorLayout>
```

Creating models

To create the models, we need to keep the same model items as the backend. But we will also include the `Gson` annotation, `@SerializedName`. The value of the `@SerializedName` annotation is used when serializing and deserializing objects. Here, `@SerializedName("username")` is stating that this is the name of the `Username` in the JSON. Though we implement the Gson, you can call these model classes as the response of the API. That means when this application requests the server and fetches the content, then this content will be returned with the help of these model classes.

Creating profile model

Create a `Profile` data class named `Profile.kt`, and here is the sample code:

```
data class Profile(
    @SerializedName("id") var userID: String,
    @SerializedName("username") var username: String,
    @SerializedName("password") var password: String,
    @SerializedName("email") var email: String,
    @SerializedName("accCreatedTime") var accCreatedTime: String,
    @SerializedName("firstName") var firstName: String,
    @SerializedName("lastName") var lastName: String,
    @SerializedName("contactNumber") var contactNumber: String,
    @SerializedName("country") var country: String
    )
```

Creating post model

Create a `Post` data class named `Post.kt`, and here is the sample code:

```
data class Post(
    @SerializedName("id") var postId: Long?,
    @SerializedName("text") var text: String?,
    @SerializedName("postedBy") var profile: Profile?,
    @SerializedName("accCreatedTime") var accCreatedTime: String?,
    @SerializedName("comments") var comment: ArrayList<Comment>?,
    @SerializedName("likes") var likes: ArrayList<Like>?
)
```

Creating a comment model

Create a comment data class named `Comment.kt`, and here is the sample code:

```
data class Comment (
    @SerializedName("id") var comment: Long?,
    @SerializedName("text") var text: String?,
    @SerializedName("postedBy") var profile: Profile?,
    @SerializedName("accCreatedTime") var accCreatedTime: String?
    )
```

Creating services

This is the most important section. This will send the GET request to the server to fetch the data from the server. First of all, we will create the services of the model classes. We will create the HTTP request functions using the Retrofit annotation, which are explained in the section called *HTTP Request Functions* in `Chapter 4`, *Spring Modules for Android*.

Creating the profile service

According to our server, we have four HTTP requests for the profile. So we will create three HTTP requests using the Retrofit annotations. Now create an interface named `ProfileService.kt`, and here is the code:

```
interface ProfileService {

    // New Profile registration
    @Headers("Content-Type: application/json")
    @POST("/profile/new")
    fun registerProfile(@Body profile: Profile): Observable<Profile>

    @Headers("Content-Type: application/json")
    @GET("/profile/login")
    fun loginProfile(@Query("username") username: String,
@Query("password") password: String): Observable<Profile>

    // Get All Profiles
    @Headers("Content-Type: application/json")
    @GET("/profiles")
    fun getUserList(): Observable<List<Profile>>

    // Get Profile by ID
    @GET("/profile/{userId}")
```

```
    fun getUserById(@Path("userId") userId: Long): Observable<Profile>
}
```

Based on the preceding code, here are the brief details of the functions:

- `registerProfile(@Body profile: Profile)` registers a new profile. You need to pass a project object.
- `getUserList()` gets all the profiles.
- `getUserById(@Query("userId") userId: Long)` gets a profile. You need to pass a user ID.

Creating the post service

According to our server, we have three `HTTP` requests for the profile. So we will create three `HTTP` requests using the Retrofit annotations. Now create an interface named `ProfileService.kt`, and here is the code:

```
interface PostService {
    @Headers("Content-Type: application/json")
    @POST("/post/{profile_id}/new")
    fun submitNewPost(@Path("profile_id") id: Long, @Query("text") text:
String): Observable<List<Post>>


    // Get all posted status
    @Headers("Content-Type: application/json")
    @GET("/posts")
    fun getPostList(): Single<List<Post>>


    // Get all posted status by Profile ID
    @Headers("Content-Type: application/json")
    @GET("/post/{id}")
    fun getPostById(@Path("id") id: Long): Observable<Post>

}
```

Based on the preceding code, here is a brief description of the functions:

- `submitNewPost(@Query("id") id: Long, @Field("text") text: String)` submits a new post, and to submit the new post, you need to pass the user ID and the text.

- `getPostList()` gets all the posts.
- `getPostById(@Query("id") id: Long)` gets a post. You need to pass a post ID.

Creating the comment service

To handle the comment REST APIs, we will create two `HTTP` requests. So we will create two `POST` and `DELETE` requests using the Retrofit annotations. Now create an interface named `PostService.kt`, and here is the code:

```
interface CommentService {
    // Post comment in a post by Profile ID and Post ID
    @POST("/comment/{user_id}/{post_id}")
    fun postCommentByPostId(@Path("post_id") postId: Long, @Path("user_id")
userId: Long,
                            @Query("commentText") commentText: String):
Observable<Post>


    // Delete comment in a post by Profile ID and Post ID
    @DELETE("/comment/{user_id}/{post_id}")
    fun deleteCommentByPostId(@Path("post_id") postId: Long,
@Path("user_id") userId: Long,
                              @Query("commentText") commentText: String):
Observable<Post>
}
```

`postCommentByPostId(@Path("post_id") postId: Long, @Path("user_id") userId: Long, @Query("commentText") commentText: String)` is a `POST` request function, and it submits a new comment. You need to pass the `user_id`, `post_id`, and the text.

`deleteCommentByPostId(@Path("post_id") postId: Long, @Path("user_id") userId: Long, @Query("commentText") commentText: String)` is a `DELETE` request function, and it deletes the comment. You need to pass the `user_id` and `post_id`.

So far, all the requests have been created, and now we need to create an API service that will hit the server and fetch the JSON.

Creating an API service

We explained this procedure in `Chapter 4`, *Spring Modules for Android*. So we will just show you the code and explain the new features. Create an object named `APIService.kt` and add `gsonConverter()` and `getOkhttpClient(username, password)`:

```
object APIService{
    fun getRetrofitBuilder(username:String, password:String): Retrofit {
        return Retrofit.Builder()
            .client(getOkhttpClient(username, password))
            .baseUrl(Constants.API_BASE_PATH)
            .addCallAdapterFactory(RxJava2CallAdapterFactory.create())
            .addConverterFactory(gsonConverter())
            .build()
    }

    fun gsonConverter(): GsonConverterFactory {
        return GsonConverterFactory
            .create(
                GsonBuilder()
                    .setLenient()
                    .disableHtmlEscaping()
                    .create()
            )
    }

    fun getOkhttpClient(profileName: String, password: String):
OkHttpClient {
        return OkHttpClient.Builder()
            .addInterceptor(BasicAuthInterceptor(profileName, password))
            .connectTimeout(30, TimeUnit.SECONDS)
            .readTimeout(60, TimeUnit.SECONDS)
            .build()
    }
}
```

If you're confused about `addInterceptor(BasicAuthInterceptor(profileName, password))`, then please go to `Chapter 5`, *Securing Applications with Spring Security*, and check out the section called *Authenticating with OkHttp interceptors*.

Now we need to initialize the `RetrofitBuilder` functions of the services. We have four service interfaces, and now we will create four `RetrofitBuilder` functions for them. Add this code in the `APIService.kt` file:

```
// get profile request builder
fun profileAPICall(username:String, password:String) =
getRetrofitBuilder(username, password)
```

```
        .create(ProfileService::class.java)

// get post request builder
fun postAPICall(username:String, password:String) =
getRetrofitBuilder(username, password)
    .create(PostService::class.java)

// get comment request builder
fun commentAPICall(username:String, password:String) =
getRetrofitBuilder(username, password)
    .create(CommentService::class.java)
```

Now we will work for the frontend, which means the activities and layouts.

Creating a login activity

This is the first activity of the app. When users enter the app it will be the first thing they see. For the user, they need to go to the register activity to register a new profile. After the registration, they will get access to the application.

Modifying the layout

Create an empty activity named `LoginActivity.kt`, and a layout named `activity_login.xml`. Here is the code in the `xml` (you will find the full version of this layout on GitHub):

```
------
------
<android.support.v7.widget.CardView
        android:layout_width="match_parent"
        android:layout_height="wrap_content"
        android:layout_alignParentEnd="true"
        android:layout_alignParentStart="true"
        android:layout_centerHorizontal="true"
        android:background="@color/reg_body"
        app:layout_constraintTop_toTopOf="parent"
app:layout_constraintStart_toStartOf="parent"
        android:layout_marginBottom="64dp"
app:layout_constraintBottom_toBottomOf="parent"
        android:layout_marginStart="32dp"
app:layout_constraintEnd_toEndOf="parent" android:layout_marginEnd="32dp"
        android:id="@+id/cardView">
```

```
        <android.support.constraint.ConstraintLayout
                android:layout_width="match_parent"
                android:layout_height="match_parent"
                app:layout_constraintEnd_toEndOf="parent"
                app:layout_constraintBottom_toBottomOf="parent"
                app:layout_constraintStart_toStartOf="parent"
                app:layout_constraintTop_toTopOf="parent"
                app:layout_constraintHorizontal_bias="0.0"
                app:layout_constraintVertical_bias="1.0"
android:layout_marginEnd="24dp"
                android:layout_marginTop="32dp"
                android:layout_marginStart="24dp"
android:layout_marginBottom="32dp">
            <TextView
                android:id="@+id/LogIn"
                android:layout_width="wrap_content"
                android:layout_height="wrap_content"
                android:layout_alignParentTop="true"
                android:layout_centerHorizontal="true"
                android:text="@string/title_login"
                android:textSize="30sp"
                android:textStyle="bold"
                android:typeface="monospace"
app:layout_constraintEnd_toEndOf="parent"
                android:layout_marginEnd="8dp"
app:layout_constraintStart_toStartOf="parent"
                app:layout_constraintTop_toTopOf="parent"
android:layout_marginStart="8dp"
                android:layout_marginTop="8dp"/>
------
------
  <Button android:layout_width="match_parent"
android:layout_height="wrap_content"
                    android:text="@string/title_login"
                    android:id="@+id/reg_submit"

app:layout_constraintTop_toBottomOf="@+id/password_title_reg"
                    app:layout_constraintStart_toStartOf="parent"
app:layout_constraintEnd_toEndOf="parent"
                    android:layout_marginEnd="32dp"
android:layout_marginStart="32dp"
                    android:layout_marginTop="64dp"/>
------
------
```

Here we have user input for Username and Password. In this layout, we have also one button to log in and one TextView to go to the RegistrationActivity.

Here is the image preview of this layout:

Modifying activity

Go to the `LogInActivity.kt` file, where we will input the login information. The user needs to provide a `username` and a `password`. Then this information will be searched in the `Profile` table of the server database. If there are the same `username` and `password` in this `Profile` table, you will be able to enter the `MainActivity`, or you will get an error message. If you are a new user, you can click **New Member?** to register a new profile.

First, we will check `SharedPreferences` to see if we have the saved `username` and `password`. It will show in the username and password fields, or it will remain blank so you can input the values. Here is the function of this logic:

```
override fun onCreate(savedInstanceState: Bundle?) {
    super.onCreate(savedInstanceState)
    setContentView(R.layout.activity_login)

    setUsernamePassword()
}

private fun setUsernamePassword() {
 if (PrefUtils.getUsername(this) != null
 || PrefUtils.getPassword(this) != null) {
 username_input_login.setText(PrefUtils.getUsername(this))
 password_input_login.setText(PrefUtils.getPassword(this))
 }
}
```

Now set the `OnClickListener()` listener function in the `TextView` named `need_reg`, which will take us to the `RegistrationActivity`. Here is the code for this function:

```
need_reg.setOnClickListener {
    val intent = Intent(this, RegistrationActivity::class.java)
    startActivity(intent)
}
```

Login request

Now we will create a function named `logInUser()`, which will send a `POST` request to the server and match the `username` and `password`. In return of failed, it gets an error and shows the error message, or it will take to to the `MainActivity`. Here is the function:

```
private fun logInUser(){

    APIClient.profileAPICall(username_input_login.text.toString(),
password_input_login.text.toString())
```

```
        .loginProfile(username_input_login.text.toString(),password_input_login.tex
t.toString() )
        .subscribeOn(Schedulers.io())
        .observeOn(AndroidSchedulers.mainThread())
        .subscribe({
                newUser ->
            if(newUser.error != null){
                Toast.makeText(applicationContext,newUser.error!!,
Toast.LENGTH_SHORT).show()
            }else {
                PrefUtils.storeUsernameID(this, newUser.userID!!)
                PrefUtils.storeUsername(this, newUser.username!!)
                PrefUtils.storePassword(this, newUser.password!!)
                username_input_login.setText(PrefUtils.getUsername(this))
                password_input_login.setText(PrefUtils.getPassword(this))
                val intent = Intent(this, MainActivity::class.java)
                startActivity(intent)
            }
        },{
            error ->
        Toast.makeText(applicationContext,R.string.err_login_msg,
Toast.LENGTH_SHORT).show()
            Log.wtf("******", error.message.toString())
        })
    }
```

Here, we store the `username`, `password`, and `userID` if we get the correct response.

Creating the registration activity

Create an activity for registration named `RegistrationActivity.kt`, where we will register a new account. Before modifying the code, we need to modify the layout.

Modifying layout

Create a layout for `RegistrationActivity.kt` named `activity_registration.xml`. Here I have added a UI, so please look at the full version of this file on GitHub. Here is a piece of code from this file:

```
    <Button android:layout_width="match_parent"
    android:layout_height="wrap_content"
                            android:text="@string/title_reg"
                            android:id="@+id/reg_submit"
    android:layout_marginTop="32dp"
```

```
app:layout_constraintTop_toBottomOf="@+id/country_title_reg"
                    app:layout_constraintStart_toStartOf="parent"
android:layout_marginStart="32dp"
                    app:layout_constraintEnd_toEndOf="parent"
android:layout_marginEnd="32dp"/>

            -----
            -----

        </android.support.constraint.ConstraintLayout>
    </ScrollView>
  </android.support.v7.widget.CardView>

</android.support.constraint.ConstraintLayout>
```

Here is the image preview of this layout:

Modifying the activity

Here is the code for RegistrationActivity:

```kotlin
class RegistrationActivity : AppCompatActivity() {

    override fun onCreate(savedInstanceState: Bundle?) {
        super.onCreate(savedInstanceState)
        setContentView(R.layout.activity_registration)


    }
}
```

Now add some logic to validate the username, password, and email id. Here is the code:

```kotlin
private fun validateName(): Boolean {
    if (username_input_reg.text.toString().trim().isEmpty()) {
        username_title_reg.error = getString(R.string.err_msg_name)
        requestFocus(username_input_reg)
        return false
    } else {
        username_title_reg.isErrorEnabled = false
    }

    return true
}

private fun validateEmail(): Boolean {
    if (email_input_reg.text.toString().trim().isEmpty() ||
!isValidEmail(email_input_reg.text.toString().trim())) {
        email_title_reg.error = getString(R.string.err_msg_email)
        requestFocus(email_input_reg)
        return false
    } else {
        email_title_reg.isErrorEnabled = false
    }

    return true
}

private fun validatePassword(): Boolean {
    if (password_input_reg.text.toString().trim().isEmpty()
    || con_password_input_reg.text.toString().trim().isEmpty()) {

        if (password_input_reg.text.toString().trim()
            == con_password_input_reg.text.toString().trim()){
            password_title_reg.error =
getString(R.string.err_match_password)
```

```
        requestFocus(password_title_reg)
    }

    password_title_reg.error = getString(R.string.err_msg_password)
    requestFocus(password_title_reg)
    return false
} else {
    password_title_reg.isErrorEnabled = false
}

    return true
}
```

Add a `TextWatcher` inner class, which will send an alert if there is any invalid input:

```
private inner class MyTextWatcher (private val view: View) : TextWatcher {

    override fun beforeTextChanged(charSequence: CharSequence, i: Int, i1:
Int, i2: Int) {}

    override fun onTextChanged(charSequence: CharSequence, i: Int, i1: Int,
i2: Int) {}

    override fun afterTextChanged(editable: Editable) {
        when (view.id) {
            R.id.username_input_reg -> validateName()
            R.id.email_input_reg -> validateEmail()
            R.id.input_password -> validatePassword()
        }
    }
}
```

When the `username`, `password,` or the `email id` is invalid, it will show an alert.

Registering a new profile

Now we will create a function called `registerUser()`, which will help you to send requests to the server and fetch the output from the server. We will show you how to use RxJava in Chapter 8, *Reactive Programming*, and Retrofit in Chapter 4, *Spring Modules for Android*. Here is the code for `registerUser()`:

```
private fun registerUser(){
    val newProfile = Profile(null,
        username_input_reg.text.toString(),
        password_input_reg.text.toString(),
        email_input_reg.text.toString(),
```

```
            null,
            first_name_input_reg.text.toString(),
            last_name_input_reg.text.toString(),
            contact_input_reg.text.toString(),
            country_input_reg.text.toString())
            APIClient.profileAPICall("","")
            .registerProfile(newProfile)
            .subscribeOn(Schedulers.io())
            .observeOn(AndroidSchedulers.mainThread())
            .subscribe({
                    newUser ->
                if(newUser.duplicate != null){
                        Toast.makeText(applicationContext,newUser.duplicate!!,
    Toast.LENGTH_SHORT).show()
                    }else {
                        PrefUtils.storeUsernameID(this, 1)
                        PrefUtils.storeUsername(this, username)
                        PrefUtils.storePassword(this, password)
                        val intent = Intent(this, LoginActivity::class.java)
                        startActivity(intent)
                    }

            },{
                    error ->
    Toast.makeText(applicationContext,error.message.toString(),
    Toast.LENGTH_SHORT).show()


            })
    }
```

Here, we will take the contents from `EditText` and create a `Profile` object. Then we take an observer that will fetch the profile list as JSON type and handle the updated list in the `subscribe()` function. If the result is complete, it will return in the first parameter, and then we will save the `username`, `password`, and `userID` locally using `SharedPreferences` and return to `LoginActivity`. If it throws an error, it will go to the second parameter.

Modifying the main activity

This is our home page. Here, you can see all the posts. We need to modify our layout and the activity class.

Modifying the layout

The layout of `MainActivity` is in the `activity_main.xml` file. Here, we have added `RecyclerView` to show the list, one `FabButton` to submit the post, and a `TextView` to show if there is no post available. Here is a piece of the code:

```xml
<?xml version="1.0" encoding="utf-8"?>
<android.support.design.widget.CoordinatorLayout
        xmlns:android="http://schemas.android.com/apk/res/android"
        xmlns:app="http://schemas.android.com/apk/res-auto"
        xmlns:tools="http://schemas.android.com/tools"
        android:layout_width="match_parent"
        android:layout_height="match_parent"
        tools:context=".ui.MainActivity">
-----
-----

<android.support.v7.widget.RecyclerView
 android:id="@+id/displayList"
 android:layout_width="0dp"
 android:layout_height="0dp"
 app:layout_constraintEnd_toEndOf="parent"
 app:layout_constraintStart_toStartOf="parent"
 tools:listitem="@layout/post_item"
 app:layout_constraintBottom_toBottomOf="parent"
 app:layout_constraintHorizontal_bias="0.0" android:layout_marginTop="8dp"
 app:layout_constraintTop_toBottomOf="@+id/appBarLayout"/>
</android.support.constraint.ConstraintLayout>
    <android.support.design.widget.FloatingActionButton
    android:id="@+id/fabMain"
    android:layout_width="wrap_content"
    android:layout_height="wrap_content"
    android:layout_gravity="bottom|end"
    android:layout_margin="@dimen/fab_margin"
    app:srcCompat="@android:drawable/ic_dialog_email"/>
</android.support.design.widget.CoordinatorLayout>
```

Modifying the activity

Go to `MainAcitivty.kt`. Here, we have `RecycleView` and the post adapter. We will add a global `List<Post>` and set the `recycleView` in the `onCreate()` function like this:

```
private var postList: List<Post> = listOf()

override fun onCreate(savedInstanceState: Bundle?) {
    super.onCreate(savedInstanceState)
```

```
setContentView(R.layout.activity_main)
    displayList.layoutManager = LinearLayoutManager(this)
    displayList.setHasFixedSize(true)
    postRecycleViewAdapter = PostRecycleViewAdapter(this, postList)
    displayList.adapter = postRecycleViewAdapter
}
```

Here, we have initialized
the `PostRecycleViewAdapter` named `postRecycleViewAdapter` and set the adapter
into the list named `displayList`.

Fetching a post

We will fetch all the posts using the `getAllPosts()` function. This function will send a
request to the server to get all the post list. In return, we will get the updated list
named `newPostList` and pass using `setItems(newPostList)` to
`PostRecycleViewAdapter` and notify with `notifyDataSetChanged()`. For the error
handling, we have used toast. Here is the code of the `getAllPosts()` function:

```
private fun getAllPosts() {
        APIClient.postAPICall(PrefUtils.getUsername(this)!!,
PrefUtils.getPassword(this)!!)
        .getPostList()
            .subscribeOn(Schedulers.io())
        .observeOn(AndroidSchedulers.mainThread())
        .subscribe({
            newPostList ->
            postRecycleViewAdapter.setItems(newPostList)
            postRecycleViewAdapter.notifyDataSetChanged()
        },{
                error ->
        Toast.makeText(applicationContext, error.message.toString(),
Toast.LENGTH_SHORT).show()
        })
}
```

Submitting a post

When you press the **fab** button we will see an alert box where you can input your status
using `submitPost()`. In return, we get the post list named `newPostList` and pass the list
to the `setItems(newPostList)` of the `PostRecycleViewAdapter` to replace with the
older post list with the new one. Lastly, notify with `notifyDataSetChanged()`, and the
`RecycleView` list will be updated.

Here is the code for the `submitPost()` function:

```
private fun submitPost(id: Long, text: String){
    APIClient.postAPICall(PrefUtils.getUsername(this)!!,
PrefUtils.getPassword(this)!!)
        .submitNewPost(id, text)
        .subscribeOn(Schedulers.io())
        .observeOn(AndroidSchedulers.mainThread())
        .subscribe({
            newPostList ->
            postRecycleViewAdapter.setItems(newPostList)
            postRecycleViewAdapter.notifyDataSetChanged()
        },{
            error ->
    Toast.makeText(applicationContext, error.message.toString(),
Toast.LENGTH_SHORT).show()
        })
}
```

Implementing the menu

To show the profile details and update a post, we will add two icons on the `Toolbar`. To do this, we need to create a toolbar file. Create a menu file in `res > menu` named `menu_main.xml`. There we will add two items, one for profile and one for updating a post.

Here is the code for `menu_main.xml`:

```
<?xml version="1.0" encoding="utf-8"?>
<menu xmlns:android="http://schemas.android.com/apk/res/android"
xmlns:app="http://schemas.android.com/apk/res-auto">
    <item
        android:id="@+id/profileMenu"
        android:icon="@drawable/ic_face_white_24dp"
        app:showAsAction="always"
        android:title="@string/title_profile">
    </item>
    <item
        android:id="@+id/postUpdate"
        android:icon="@drawable/ic_autorenew_white_24dp"
        app:showAsAction="always"
        android:title="@string/title_update">
    </item>
</menu>
```

We have used `app:showAsAction="always"`, and it means the items will always show on the toolbar.

Now implement it in `MainAcitivy.kt`. To do this, we need to override two functions, and these are `onCreateOptionsMenu()` and `onOptionsItemSelected()`.

We will bind the `menu_main` menu XML file using `menuInflater.inflate()` in `onCreateOptionsMenu()`, and we will write down the logic for every menu item in the `onOptionsItemSelected()`:

```kotlin
override fun onCreateOptionsMenu(menu: Menu): Boolean {
    menuInflater.inflate(R.menu.menu_main, menu)
    return true
}

override fun onOptionsItemSelected(item: MenuItem?): Boolean {
    when (item!!.itemId) {
        R.id.profileMenu -> {
            val intent = Intent(this, ProfileActivity::class.java)
            startActivity(intent)
        }
        R.id.postUpdate -> {
            getAllPosts()
        }
    }
    return true
}
```

`R.id.profileMenu` will take you to the `ProfileActivity` class.

`R.id.postUpdate` will update the post using `getAllPosts()`.

Modifying the post adapter

Now we need to modify our post adapter class. It will help us to show the post in a nice structure. Our post adapter name is `PostRecycleViewAdapter`, and the layout name is `post_item`.

Modifying post adapter layouts

To utilize the post adapter, we need to create an `xml` file named `post_item.xml`, and here we will implement the UI. Here is a piece of the code (the entire code can be found on GitHub):

```
----
----
        <TextView android:layout_width="wrap_content"
android:layout_height="wrap_content"
                tools:text="@tools:sample/date/ddmmyy"
                android:id="@+id/postedDate"
                android:textAppearance="?android:textAppearanceSmall"
                app:layout_constraintTop_toBottomOf="@+id/profileName"
                app:layout_constraintStart_toStartOf="@+id/profileName"
                android:layout_marginTop="4dp"
                app:layout_constraintBottom_toBottomOf="parent"
android:layout_marginBottom="4dp"/>
    </android.support.constraint.ConstraintLayout>

    <TextView android:layout_width="0dp"
android:layout_height="wrap_content"
                tools:text="@tools:sample/lorem"
                android:id="@+id/postText"
                android:padding="4dp"
                android:textAppearance="?android:textAppearanceSmall"
                app:layout_constraintStart_toStartOf="parent"
                app:layout_constraintEnd_toEndOf="parent"
android:layout_marginTop="4dp"
                app:layout_constraintTop_toBottomOf="@+id/constraintLayout"/>
----
----
```

We have four `TextView` for user full name, username, posted time, and the post text.

Here is a sample image from the preview option of the layout:

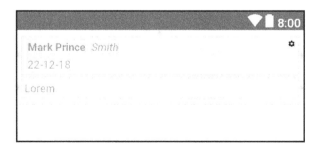

Creating the adapter for posts

Let's create a custom `RecycleView` adapter named `PostRecycleViewAdapter.kt` to display the post list. We have shown you how to create custom adapters in Chapter 4, *Spring Modules for Android,* so we won't repeat it. Here is the `PostRecycleViewAdapter` class:

```
class PostRecycleViewAdapter(private var context: Context,
                       private val postList: List<Post>):
RecyclerView.Adapter<PostRecycleViewAdapter.ViewHolder>() {
-----
-----
}
```

Now create the `ViewHolder` class and initialize all the content of the `post_item` layout in `PostRecycleViewAdapter.kt`, as shown in the following code:

```
class ViewHolder(view: View): RecyclerView.ViewHolder(view){
    val postRoot = view.findViewById(R.id.postRoot) as ConstraintLayout

    val profileFullName = view.findViewById(R.id.profileFullNamePost) as
TextView
    val username = view.findViewById(R.id.usernamePost) as TextView
    val postedDate = view.findViewById(R.id.postedDate) as TextView
    val postText = view.findViewById(R.id.postText) as TextView
}
```

Now override `onCreateViewHolder()` and return the `ViewHolder` class:

```
override fun onCreateViewHolder(viewGroup: ViewGroup, p1: Int): ViewHolder
{
    val layoutInflater -
LayoutInflater.from(context).inflate(R.layout.post_item, viewGroup, false)
    return ViewHolder(layoutInflater)
}
```

Now, we need to set the value in every raw of the list based on its position. To do this, override the `onBindViewHolder()` function and add this code:

```
override fun onBindViewHolder(viewHolder: ViewHolder, position: Int) {

    val userDetails = postList[position]

    viewHolder.profileFullName.text = "${userDetails.profile!!.firstName}
${userDetails.profile!!.lastName} "
    viewHolder.username.text = userDetails.profile!!.username
    viewHolder.postedDate.text = userDetails.postCreatedTime
```

```
        viewHolder.postText.text = userDetails.text

}
```

Modifying the profile layout

This layout will help to get the profile details from the users. Open
`activity_profile.xml` and modify it as follows (please check GitHub for the full layout
code):

```xml
<?xml version="1.0" encoding="utf-8"?>

    <!--full name-->

    <TextView android:layout_width="wrap_content"
android:layout_height="wrap_content"
                android:id="@+id/profileFullNameTitlePro"
                android:textStyle="bold"
                android:text="@string/title_full_names"
                android:textAppearance="?android:textAppearanceSmall"
                android:layout_marginStart="8dp"
                app:layout_constraintStart_toStartOf="parent"
android:layout_marginTop="32dp"
                app:layout_constraintTop_toBottomOf="@+id/usernamePro"
android:layout_marginEnd="8dp"
                app:layout_constraintEnd_toEndOf="parent"
app:layout_constraintHorizontal_bias="0.0"/>

    <TextView android:layout_width="wrap_content"
android:layout_height="wrap_content"
                tools:text="@tools:sample/full_names"
                android:id="@+id/profileFullNamePro"
                android:textAppearance="?android:textAppearanceSmall"
app:layout_constraintTop_toTopOf="@+id/profileFullNameTitlePro"
app:layout_constraintBottom_toBottomOf="@+id/profileFullNameTitlePro"
                app:layout_constraintEnd_toEndOf="parent"
                android:layout_marginEnd="160dp"
                app:layout_constraintVertical_bias="1.0"/>
------
------
</android.support.constraint.ConstraintLayout>
```

Here we have one `TextView` for the username, a `TextView` for each profile item label
name, and four for the profile contents of `Full Name`, `Email`, `Contact Number`,
and `Country`.

Here is the preview of the **Profile** details:

Modifying a profile activity

Create a new activity called `ProfileActivity.kt`, and here is the code:

```
class ProfileActivity : AppCompatActivity() {

        private var username: String = ""
    private var password: String = ""

    override fun onCreate(savedInstanceState: Bundle?) {
        super.onCreate(savedInstanceState)
        setContentView(R.layout.activity_profile)
        setTitleName()

        username = PrefUtils.getUsername(this)!!
        password = PrefUtils.getPassword(this)!!
    }
}
```

Fetching the profile details

To fetch the profile details, we need to create a function named `getUser()` in which we will call `getUserById()` from the `Profile` services. In return, it will provide the user details, or if there is an error, it will show the error message. Here is the code of the `getUserById()` function:

```
private fun getUser(){
        APIClient.profileAPICall(username,password)
            .getUserById(PrefUtils.getUsernameID(this)!!)
            .subscribeOn(Schedulers.io())
            .observeOn(AndroidSchedulers.mainThread())
            .subscribe({
                    myUser ->

                usernamePro.text = myUser.username
                profileFullNamePro.text = "${myUser.firstName}
${myUser.lastName}"
                emailPro.text = myUser.email
                contactNumberPro.text = myUser.contactNumber
                countryPro.text = myUser.country
            },{
                    error ->
                UtilMethods.hideLoading()
                Log.wtf("******", error.message.toString())
            })
    }
```

Post details activity

Now we will need our last activity, `PostDetailsActivity.kt`, and the layout is in `activity_post_details.xml`. In this activity, you will see a specific post and its comments. You can also post a comment.

Modifying the post details layout

This view will show specific post details. Here is a piece of code from `activity_post_details.xml`:

```
-----
----
<android.support.v7.widget.RecyclerView
        android:id="@+id/displayList_com"
        android:layout_width="0dp"
        android:layout_height="0dp"
        tools:listitem="@layout/post_item"
        app:layout_constraintStart_toStartOf="parent"
        app:layout_constraintEnd_toEndOf="parent"
app:layout_constraintTop_toBottomOf="@+id/postRoot_pd"
        android:layout_marginBottom="8dp"
app:layout_constraintBottom_toBottomOf="parent"
        android:layout_marginStart="16dp"  android:layout_marginEnd="16dp"
android:layout_marginTop="8dp"/>

<android.support.constraint.ConstraintLayout
        android:layout_width="match_parent"
        android:id="@+id/postRoot_pd"
        android:layout_height="wrap_content"
        android:layout_marginTop="8dp"
        app:layout_constraintTop_toBottomOf="@+id/appBarLayout_pd"
app:layout_constraintEnd_toEndOf="parent"
        app:layout_constraintStart_toStartOf="parent"
android:layout_marginEnd="8dp"
        android:layout_marginStart="8dp">
-----
----
```

Here we have a post's details and its list of comments.

The preview of this layout is as follows:

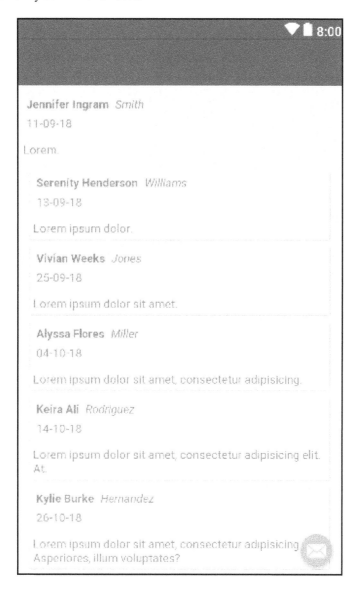

Modifying the post details activity

This is an activity where will handle a specific post. This post will be fetched by a `postId`, and we will get this through the intent that is sent from `PostRecycleViewAdapter`. To get the intent view, we need to use `intent.extras`. We use `Long` with the *key name* of `"postId"`, as shown in the following code:

```
private var postId:Long = -1

if(intent.extras!=null){
    postId = intent.extras.getLong("postId")
}
```

Fetching post details

Now create a function called `getPostById(id: Long)`, and we will pass the given `postId` from `MainActivity`. We will handle all the value in the specific `TextView`, such as `MainActivity`:

```
@SuppressLint("CheckResult")
private fun getPostById(id: Long){
    UtilMethods.showLoading(this)
    APIClient.postAPICall(PrefUtils.getUsername(this)!!,
PrefUtils.getPassword(this)!!)
        .getPostById(id)
        .subscribeOn(Schedulers.io())
        .observeOn(AndroidSchedulers.mainThread())
        .subscribe({
                post ->
            postText_pd.text = post.text
            profileFullNamePost_pd.text = "${post.profile!!.firstName}
${post.profile!!.lastName}"
            usernamePost_pd.text = post.profile!!.username
            postedDate_pd.text =
SimpleDateFormat(Constants.TIME_FORMAT).format(post.postCreatedTime!!)

            commentList = post.comment!!

            Log.wtf("******", commentList.toString())
            commentRecycleViewAdapter.setItems(commentList)
            commentRecycleViewAdapter.notifyDataSetChanged()

            UtilMethods.hideLoading()
        },{
                error ->
            UtilMethods.hideLoading()
```

```
        Log.wtf("******", error.message.toString())
        Toast.makeText(applicationContext, error.message.toString(),
Toast.LENGTH_SHORT).show()
        })
}
```

Submitting comment

To submit a comment, click `fabButton` and enter a comment. The system of comment submission is similar to the post submission system. We create a function named `submitComment(id: Long, text: String)` and use it to submit the comment. Here is the `submitComment()` function:

```
@SuppressLint("CheckResult")
private fun submitComment(id: Long, text: String){
    UtilMethods.showLoading(this)
    APIClient.commentAPICall(PrefUtils.getUsername(this)!!,
PrefUtils.getPassword(this)!!)
        .postCommentByPostId(id, PrefUtils.getUsernameID(this)!!,text)
        .subscribeOn(Schedulers.io())
        .observeOn(AndroidSchedulers.mainThread())
        .subscribe({
            newPostList ->
            commentList = newPostList.comment!!

            Log.wtf("******", commentList.toString())
            commentRecycleViewAdapter.setItems(commentList)
            commentRecycleViewAdapter.notifyDataSetChanged()
            UtilMethods.hideLoading()
        },{
            error ->
            UtilMethods.hideLoading()
            Log.wtf("******", error.message.toString())
            Toast.makeText(applicationContext, error.message.toString(),
Toast.LENGTH_SHORT).show()
        })
}
```

Modifying the comment adapter

This adapter is the same as the Post adapter. Check the Modifying Post Adapter, Modifying Post Adapter Layouts to modify this comment adapter. The name of this adapter is `CommentRecycleViewAdapter.kt` and the layout is `comment_item.xml`.

Our project is complete! Now it's time to check the output of the server and the client.

Checking the output

To check our output, first, run the server from the `Social_Network` Spring project. Then you can run two different emulators or Android devices as client users.

Now open the Android app. Click the **New Member?** button to create a new account. Fill in all the required details and click the **Registration** button:

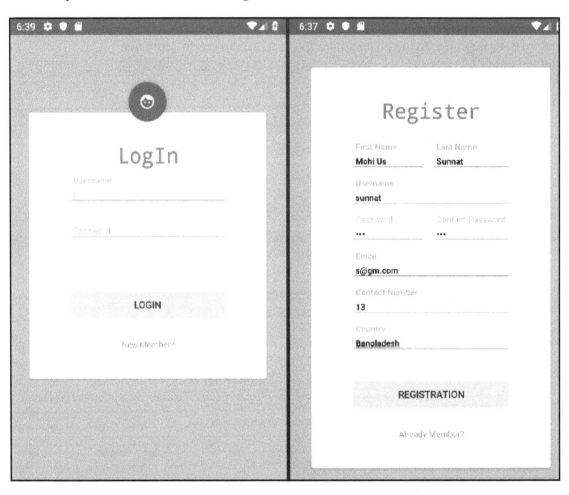

If the username is already taken, then it will alert you like this:

Now if you press the **Profile** button, the second left on the toolbar, you will see the **Profile** details. If you press the **Update** button, the top-left icon of the toolbar, your post will update, as you can see in the following screenshot:

Click on any post and you will see the specific post, and you can add a comment using the **Fab** button:

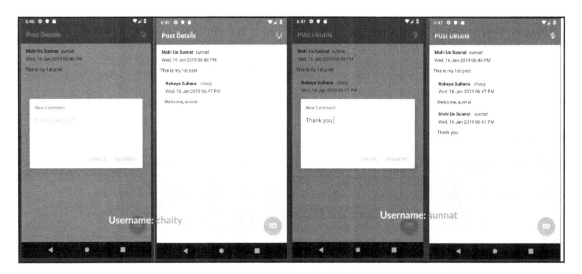

We are at end of this long journey. Now your client application is ready to use. Here you can post a status, see the posted status, check the details of the post, and put comments on that post. We have shown you how to use the server and handle the resources from the server in an Android application. You can find some minor functions and layouts on GitHub that may be helpful with this application. We recommend you create another application with your own imagination and deploy it. That will be more effective, and you can learn more about what you want to learn. There are lots of alternative ways to handle HTTP requests, and so you can learn more. If you want to learn more, have a look at the *Further reading* section.

Summary

After a long journey, we have finished this chapter. Here we have seen how to create a server side and a client side complete application using all the modules of the previous chapters, such as Spring Security and database. You can modify this project in your own style. You can implement new architecture and implement new frameworks. In this chapter, first, we learned about the design of a project. Then we created the database model for our project. After creating the database model, we created our server-side project and implemented the dependencies. Then we created the models based on the database model. Then we created the repositories and the controller. In the controller, we created the HTTP request functions. Then we implemented the security. We used basic authentication from Spring Security. Then we modified application.properties to connect to the MySQL database. After finishing the server side, we started to create the Android application. We created the workflow of the application. Then we created the models of the users, posts, and comments. Then we created the API services and requests. After the backend, we developed the layouts and activities. In the activities, we called the HTTP request using Retrofit and RxJava. Then we modified the UI classes and layouts of the application. Lastly, we tested the output of the project.

In Chapter 10, *Testing an Application*, you will learn how to use the JUnit framework to unit test the Spring project and the UI testing using the Espresso in the Android application.

Questions

1. What is the EER diagram?
2. What are CRUD operations?
3. What type of tools can be used as the HTTP client?
4. Currently, what are the minimum, maximum, and targeted API versions for Android?
5. What are the common names of the Android architecture?
6. What are the names of emulators to develop Android applications?

Further reading

- *Building Applications with Spring 5 and Kotlin* (`https://www.packtpub.com/application-development/building-applications-spring-5-and-kotlin`) by Miloš Vasić

- *Spring MVC – Beginner's Guide - Second Edition* (`https://www.packtpub.com/application-development/spring-mvc-beginners-guide-second-edition`) by Amuthan Ganeshan

- *Android Development with Kotlin* (`https://www.packtpub.com/application-development/android-development-kotlin`) by Marcin Moskala, Igor Wojda

- *Kotlin for Android Developers [Video]* (`https://www.packtpub.com/application-development/kotlin android developers-video`) by Yusuf Saber

Testing an Application

10

To make an application more usable and attractive, we always concentrate on the logos, contents, UI, experiences, and so on, besides we also take care of the coding style. We use the latest architectures and frameworks to reduce code lines and boiler codes in order to make a robust, simple, and fast application. However, many developers forget about the testing phase. Some might not realize there's an issue until a crash report generates during application use, because they didn't adequately test during the project. Generally, some developers skip testing, as they don't want to spend some extra time on writing test cases that are not directly used in the project. This is a common mistake and results in falling quality.

Applications that randomly crash will always be disliked by the user, which is why the most successful Android apps always undergo thorough testing. In-depth testing can iron out an app's bugs, and optimize memory use, as well as allowing you to improve the condition of an app in regards to functional behavior, usabilities, and correctness.

In this chapter, we will walk through testing and its use in both Spring and Android. This chapter covers the following topics:

- Software testing
- Fundamental of testing
- Unit testing on Spring Boot
- Creating a project
- JUnit
- UI testing on Android
- Espresso

Technical requirements

You will need to import some dependencies for both Spring and Android. Here are the dependencies.

- **Spring**

To implement the dependency for testing, you need to add the testing dependency in the pom.xml file:

```
<!-- This is to implement the testing functions for the spring project -->
<dependency>
    <groupId>org.springframework.boot</groupId>
    <artifactId>spring-boot-starter-test</artifactId>
    <scope>test</scope>
</dependency>
```

- **Android**

To test an Android project, we need to implement the testing dependencies in the gradle file. To add the dependencies, we need to implement in the dependencies { ... } of build.gradle (app module) file. Here is a snippet code of this build.gradle file:

```
// Dependencies for local unit tests
dependencies{
testImplementation "junit:junit:$rootProject.ext.junitVersion"

// Espresso UI Testing dependencies.
androidTestImplementation "com.android.support.test.espresso:espresso-
core:$rootProject.ext.espressoVersion"
androidTestImplementation "com.android.support.test.espresso:espresso-
contrib:$rootProject.ext.espressoVersion"
androidTestImplementation "com.android.support.test.espresso:espresso-
intents:$rootProject.ext.espressoVersion"
}
```

The source code with an example for this chapter is available on GitHub at the following link: https://github.com/PacktPublishing/Learn-Spring-for-Android-Application-Development/tree/master/Chapter10.

Software testing

Software testing is one of the most essential parts of any project. Testing evaluates the stability, usability, quality assurance, functionality of components, and ensures that the software is ready to publish in the market. It also helps to find out the errors, missing requirements of a project, and so on. Testing uses techniques to execute some processes in an application or program with the intent to find bugs.

In `Chapter 6`, *Accessing the Database* and `Chapter 9`, *Creating an Application*, we created Spring applications and implemented REST APIs. Then we tested with a third-party tool called Insomnia. After this, we mentioned the URL path with the HTTP CRUD request functions and checked the output. This system was fine and we could see the output directly. However, it can often be difficult to find the errors and bugs, as it can't show you the errors or any abnormal behavior. Though this project is running, it's not necessarily safe to release to the market. Therefore, we need to further test its stability. Let's run through two popular testing tools and frameworks, JUnit and Espresso.

JUnit

JUnit is the most popular testing framework, built for Java, and is open source. It has almost all the features and modules necessary to test a Java-based application in a test-driven development environment. JUnit mainly focuses on writing tests that are automated for a certain class or function. It helps to call a function and check for the expected output. Before seeing some examples of JUnit in use, let's learn about its advantages.

Advantages of JUnit

JUnit is widely used for testing Java applications because of its user-friendly functionalities. It has some powerful advantages, such as the following:

- The JUnit framework is open source
- It provides text-based command lines as well as AWT-based and Swing-based graphical test mechanisms
- It has some annotations to utilize test functions
- It has a test runner to test running applications
- It allows you to write code
- It can test automatically and provide feedback

Basic annotations of JUnit

JUnit has some basic and important annotations, such as the following:

- The `@BeforeClass`: This runs once before any test functions in the class. In this function, you can connect the database or connection pool. This function has to be a static method.
- The `@AfterClass`: This runs once after any test functions in the class. In this function, you can close the database connection and cleanup.
- The `@Before`: This can run before `@Test` annotated functions. Here you create some objects and share to all `@Test` annotated testing functions.
- The `@After`: This can run after `@Test` annotated functions. Here, you modify or clean the objects and share to all `@Test` annotated testing functions.
- The `@Test`: This annotated function is the test function.

Now we'll look at an example of how to test a project with JUnit. Here, you can learn about the life cycle of the testing annotations and the use of these annotations.

Creating a project

Let's create a project where we will create REST APIs using a database for users, and show a list of the user details. In this project, we will use JDBC, MySQL, and Spring Boot.

To create a project, go to `https://start.spring.io` and create a Kotlin-based project with the following given dependencies:

- Web
- JDBC
- MySQL
- DevTools

Now we'll create some demo code, and we can test them.

Test a project using JUnit

Open your project that we generated previously and follow these steps:

1. Go to the **test** | **kotlin** | **com.packtpub.sunnat629.testing_application**, as in this screenshot:

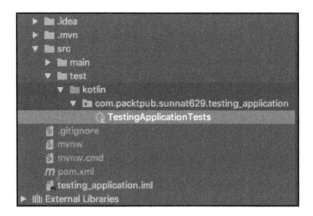

2. Now create a class named `JUnitTestClass.kt` where we will create some test cases using the annotations. Here is the sample code:

```kotlin
class JUnitTestClass {

    companion object {
        @BeforeClass
        @JvmStatic
        fun runBeforeClass(){
            println("============ @BeforeClass ============\n")
        }

        @AfterClass
        @JvmStatic
        fun runAfterClass(){
            println("=========== @AfterClass ===========")
        }
    }

    @Before
    fun runBefore(){
        println("=========== @Before ===========")
    }

    @After
```

```
        fun runAfter(){
            println("============ @After ============\n")
        }

        @Test
        fun runTest1(){
            println("============ @TEST One ============")
        }

        @Test
        fun runTest2(){
            println("============ @TEST Two ============")
        }
    }
```

You can see that we have written the `@BeforeClass` and `@AfterClass` annotated function in the `companion object {}`, which means these functions are static. In Kotlin, you have to write the static variables and functions in the `companion object {}`.

We have used the `@JvmStatic` annotation. This is especially used in Kotlin to specify that this function is static and needs to be generated in the element of this function.

3. Now run this test by clicking the **Run Test** icon beside the function name, as in the following screenshot:

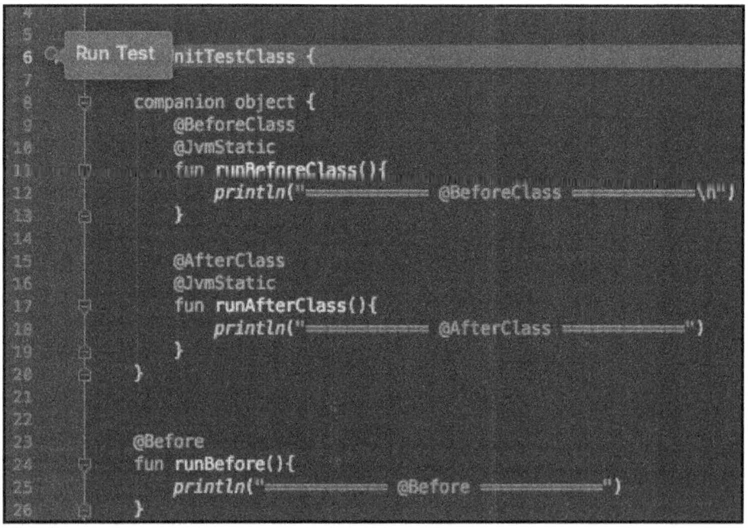

After running the test on all the test cases, it will show the results; namely, pass or fail. Here is the output:

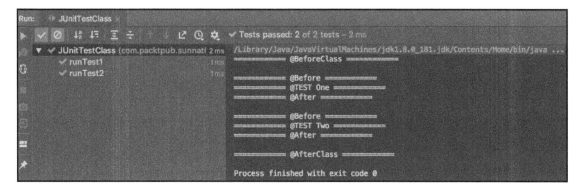

Here you can see that we had two test cases named `runTest1` and `runTest2` that have passed the test.

4. Now modify our `runTest1` function and write logic:

```
@Test
fun runTest1(){
    println("============ @TEST One Start ============")
    assertEquals(6, doSum(3,2))
    println("============ @TEST One End ============")
}

private fun doSum(num1: Int, num2: Int): Int{
        return num1 + num2
    }
```

Here, we have done a very simple equation to check the testing function. We have used a method of `Assert` class. The `assertEquals()` is a method of assert, and mainly checks the equality with the two inputs. Here, for example, we provide 6 and (2+3), which is not true and it will show an error.

If the equation is correct, then you will see the test is passed or it will show an error with the expected result. Here is what the result looks like:

There are a lot of Assert methods. Here are some of them:

- The `assertArrayEquals`: This will return the equality of two array types input
- The `assertEquals`: This will return the equality of two same types of input such as `int`, `long`, `double`, `String`, and so on
- The `assertTrue`: This will assert that the given condition is `true`
- The `assertFalse`: This will assert that the given condition is `false`
- The `assertNotNull`: This will assert that the given object is not null
- The `assertNull`: This will assert that the given object is null

Creating a test case for a Rest API

Now we will see how to test the database using the JPA and Hibernate of a Spring project. Here are the steps of how to test the database using JPA:

1. Open the social_network project. The link is here: `https://github.com/PacktPublishing/Learn-Spring-for-Android-Application-Development/tree/master/Chapter09/social_network`.

2. Now go to the **test** | **kotlin** | **com.packtpub.sunnat629.social_network** package and create a file named `ProfileRepositoryTest.kt` with two annotations named `@RunWith(SpringRunner::class)` and `@DataJpaTest`.

Here is the code of the `ProfileRepositoryTest.kt`:

```
@RunWith(SpringRunner::class)
@DataJpaTest
class ProfileRepositoryTest {

    @Autowired
    private lateinit var entityManager: TestEntityManager

    @Autowired
```

```
    private lateinit var profileRepository: ProfileRepository

    @Test
    fun getUserTesting(){
        val newProfile = getNewProfile()
        val saveProfile = entityManager.merge(newProfile)

        val foundProfile = profileRepository.getOne(saveProfile.id!!)

        assertThat(foundProfile.username)
                .isEqualTo(saveProfile.username)
    }

    private fun getNewProfile(): Profile {
        return Profile( "naruto",
                "12345",
                "naruto123@gmail.com",
                "Naruto",
                "Uzumak")
    }
}
```

The following is an explanation of the preceding code:

- The `@RunWith(SpringRunner::class)` is the annotation in the connector between the Spring and JUnit. It uses the Spring's testing support to run JUnit.
- The `@DataJpaTest` enables the JPA testing features.
- We autowired the TestEntityManager, which is mainly designed for JPA testing and JPA EntityManager's alternative.
- The `getUserTesting()`, which has the `@Test` annotation and is the main testing function.

Now, we will insert a demo `Profile` object and check if the insertion is working or not. To begin with, we have to create a Profile object using the `getNewProfile()` function.

After this we save this profile as a new variable, such as this:

```
val saveProfile = entityManager.merge(newProfile)
```

Here, we used the `entityManager.merge()`, which will insert the profile in the database.

We also autowired the `profileRepository` now use this line to fetch the inserted profile by the ID:

```
val foundProfile = profileRepository.getOne(saveProfile.id!!)
```

Now we have used the `assertThat()` to check the given logic is correct or not. In this function, we have checked the created profile and the fetched profile:

```
assertThat(foundProfile.username).isEqualTo(saveProfile.username)
```

Now, if there are any errors regarding insertion or communication with the database, it will return an error.

Here is the output of our test:

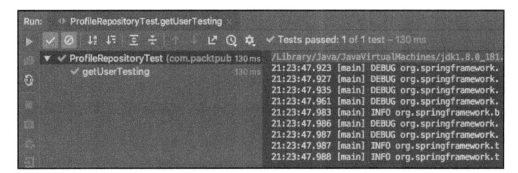

If you provide something as a false value, or the test encounters an error, it will output the following:

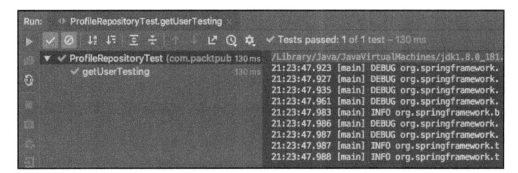

We have entered a profile name as `naruto`, but we tested the name `Uzumak`, which is why it didn't match. The result subsequently failed.

UI testing on Android

Nowadays, people are more dependent on mobile than desktop. If we consider Android, millions of applications are on the Play Store and other app stores. So, it is very important to test the UI to make a UI bug free and stable product in the app store. You need to be very careful during testing as there are myriad devices with various display sizes. For the backend, you can test with the JUnit and the system is same. But now our test will be UI-based and so we will use Espresso. This is the most popular framework for UI testing.

Espresso

Espresso is an open source framework and an instrumentation-based API, designed by Google. It is good practice to create some test cases of various scenarios of the project. It helps to find out the unexpected results or bugs of the UI, as well as the use case. It automatically syncs the actions of the test with the UI of the application. It allows you to test on both real devices and emulators. But there is a disadvantage of the use in a real device due to its high price to test various size of displays and manufacturers. So an emulator is the best solution to reduce the cost and time for testing. According to the Espresso testers, almost 99% of bugs on an Android application can be detected by this framework. The APIs of Espresso are very small, predictable, and easy to learn. You can also customize these APIs if you want.

Let's create a project and test it with Espresso.

Creating an application

Let's create a simple Android app as a client that will retrieve the REST API using the GitHub API:

1. First of all, we need to create an app from Android Studio and put down your project and the company domain. Don't forget to check **Include Kotlin support**. The following screenshot shows the **Create Android Project** window:

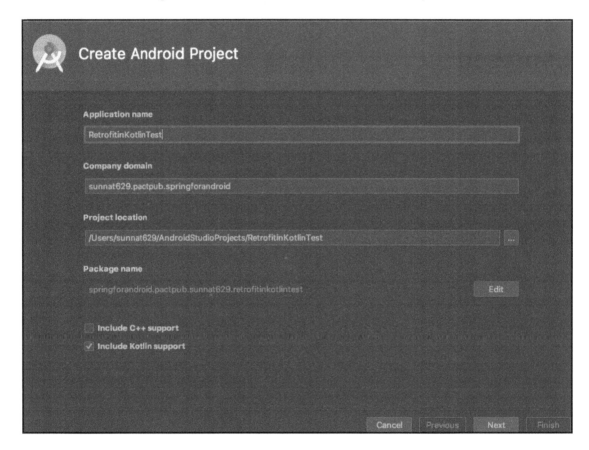

2. Then select the **minimum API version** from the **Phone and Tablet** option. There is no need to add other options for this project. After clicking **Next**, in the **add an Activity to mobile** field, you can select **Empty Activity** and then, after renaming the activity name and layout, click **Finish**. After the build, you will be ready to start creating an Android app.

After creating the project, we need to implement the dependencies to test.

Injecting dependencies

This project is mainly to test UI the application and so we need to implement Espresso. Write down the given lines to implement Espresso in the `dependencies{}` block of `build.gradle` (Module—app):

```
testImplementation 'junit:junit:4.12'
androidTestImplementation 'com.android.support.test:runner:1.0.2'

// Espresso UI Testing dependencies.
androidTestImplementation "com.android.support.test.espresso:espresso-core:3.0.2"
androidTestImplementation "com.android.support.test.espresso:espresso-contrib:3.0.2"
androidTestImplementation "com.android.support.test.espresso:espresso-intents:3.0.2"
```

Then in the same file, add the code to implement the JUnit3 and JUnit4 tests against an Android package in the `android{}` block:

```
testInstrumentationRunner "android.support.test.runner.AndroidJUnitRunner"
```

`AndroidJUnitRunner` is the instrumentation runner. It mainly controls the test APK, the environment, and all of the test launches.

Now sync the project to download and add the dependencies to the project.

Modifying the application

We have learned how to create an app based on `RecyclerView` in Chapter 9, *Creating an Application,* so we can just run through the concept of this app. We have a user data class with the ID and username. We will insert 100 users in the database and show in a custom `RecyclerView`. We also use a `UserItemAdapter` to customize the `RecyclerView`.

Clone this project if you want: `https://github.com/PacktPublishing/Learn-Spring-for-Android-Application-Development/tree/master/Chapter10/TestingWithEspresso`.

In this project, you find the `MainActivity.kt` where you can find a list view. Here is a piece of code from this class:

```
----
----
 userLists.adapter = UserItemAdapter(this, userList)
----
----
```

Here, the `userLists` is the RecyclerView and we have the `UserItemAdapter` custom adapter of a `UserModel`. Here, the `UserModel` code is where we take the ID and name of a user:

```
data class User(var userID: Int, var username: String)
```

Now, we will test this list view using Espresso with some major functions that are frequently used in our projects.

Creating testing files

Let's write some test cases. To write this code, we need to create new files in the **androidTest** package. To do this, follow the steps:

1. Now go to **src** | **androidTest** | **java** | `module_name` of the project. Here is a screenshot of this directory:

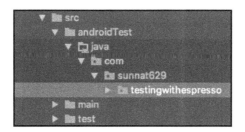

2. Create a class
   named `MainActivityTest.kt` with `@RunWith(AndroidJUnit4::class)` annotation. This annotation will link the test and the app features.

Let's create our very first Espresso test:

First of all, we need to connect our `MainActivity` class. To do this, we will initialize a variable of `ActivityTestRule<MainActivity>` and it will provide all the functionalities for the `MainActivity`. It has an annotation of `@Rule`, which means testing for a single activity and here it is `MainActivity`.

This `getCountUser()` function is for checking the number of your list:

```
// User count Matching
@Test
fun getCountUser(){
    onView(withId(R.id.userLists))
        .check(matches(itemCount(20)))
}
```

In the previous code, we do the following:

- `ViewMatchers.onView()` means it will take a matcher logic.
- `ViewMatchers.withId()` uses to connect the component of your activity's layout. In our `main_activity.xml`, the ID name of the `RecyclerView` is `userLists`, so we connect it here.
- `check(..)` will return a Boolean.
- The `matches(itemCount(20)` means it will match the given number with your user list number.

We need to create the `itemCount()` manually. To do this, create a class named `CustomUserMatchers.kt`. Here, is the code of this class:

```
class CustomUserMatchers {
    companion object {
        fun itemCount(count: Int): Matcher<View>{
            return object : BoundedMatcher<View,
RecyclerView>(RecyclerView::class.java) {
                override fun describeTo(description: Description?) {
                    description!!.appendText("Total User = $count")
                }

                override fun matchesSafely(item: RecyclerView?): Boolean {
                    return item?.adapter?.itemCount == count
                }
            }
        }
    }
}
```

Here, we create a `CustomUserMatchers.kt` class where we create a static function and return a `Matcher<View>`.

`BoundedMatcher<View, RecyclerView>(RecyclerView::class.java)` have two functions named `describeTo(description: Description?)` and `matchesSafely(item: RecyclerView?)` and we have overriden these classes.

In the `matchesSafely`, we will check the equality of the list number with the given number.

In our output list, we have `100` users but here the given number is `20`. So when you run the test, it will fail, as in this screenshot:

If you provide `100` and run then you can see that the test is passed, as in this screenshot:

Now create a test case named `getUserPosition()` to get a specific position and click it:

```
// User Click with a position number
@Test
fun getUserPosition(){
    onView(withId(R.id.userLists))
        .perform(actionOnItemAtPosition
        <RecyclerView.ViewHolder>(34, click()))
}
```

The `actionOnItemAtPosition<RecyclerView.ViewHolder>` is to select a position of the `RecyclerView` list using the `RecyclerView.ViewHolder` and then we use a `click()` of row 34 of the list. That means this test will go to your given position and then it will click that item. You can see in the following screenshot that it has clicked and showed the Toast that the test case has clicked the row 34 of the list:

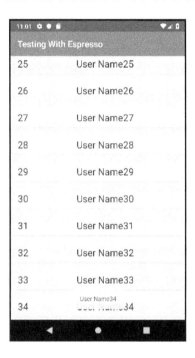

If you look at the logcat, you will also notice that the test has been passed. Here is the output of the logcat of Android Studio:

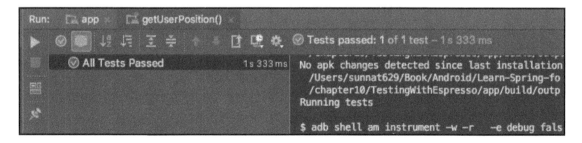

- Create a `getIsDisplayed()` function to test whether the given list is displaying or not.
- The `withId(R.id.userLists)` will get the listview of the `MainActivity`.

- The `check(matches(isDisplayed()))` checks whether the list is displaying in the device or not:

```
// User list display test
@Test
fun getIsDisplayed(){
    onView(withId(R.id.userLists))
        .check(matches(isDisplayed()))
}
```

Create a `getIsClickable()` function to test whether the given list is displaying or not. The `withId(R.id.userRoot)` will get the `ConstraintLayout` and `check(matches(isClickable()))` will match layout's clickability status of the list:

```
// User list display test
@Test
fun getIsClickable(){
    onView(withId(R.id.userRoot))
        .check(matches(isClickable()))
}
```

Create a `getScrollToBottom()` function to check how to scroll to the specific position. The `withId(R.id.userLists)` will get the list view and `perform(scrollToPosition<RecyclerView.ViewHolder>(activityTestRule.activity.userLists.adapter!!.itemCount - 1))` will scroll to the bottom of the list. Using this test case, you can see whether the list is smooth or not:

```
// User list scroll to bottom
@Test
fun getScrollToBottom(){
    onView(withId(R.id.userLists))
.perform(scrollToPosition<RecyclerView.ViewHolder>(activityTestRule.activit
y.userLists.adapter!!.itemCount - 1))
}
```

There are even more functions of Espresso. You can check this cheat sheet (`https://developer.android.com/training/testing/espresso/cheat-sheet`), which is provided by Google.

Summary

Testing is always a good way to discover errors in the UI, backend code, or logic. It helps to understand the reason for crashes. Here, we have learned about two powerful frameworks. One is JUnit and another is Espresso. In this chapter, we have seen how to add the dependencies for testing. We have learned how to implement the JUnit into a project. We saw how to use the logic in our test case and how to check to see the pass or fail result of a test case. Additionally, we have seen how to connect the database for testing. Then, we saw how to insert a demo object into a database, and subsequently, fetch it from the database, after which we have matched the object.

In Android testing, we have used the Espresso framework to test the UI. Finally, we have seen some uses of the Espresso APIs and how to handle and connect them with a specific activity. This chapter gave you a brief idea of testing so that you can use test cases to perfect your project. If you want to learn more, please see our reference book under the *Further reading* section.

If you are reading this paragraph, that means you have finished this book and are ready to build a server-based and client-based projects alone. Now you are a one-man army, able to create a server and mobile application with security, databases, and testing. I hope you enjoyed reading this book and that it will be a reference point in your upcoming projects.

Questions

1. What types of code does JUnit support?
2. Who designed Espresso?
3. In which platform, JUnit uses?
4. Why is the Espresso used in the Andriod application?
5. What is the Android testing strategy?
6. What is the standard ratio of testing?
7. How do you test different screen sizes on devices?

Further reading

- *Android Application Testing Guide* (https://www.packtpub.com/application-development/android-application-testing-guide) by Diego Torres Milano
- *Learning Android Application Testing* (https://www.packtpub.com/application-development/learning-android-application-testing) by Paul Blundell, Diego Torres Milano
- *Spring Framework Master Class - Beginner to Expert [Video]* (https://www.packtpub.com/application-development/spring-framework-master-class-beginner-expert-video) by Ranga Karanam

Assessments

Chapter 1

1. Spring is built on Java **Standard Edition** (**SE**), but can run Java **Enterprise Edition** (**EE**)
2. Almost all Java-supported IDEs where you can use Spring, such as NetBeans, and Visual Studio
3. Tomcat is a web server
4. You can also use Jetty and Undertow for Spring development
5. No. You can you use IntelliJ IDEA, Visual Studio—Xamarin, PhoneGap, Corona, and CppDroid, but Android Studio is highly recommended, and it is the official IDE for developing an Android app

Chapter 2

1. Kotlin is a statically typed programming language that compiles to the same bytecode as Java.
2. Kotlin supports all the features of object-oriented programming.
3. Kotlin supports a lot of the features of functional programming.
4. To define a read-only variable, we have to use the `val` keyword and the `var` keyword for mutability.
5. To define a function, we have to use the `fun` keyword. Functions can be defined as first-class citizens, class members, or local.

Chapter 3

1. Spring stands out as the most broadly utilized Java EE framework. Spring Framework's core ideas are *Dependency Injection* and *Aspect-Oriented Programming*. Spring Framework can also be utilized in normal Java applications to accomplish free coupling between various segments by actualizing dependency injection, and we can perform cross-cutting assignments.

2. Dependency injection configuration design enables us to expel the hardcoded dependencies and make our application approximately coupled, extendable, and viable. We can execute a dependency injection example to move the dependency goals from accumulate time to runtime. A portion of the advantages of utilizing Dependency Injection is Detachment of Concerns, Boilerplate Code decrease, Configurable segments, and simple unit testing.

3. **Aspect-oriented programming** (**AOP**) is a programming worldview that supplements **object-oriented programming** (**OOP**) by isolating the worries of a software application to enhance modularization.

4. **Inversion of Control** (**IoC**) is the instrument to accomplish free coupling among object dependencies. To accomplish free coupling and dynamic official of the objects at runtime, objects characterize their dependencies that are being injected by other constructing agent objects. Spring IoC container is the program that injects dependencies into an object and prepares it for our utilization.

5. Any normal Java class that is introduced by Spring IoC container is called Spring Bean. We utilize a Spring `ApplicationContext` to get the Spring Bean occurrence.

6. Much the same as MVC configuration design, a controller is the class that deals with all the customer requests and sends them to the arranged assets to deal with. In Spring MVC, `org.springframework.web.servlet.DispatcherServlet` is the front controller class that introduces the context-dependent on the Spring beans configurations.

7. `DispatcherServlet` is the front controller in a Spring MVC application, and it stacks the Spring Bean configuration file, stating every one of the beans that are arranged. In the event that annotations are empowered, it additionally filters the bundles and designs any beans annotated with the `@Component`, `@Controller`, `@Repository`, or `@Service` annotations.

8. `ContextLoaderListener` is the audience to fire up and close down Spring's root `WebApplicationContext`. Its important roles are to tie the life cycle of `ApplicationContext` to the life cycle of the `ServletContext`, and to robotize the production of `ApplicationContext`. We can utilize it to characterize shared beans that can be utilized across various Spring contexts.

9. Boilerplate code is repetitive code that shows up again and again for similar purposes.

Chapter 4

1. REST means REpresentational State Transfer; it is a generally new aspect of composing a web programming interface.
   RESTFUL is referred for web services composed by applying REST building idea are called RESTful services. It centers around system assets and how the condition of an asset ought to be transported over HTTP convention to various clients written in various dialects. In a RESTful web service, HTTP methods such as `GET`, `POST`, `PUT`, and `DELETE` can be utilized to perform CRUD activities.

2. The architectural style for creating a web API is as follows:
   - HTTP for client-server communication
   - XML/JSON as a formatting language
   - Simple URI as the address for the services
   - Stateless communication

3. The `SOAPUI` tool for `SOAP WS` and Firefox *poster* plugin for `RESTFUL` services.

4. Web services dependent on REST architecture are known as RESTful web services. These web services utilize HTTP methods to execute the idea of REST architecture. A RESTful web service more often than not characterizes a URI (Uniform Asset Identifier), a service, gives asset portrayal, for example, JSON and set of HTTP methods.

5. URI stands for Uniform Resource Identifier. Every asset in REST architecture is recognized by its URI. The motivation behind a URI is to find a resource on the server facilitating the web service.

6. It is an HTTP success code: `OK`.

7. It is an HTTP client error code: `Not Found`.

Chapter 5

1. There are two areas that Spring Security mainly targets, and these are authentication and authorization.

2. The `SecurityContext` and `SecurityContextHolder` classes, which are Spring security.

3. The `DelegatingFilterProxy` class is required for Spring security, and this class is from `package org.springframework. web.filter`.

4. Yes. Spring Security supports password hashing.

5. Authorization Code, Implicit, Password, Client Credentials, Device Code, Refresh Token.

Chapter 6

1. H2 is an open source Java database that is very lightweight. It can be embedded in Java applications. It also runs on the client-server model.

2. A *resource* means how data will be represented in *REST* architecture. It allows a client to read, write, modify, and create resources using HTTP methods, for example GET, POST, PUT, DELETE, and so on.

3. CRUD stands for Create, Read, Update, and Delete.

4. DAO is an abstraction of data persistence. *Repository* is an abstraction of a collection of objects.

5. SQLite uses dynamic typing. Content can be stored as INTEGER, REAL, TEXT, BLOB, or NULL.

6. Alternatives to the SQLite database are OrmLite, Couchbase Lite, and Snappy DB.

7. The standard SQLite commands are SELECT, CREATE, INSERT, UPDATE, DROP, and DELETE.

8. There are some disadvantages of SQLite. They are as follows:
   - It is used to handle low-to-medium traffic HTTP requests.
   - The size of SQLite is restricted to 2 GB in most cases.

Chapter 7

1. The call stack is a part of memory that is allocated by a thread or a coroutine and contains a stack of functions that were invoked in the context of the thread and local variables.

2. Thread pool is a pattern that uses a set of threads that are waiting for a job from a queue.

3. Callback is a pattern used for delivering the result of an asynchronous operation.

4. Coroutines are lightweight threads, because the creation of a coroutine doesn't require as many resources as the creation of a thread.

Chapter 8

1. Reactive programming is an approach to asynchronous events handling.
2. Mono is a publisher that can emit zero or one event.
3. Observable is a class from RxJava that emits a stream of values.
4. Scheduler is an abstraction over thread pools.

Chapter 9

1. EER stands for **E**nhanced **E**ntity-**R**elationship. It is a high-level model to a modified and transitive version of an ER model. It helps to create database schemas with more accuracy.
2. CRUD stands for create, read, update and delete.
3. Postgresql, MySQL, MongoDB, and so on.
4. Postman. Insomnia is easy to use and powerful.
5. The minimum API is 21; target and max will be the latest API (the current latest API is 28).
6. MVC, MVP, and MVVM.
7. Android Studio, Genymotion (free/pain), Remix OS, and Nox Player.
8. ANR is short for **A**pplication **N**ot **R**esponding. When the application is stuck the UI because of some bugs in the background, then it occurs.
9. Sketch is the best, and Adobe XD is also a powerful app for designing prototypes.

Chapter 10

1. Text-based command lines, and also AWT-based and Swing-based graphical test mechanisms.
2. Google.
3. In Java-based applications.
4. Unit test, integration test, and UI test.
5. 70% small (unit tests), 20% medium (integration tests), and 10% large (UI tests).
6. The best way to handle it is to use emulators.

Other Books You May Enjoy

If you enjoyed this book, you may be interested in these other books by Packt:

Building Applications with Spring 5 and Vue.js 2
James J. Ye

ISBN: 9781788836968

- Analyze requirements and design data models
- Develop a single-page application using Vue.js 2 and Spring 5
- Practice concept, logical, and physical data modeling
- Design, implement, secure, and test RESTful API
- Add test cases to improve reliability of an application
- Monitor and deploy your application to production

Hands-On Full Stack Development with Spring Boot 2.0 and React
Juha Hinkula

ISBN: 9781789138085

- Create a RESTful web service with Spring Boot
- Understand how to use React for frontend programming
- Gain knowledge of how to create unit tests using JUnit
- Discover the techniques that go into securing the backend using Spring Security
- Learn how to use Material UI in the user interface to make it more user-friendly
- Create a React app by using the Create React App starter kit made by Facebook

Leave a review - let other readers know what you think

Please share your thoughts on this book with others by leaving a review on the site that you bought it from. If you purchased the book from Amazon, please leave us an honest review on this book's Amazon page. This is vital so that other potential readers can see and use your unbiased opinion to make purchasing decisions, we can understand what our customers think about our products, and our authors can see your feedback on the title that they have worked with Packt to create. It will only take a few minutes of your time, but is valuable to other potential customers, our authors, and Packt. Thank you!

Index

X

www.ingramcontent.com/pod-product-compliance
Lightning Source LLC
Chambersburg PA
CBHW080609060326
40690CB00021B/4637